T
RESU
LIBERAL
(And Other
Unfashionable Prophecies)

Also by the Author

THE RESURGENT LIBERAL

(And Other Unfashionable Prophecies)

ROBERT B. REICH

VINTAGE BOOKS

A DIVISION OF RANDOM HOUSE, INC.

NEW YORK

FIRST VINTAGE BOOKS EDITION, FEBRUARY 1991

Copyright © 1981, 1982, 1983, 1984, 1985, 1986, 1987, 1988, 1989 by Robert B. Reich

Library of Congress Cataloging-in-Publication Data

Reich, Robert B.
    The resurgent liberal (and other unfashionable prophecies)/
Robert B. Reich.—1st Vintage Books ed.
        p.   cm.
    Reprint. Originally published: New York: Times Books,
1989.
    Includes index.
    ISBN 0-679-73152-0
        1. United States—Economic policy—1981–   2. United
States—Politics and government—1989–   3. United States—
Social policy—1980–   4. Liberalism—United States.
I. Title.
HC106.8.R454   1991
338.973—dc20   90-50146
                                CIP

Manufactured in the United States of America

10 9 8 7 6 5 4 3 2 1

PERMISSIONS
ACKNOWLEDGMENTS

Some essays in this work were originally published in the following publications: *Across the Board, The American Oxonian, Foreign Affairs, Harper's Magazine, The New Republic, The New York Times, The Washington Post, Working Mother,* and *Yale Journal of Law and Policy.*

"Toward a New Philosophy" ("The Once and Future Liberal"), April 1985, "The Rise of Techno-Nationalism," April 1987, and "The Corporation and the Nation," May 1988, were originally published in *The Atlantic Monthly.*

Grateful acknowledgment is made to the following for permission to reprint previously published material: *Harper & Row Publishers, Inc.:* Introductory essay from The *Power of Public Ideas* by Robert B. Reich. Copright © 1988 by Robert B. Reich. Reprinted by permission of the Ballinger Division, Harper & Row Publishers, Inc.

Harvard Business Review: "Regulation by Confrontation or Negotiation" ("The Origins of Red Tape") and "The Team as Hero" by Robert B. Reich from the May/June 1981 and May/June 1987 issues of *Harvard Business Review.* Copright © 1981, 1987 by the President and Fellows of Harvard College. Reprinted by permission of Harvard Business Review. All rights reserved.

National Education Association: "Education and the Next Economy" ("Dick and Jane Meet the Next Economy") by Robert B. Reich. Copyright © 1988 by National Education Association of the United States. Reprinted by permission of N.E.A.

The New York Times: "Entrepreneurialism" and "Loophole Mentalities" ("The Spirit of Law") by Robert B. Reich from the May 23, 1980, and September 13, 1987, issues of *The New York Times.* Copyright © 1980, 1987 by The New York Times Company. Reprinted by permission. All rights reserved.

Harcourt Brace Jovanovich, Inc.: Excerpts from *Revolution* by Martin Anderson. Copyright © 1988 by Martin Anderson. Excerpts from *For the Record* by Donald T. Regan. Copyright © 1988 Donald T. Regan. Reprinted by permission of Harcourt Brace Jovanovich, Inc.

For Sam

CONTENTS

PREFACE

MY REPUTATION AS A SOOTHSAYER BEGAN IN OCTOBER 1987, TWO WEEKS before the Dow Jones Industrial Average plunged five hundred points, when I appeared on a nationally televised talk show opposite a conservative economist who assured viewers that the bull market would continue. I demurred. My advice to viewers was to get out of the market before the coming crash. I had the temerity to predict that the crash would occur within the month. In the weeks following the crash I was inundated with letters from people wanting to subscribe to my investment letter. Politely but regretfully, I informed each of them that I did not publish an investment letter. I did not tell them, however, that I had been making precisely the same prediction for five years.

I have been predicting the resurgence of liberalism for many more years than that, and no doubt someday my clairvoyance will be appreciated in similar fashion. There are eventual benefits to tenacity. When the day comes, and my political prognostications are a valued commodity, you, dear reader, may justly share in the acclaim. After all, you were reading this before it became fashionable.

The following pages are especially designed for those who may feel the need for some companionship and fortification in the meantime. The true triumph of conservatism has come in making some of us feel defensive, even slightly embarrassed, about our liberal tendencies. (The most recent Democratic candidate for President tried for months to dodge the label, confessing to his liberal beliefs only under duress.) Under these circumstances, a firm assurance that such inclinations are essentially healthy, natural, and even socially beneficial may relieve the abashment and give courage to discuss them openly in mixed company.

Self-confidence is necessary but not sufficient. There must also be something to be confident about. Thus, a second purpose of this book. Modern liberalism should stand squarely for, and against, certain things. The following essays do not lack a point of view.

Conservative orthodoxy places great faith in the social utility of fear and avarice. Fear of unpleasant consequence, argues the conservative, keeps would-be criminals at bay, foreign aggressors in line, and the lazy and indolent off the streets. Avarice, meanwhile, inspires geniuses to new invention, mavericks and risk takers to new enterprise, and nations to new greatness. That few facts can be found to support these propositions is beside the point. They rest on faith, grounded in a mixture of strict child rearing, social Darwinism, and neoclassical economics.

Future historians who examine the late 1970s and 1980s will discover a different set of consequences flowing from the prevailing fear and avarice. They will find that excessive greed inspired clever criminals, on and off Wall Street, to ever more ingenious circumnavigations of law. Audacious displays of avarice also demoralized average working people who came to believe that the path to success lay in selfish opportunism rather than in loyalty to company and country. Greed on a grander scale led an entire nation into debt and thus into precarious financial dependence on foreign powers, oblivious to the burden placed on future generations. As lawfulness, loyalty, and national security so declined, society was forced to develop ever larger and more elaborate ways to deter criminality, opportunism, and foreign domination. This vicious spiral provoked conservative demands for even greater financial reward and more draconian punishment; if carrots and sticks failed to elicit the intended behavior, they argued, it was because the carrots were too meager and the sticks too frail.

What will history conclude finally reversed the trend? A financial crisis? A particularly revolting scandal? A generation of graying baby boomers, sated and sedated, despised by their children and grandchildren, who finally repented? The unanticipated bleeding heart of a President Quayle? My crystal ball fails me on these finer points. But of this I am reasonably certain: With the liberal resurgence will come a new appreciation of the importance to society of loyalty, collaboration, civic virtue, and responsibility to future generations. Such altruistic inclinations are unlikely to grow in a society organized around fear and greed. Resurgent liberals will adopt a different set of organizing principles. Avarice will be discouraged (there will be no shame, for example, in enacting a very high marginal tax rate on princely incomes). The pain and fear of economic dislocation will be eased (through extended unemployment insurance, job training coupled with day care, health insurance for the unemployed and working poor, and similar programs). American enterprises will become owned and controlled by all their employees (rather than solely by their overleveraged executives, per the latest fashion in corporate finance). And neither military jingoism nor economic mercantilism will any longer be the measure of patriotism. True patriotism will be founded instead on a common concern for, and investment in, the well-being of our future citizens.

A final prediction. As a by-product of the liberal resurgence, liberals will no longer feel embarrassed by their inclinations. In fact, fueled by renewed confidence and exuberance, liberals eventually will display the same grandiosity that got them into trouble last time. And the cycle will repeat.

* * *

The following ruminations span the decade or so before the coming liberal resurgence. The first set of essays concerns the rise of the paper economy—the substitution of paper for product in American managers' hearts and minds, and the attendant consequences for our politics and economics. A second group of essays deals with the larger incapacity of the economy to generate new wealth, due in part to the failure to invest in, and give meaningful voice and responsibility to, the American work force. I include here a summary of my ideas about the work force of the future and the challenge it poses to the American corporation and American education.

The next few essays are on economic nationalism. It is by now a commonplace that the nation is involved in two global contests—one, a political contest with the Soviet Union and its allies; the other, an economic contest with Japan. But there is confusion about which contest is the more important, how the two contests affect one another, and more generally, the appropriate role for economic nationalism in policy making. My arguments on these questions should be clear, if not convincing.

The final two sections are on American politics, social trends, and political thought. Economics cannot be divorced from politics (although many economists make valiant efforts in this direction). These essays seek some new connections, and directions.

In sum, as these essays reveal, the 1980s have provided abundant material for rumination. Nothing inspires the dissident imagination quite as well as prevailing orthodoxy; nothing emboldens it as well as excess in high places. In this respect I am deeply indebted to Ronald Reagan, George Bush, Ivan Boesky, Michael Deaver, Edwin Meese, George Steinbrenner, Donald Regan, Oliver North, Donald Trump, Frank Lorenzo, and many of the fine people who still inhabit the upper reaches of American business, finance, and government. Without their stout conviction and audacious conduct, these essays would not have been written.

Robert B. Reich
Cambridge, Massachusetts

I

THE
PAPER
ECONOMY

1

THE SECRET
OF HIS SUCCESS

GEORGE HAD BEEN ONE OF MY BEST STUDENTS WHEN I CAME TO HAR-vard. I hadn't seen him since graduation. The wedding reception for one of his classmates gave me a chance to catch up.

"What have you been up to, George?" I asked.

"Doing M and A deals," he said, a bit sheepishly.

"M and A deals?"

"Mergers and acquisitions," he explained. "You know—putting them together, financing them, the whole bit. I'm an investment banker."

I tried to look enthusiastic. "Enjoying it?"

"Yeah. Made half a million last year. This year I'll top a million for sure."

I was astounded, not only at the amount of money, but also at George's overwhelming desire to tell me about it. "You mean, you actually earned half a million dollars?"

Now George became animated. "Base pay of one hundred and twenty-five thousand dollars, bonus of three hundred seventy-five thousand dollars. There's no limit. I'll be earning two million dollars a year by the time I'm thirty."

I remembered George equally animated, in the classroom six years earlier. It was a course on American political economy, and George had been an active contributor. He had the ability to get to the heart of the matter, to cut through conventional economic theory and its idealized view of markets, and to focus instead on the real frailties and foibles of the American system. Now I was going to find out what he had learned since then.

"Half a million dollars is a lot of money," I said with a smile. "You sure you're worth that much?"

George smiled back. "Of course not." Then he pointed to several of his classmates sitting at other tables. "And neither are Tim or Fred or Jane. They all made as much as I did last year, doing deals."

"How do you explain it, you and all the others pulling down that kind of money in your twenties?" I asked. "Economic theory says that people get paid according to their marginal product—what they contribute to society. You're earning more than most top executives of Fortune 500 companies, more than heart surgeons, nuclear physicists, more than university presidents, judges, the President of the United States. And much, much more," I added wistfully, "than Harvard professors. What gives?"

George's smile turned into a broad grin. His eyes lit up the way I remembered in the classroom. "Some say that we're worth every penny because we're restructuring America, making it more competitive." He laughed. "That's bull. We're just moving financial assets from one pocket to another. Unfriendly takeovers have been a big thing since the mid-1970s. What's happened with productivity growth since then? Zip."

"OK, OK. So tell me—why are you guys earning so much?"

"Look, there are two ways to make a bundle in this business," said George, his eyes narrowing in mock conspiracy. "The first is to move a huge sum of money. We work on a percentage basis, so the more money we move, the more we make."

George took out his pen and began drawing circles and numbers on a napkin. "Institutions like mutual funds, pension funds, bank trust departments, insurance companies—they're managing billion-dollar portfolios, more than a third of all the outstanding equity in the nation. And they're shifting big hunks of stock here and there at the slightest provocation."

George drew a line on the napkin, as if to add up the total. "The more action, the better for us. In 1980 the twenty biggest investment banks earned about eleven billion dollars. Last year, revenues topped thirty-five billion dollars."

George put down his pen. "Think about it—all this money moving around faster and faster. We grab a tiny piece of every dollar that's moved. The big institutions don't even miss it. I mean, what's a few million dollars when you're shifting billions every day?"

George grinned, eyebrows raised—the same mischievous expression I remembered from years before, when he was homing in on some core economic truth. "You have to remember that we're the ones who are advising the big institutions about whether they should move their money," he continued. "We're advising the corporate raiders about whether they should undertake a raid. We're advising everyone else about whether they should buy or sell or go private. And you know, it's just amazing how often our fancy analysis boils down to the same advice: Move your money! Quick!"

I was beginning to understand. "You said there were two ways to make a bundle. What's the second way?"

George paused, then leaned in toward me. "Remember, the first is to move a lot of money. The second way is to move it to where a lot of other money is heading, before the other money gets there." He lowered his voice. "You've been following the scandals—the insider-trading stuff?"

"George, I don't think you should tell me anything that . . ."

He stopped me. "No, no, no. Don't worry. I'm clean. Those guys that got indicted—they got greedy. They traded on inside information. They broke the law. My point is that you can move your money to where other money is heading without breaking the law."

George again picked up his pen and drew a big box on the napkin. "Let's call this an investment banking firm," he said. He divided the box into four squares. "Over here are the guys who help companies raise money. In the next box are the M and A specialists, the ones who do all the mergers and acquisitions and buyouts. In this third box are the guys who trade for the big institutions, the block traders. And in this last box are the guys who speculate on our own account, the arbitrageurs. In the gentlemanly days of investment banking most of the revenues came from the first box, from the guys who helped corporations get financing. But these days the really big earnings come from the other three boxes."

George drew dotted lines connecting the M and A specialists, the block traders, and the arbs. "Now, it would be illegal for us to trade on inside information; the arbs aren't allowed to buy into a company that's the target of one of our clients, for example. But you've got to remember how much information there is of a slightly more general character that's shared between these boxes all the time. I mean, you've got to talk about something at lunch, right?"

George again put on his mock conspiratorial expression. "Say the M and A guys have a client who's considering whether to take over CBS. Then they hear of another company that's interested in taking over ABC. Well, it doesn't take a rocket scientist to figure out that television networks are getting hot, so the M and A specialists tell the arbs to start buying NBC. Sure enough, network stocks take off, the firm makes a bundle. Illegal? Not at all. Done all the time."

George warmed to the topic. "Or suppose a prospective client comes in and says he's interested in taking over a car company, but the M and A guys have too much work and turn him down, and he goes to another investment bank. Still, you're pretty sure—given the client's size and history—that he's hot to make a bid for Chrysler. You also know that a lot of other investment bankers will soon figure out the same thing, as the client moves down the street trying to hire some muscle. So you tell the arbs to get into Chrysler fast. Sure enough, Chrysler's share price starts moving up in anticipation of a bid, and the firm makes a bundle. Illegal? No way. Done all the time.

"You see," he said, striking his pen on the table, "valuable information circulates all over every investment banking firm, all over Wall Street. It's not inside information, because it's not very specific, and nobody trades directly upon it. You profit indirectly from it. Call it *insidious* information." George laughed, proud of his neologism.

By now, the party was almost over. The bride and groom had already left. My wife mentioned something about baby-sitters and went to get our coats. I rose and extended my hand to George. "I'm afraid we have to get going, George. I would have liked to hear more, but I've got the idea. You've explained a great deal."

George gave me an iron grip. "It's all a big, speculative bubble," he said, rising. "I'm getting out before I'm thirty-five, before it bursts."

"That sounds wise," I said. "You'll be a rich man. What will you do then?"

George smiled broadly. "Politics."

2

THE NEW
AMERICAN ENTREPRENEUR

When the capital development of a country becomes a by-product of the activities of a casino, the job is likely to be ill-done. The measure of success attained by Wall Street . . . cannot be claimed as one of the outstanding triumphs of laissez-faire capitalism.

—*John Maynard Keynes*
**General Theory of Employment,
Interest and Money** *(1936)*

THE PAPER ENTREPRENEURS ARE WINNING OUT OVER THE PRODUCT entrepreneurs.

Paper entrepreneurs—trained in law, finance, accountancy—manipulate complex systems of rules and numbers. They innovate by using the systems in novel ways: establishing joint ventures, consortia, holding companies, mutual funds; finding companies to acquire, "white knights" to be acquired by, stock-index and commodity futures to invest in, tax shelters to hide in; engaging in proxy fights, tender offers, antitrust suits, stock splits, leveraged buyouts, divestitures; buying and selling notes, junk bonds, convertible debentures; going private, going public, going bankrupt.

Product entrepreneurs—inventors, design engineers, production engineers, production managers, marketers, owners of small businesses—produce goods and services people want. They innovate by creating better products at less cost; establishing more-efficient techniques of manufacture, distribution, sales; finding cheaper sources of materials, new markets, consumer needs; providing better training of employees, attention-getting advertising, speedier consumer service and complaint handling, more-reliable warranty coverage and repair.

Our economic system needs both. Paper entrepreneurs ensure that capital is allocated efficiently among product entrepreneurs. They also coordinate the activities of product entrepreneurs, facilitating readjustments and realignments in supply and demand.

But paper entrepreneurs do not directly enlarge the economic pie; they only arrange and define the slices. They provide nothing of tangible use. For an economy to maintain its health, entrepreneurial rewards should flow primarily to product, not paper.

Yet paper entrepreneurialism is on the rise. It dominates the leadership of our largest corporations. It guides government departments and agencies. It stimulates platoons of lawyers and financiers. It preoccupies some of our best minds, attracts some of our most talented graduates, embodies some of our most creative and original thinking, spurs some of our most energetic wheeling and dealing. Paper entrepreneurialism also promises the best financial rewards, the greatest employment security, the highest social status.

The ratio of paper entrepreneurialism to product entpreneurialism in our economy—measured by total earnings flowing to each, or by the amount of news in business journals and newspapers typically devoted to each—is about two to one.

Our economic system has become so complex and interdependent that capital must be allocated according to symbols of productivity rather than according to productivity itself. These symbolic rules and numbers lend themselves to profitable manipulation far more readily than do the underlying processes of production. It takes time and effort to improve product quality, exploit manufacturing efficiencies, develop distribution and sales networks, thus enlarging market share and profitability. But through the strategic use of accounting conventions, tax rules, stock and commodity exchanges, exchange rates, and litigation, enormous profits are possible with relatively little effort.

Paper entrepreneurialism is also cleaner than product entrepreneurialism. The paper entrepreneur needs only a phone, a Telex, a fax machine, a good secretary. The product entrepreneur depends on a complex web of raw materials, suppliers, employees, machines, distributors, advertisers, consumers—any of which can cause unexpected problems, at any time.

When paper entrepreneurs look for solutions to America's slowing productivity and its loss of international competitiveness, they come up with paper remedies to stimulate capital investment: accelerated depreciation, tax credits, cuts in capital-gains tax rates, relaxation of antitrust laws. Product entrepreneurs focus on techniques for improving output: better quality controls, improved labor-management relations, more-effective incentives for managers and employees, more-aggressive marketing and sales.

We may need to choose from between both sets of strategies. But in evaluating them, we should consider carefully their likely effects. If we are to increase the economic pie, we will need to redress the balance of entrepreneurial effort. Which strategies will stimulate more paper and which more product?

* * *

The most obvious example of the dominance of paper over product is to be found in the continuing urge to merge and then unmerge. Over the last decade billions of dollars have been spent to acquire existing corporate assets. Only a small percentage of this sum was actually consumed in the takeover process, in the necessary costs of transacting the deals. Most of the money repeatedly circulated among investment bankers, arbitrageurs, portfolio managers, brokers, and other financial intermediaries, as they traded shares of stock in companies about to be taken over, or about to be disassembled, or they made bets on whether *other* financial intermediaries would expect such companies to be taken over or disassembled, and so on, in an almost infinite regression of trades and takeover bets, and bets on takeover bets, and trades on bets on takeover bets.

The language through which all this has been accomplished is colorful and childlike, featuring "golden parachutes," payments of "greenmail," "white knights," and poison pills of all hues. The bright colors mask darker realities, calling into question the purpose of the American corporation in the latter decades of the twentieth century. For at least fifty years it had been assumed that public ownership of stocks assured that America's major corporations were well managed and that public trading in such stocks guaranteed that investors received fair value. No longer.

Golden parachutes are nothing more than generous severance payments, often totaling large multiples of an executive's annual salary and bonus, which are awarded—the parachute automatically opens, as it were—when the takeover becomes successful. The proffered justification is dubious: Such insurance is thought essential to preserve the executive's impartial judgment about hostile takeover bids. Without the parachute, so the argument goes, the executive would be tempted to fight the takeover even if it were in the best interests of the stockholders. The logic suggests that the only way stockholders can trust corporate executives not to feather their nests at the stockholders' expense is to provide them a prefeathered nest at the stockholders' expense.

Greenmail is ransom, paid to those who are trying to take over the company, to get them to stop offering the company's stockholders high prices for their stock. The ransom is paid by corporate executives and directors, who presumably would lose their jobs if the predator succeeded. The ransom money comes ultimately from the same stockholders who are being courted by the predator. The justifications for greenmail are equally suspect: Executives and directors argue that predators don't understand the business and, once in control, would diminish its value. Alternatively, they argue that the stockholders don't know how much their stock is *really* worth, and they are being duped by the low bids of predators. Either way, the logic suggests that the current executives and directors are doing a superb job and only they are fit to judge how superb.

White knights, poison pills, and further exotica also help incumbent management ward off unfriendly predators. By the late 1980s managers who sensed the possibility of a hostile takeover employed a technique known as the "leveraged buyout." The financial complexities were dazzling, but the underlying principle was straightforward. The corporate managers borrow money, often at high interest rates, to buy up their company's stock. These loans are backed by the company's assets. The managers who now own the company thereupon make it more valuable, either by increasing its productivity or by selling off its divisions. They thus make a bundle. With high leverage, small improvements in operating performance can dramatically increase the value of a tiny equity base.

Here again, the proffered justification is oddly inconsistent with our inherited notions about the function and purpose of the corporation. The argument is that once managers' wealth is tied up in the company, they will become more efficient and improve the firm's performance; that is, managers who own their company work harder and better. But this logic suggests that the same managers have been grossly deficient in the past, failing to act in the stockholders' best interests.

All of these asset-rearranging techniques require the ubiquitous skills of accountants and lawyers. A new field of consultancy has grown up in recent years, euphemistically deemed "earnings management," which consists of the strategic use of accounting conventions—redistributing income from good years to bad, recognizing profits in advance of sales, and similar innovations. The leading edge of American jurisprudence is found in such fields as securities and tax law, where piles of arcane pleadings and truckloads of depositions now inundate our courtrooms and preoccupy squadrons of lawyers, overworked clerks, and despairing judges.

*   *   *

Apologists of such antics argue that they are justified by economic fundamentals. (When you hear an argument based on "economic fundamentals," you would be wise to place a hand firmly over your wallet and keep it there until the perpetrator has moved on.) Faced with the alternatives of investing in new plants, equipment, or research (risky propositions the payoffs of which are likely to be in the distant future), or of distributing the earnings to shareholders (who are immediately taxed on such largesse), corporate managers instead see considerable attraction in snapping up profitable, well-run companies with established market positions—even their own. They speak of wondrous gains from "synergy," the dynamic effects of pooled management on what were formerly independent firms, making the whole greater than the sum of the parts. They wax with equal enthusiasm over the gains to be had from disassembling and selling off piecemeal such parts, thus making the sum of the parts greater than the whole. And through it all, they exhibit faith—endless faith, indomitable faith—in the hidden, *potential* value of the assets being purchased, relative to the price they currently fetch on the stock market.

Most of this is nonsense, or worse. The record of the 1970s and 1980s is dismally clear. Acquiring companies rarely have done well for their stockholders. Despite all the claims for synergy, there is little evidence to suggest that mergers have on the average enhanced the basic profitability of merging enterprises. The subsequent rush to dismember suggests, in fact, just the reverse.

A case in point. R. J. Reynolds, the giant tobacco company, merged with Nabisco, the giant food processor, in 1985. The merger was then hailed as a brilliant strategy, through which the tobacco company would diversify into foods. Just three years later, the newly merged company became the object of a mammoth contest between armies of investment bankers pledging billions of dollars for the privilege of breaking it up once again.

Another. In the 1960s Avis Rent-A-Car was a part of ITT's conglomerate empire. Synergies notwithstanding, ITT sold Avis to Norton Simon. Norton Simon, in turn, was taken over by Esmark. One year later, Esmark succumbed to the blandishments of Beatrice Foods. In 1986 Beatrice itself was taken over by a group of investors that included several former Esmark executives. They promptly dismembered Beatrice, selling off Avis to its own managers. A mere fourteen months later, Avis's managers sold the erstwhile company to its employees. Over the years the only predictable aspect of Avis Rent-A-Car has been its penchant for changing hands.

Defenders of such escapades claim nevertheless that asset rearranging is no mere speculative game but a means by which the financial market ensures that resources are available for new enterprise. Close examination belies this comforting view. Wall Street's dynamism has little to do with the financing of new commercial venture. During most of the 1980s, new issues of common stock averaged only about 1 percent of the total stock outstanding. Ninety-nine percent of Wall Street's exuberance pertained to shares of stock already in circulation, which became objects of titillating rumor. Portfolio managers frantically bid against one another to take advantage of small upticks or downblips in this vast casino, betting pension funds or mutual funds in which Americans had placed their savings. In effect, most Americans unknowingly were engaged in continuous bidding against one another (and, if their money was entrusted to more than one fund manager, as was often the case, against themselves). It was exactly as if we had all crowded into Vegas for a long binge.

The American economy as a whole has not benefited demonstrably. Since the mid-1970s, when most of this began, productivity gains have slowed. Average real wages (controlled for inflation) have stagnated. Average stock prices have barely risen. And only the public-relations office of the United States Chamber of Commerce would contend that American firms have stayed competitive with those of Japan, West Germany, South Korea, and other places around the globe, where, incidentally, hostile takeovers and leveraged buyouts rarely if ever occur.

* * *

Then why did it happen? If there is no economic justification, why does it continue?

Let us go back to 1974. That year, the International Nickel Company decided to buy up enough shares in Electric Storage Battery Company to give International Nickel control over the board of directors of Electric Storage and thus allow International Nickel to run the company effectively. The managers of Electric Storage Battery did not want International Nickel to run the company, because they didn't believe that International Nickel could do a very good job of it, and they didn't want to lose their jobs. They thus regarded International Nickel's act as hostile, as it in fact was—the first in a long and not-so-distinguished line of such unfriendly initiatives.

Before International Nickel did this dirty deed, Wall Street had viewed such aggression as unseemly, if not unethical. One didn't just *take over* a company. A company was its managers and employees, its trademark and reputation. These attributes could not be purchased *against its will,* or so it was assumed. Besides, there was no reason for such shenanigans. The American economy, then run along more gentlemanly lines, had grown quite large, and at a rapid clip, without stooping to such behavior.

Then Wall Street's other shoe fell. In 1975 the Securities and Exchange Commission decreed that commissions paid on stock transactions were no longer to be based on fixed rates but were to be negotiable. Henceforth, brokers' commissions were to be subject to the free market, to ungentlemanly *competition*! Within a year revenues in Wall Street brokerage houses plunged $600 million. This was no time for squeamishness. Forget the niceties. The Street had to forage for new sources of earnings, and hostile takeovers looked like just the place to start.

The supply of investment bankers, as it were, created its own demand. There were twelve hostile takeovers of $1 billion or more in the remainder of the 1970s; between 1981 and 1984 there were forty-five. Then came the leveraged buyouts, culminating in the last days of the Reagan Administration, appropriately enough, with the $25 billion buyout of RJR-Nabisco. In 1978 mergers and acquisitions accounted for less than 5 percent of the profits of Wall Street brokerage houses. By 1988 the "M&A business," as it was affectionately called on the Street, accounted for more than 50 percent of their profits.

And profitable it has been. Over the decade the average incomes of paper entrepreneurs grew 21 percent, compared with a 7 percent rise in the incomes of everyone else.

The demand for paper entrepreneurs, in turn, generated more of a supply. Between 1977 and 1987 employment in the securities industry doubled—increasing by an average of 10 percent a year—compared to average yearly job growth of 1.9 percent in the rest of the economy. The stock market crash of October 19, 1987, slowed things down a bit. For several months there were poignant stories of $200,000-a-year investment bankers suddenly forced to sell their East Side duplexes. But within a year the forward thrust of the M&A business had been fully restored. By the end of 1988 one quarter of all new private-sector jobs in New York City, and more than a third of all the new office space in that industrious town, were devoted to paper professionals engaged in rearranging assets.

Deal making has proved particularly lucrative, because every time industrial assets are rearranged, paper professionals earn money. The larger and more complex the escapade, the more money they earn. If they handle the legal complexities, they are paid according to the amount of time they put in. If they manage the financial niceties, they are paid a small percentage of the deal. Thus, there has emerged a strong interest in doing deals.

And here, the most critical point: Paper entrepreneurs not only do the deals but also advise their clients (corporate directors, chief executives, pension-fund managers) about when and whether such deals *should* be done. Like doctors and automobile mechanics, who occupy equally enviable positions both of advising about the need for their services and supplying the needed services, paper entrepreneurs have discovered that there is no necessary limit to the amount of service they can urge on their customers and thereupon provide. Deals thus have become more plentiful, and larger.

More plentiful: In 1960 an average of three million shares of stock were traded daily on the New York Stock Exchange. During the entire year, some 12 percent of the listed shares were exchanged and, on average, held eight years before being resold. During an average day in 1988, by contrast, two hundred million shares exchanged hands. For the year as a whole, 95 percent of the listed shares were traded, and most remained with their owners for only a few hours. The dollar value of trading in stock-index options and futures—bets on how bundles of stocks will move—was five times that of the trades in shares of stock.

Larger: The RJR-Nabisco deal of 1988 generated close to $1 billion in paper-entrepreneurial fees. Like the obscure services listed on hotel bills and automobile stickers, those that comprised this sum were not self-evident: some $200 million for what was called a "buyout fee"; $400 million for "junk-bond underwriting and bank commitment."

"Merger and advisory fees" added another $150 million. The prospective sales of the food and tobacco businesses would earn investment bankers an additional $100 million. The platoon of lawyers and legal advisers reaped at least $50 million.

Deal making also has created abundant work for lawyers, especially when deals turn sour. Texaco and Pennzoil feuded over Getty Oil Company for almost three years. By the end, Texaco had paid over $60 million to lawyers; Pennzoil, $400 million.

Should the economy suddenly fall into recession or worse, no matter. By the close of the 1980s paper entrepreneurs were preparing to make money on the pending collapse. Investment banks had already amassed funds for "deleveraged buyouts," the purpose of which would be to do the reverse of what had been done during boom times—this time, reduce the debt load and increase the shares of stock. It was happily anticipated that the bonds of newly bankrupt companies could be purchased for a small fraction of their face values and new shares issued to the remaining creditors. The newly reorganized company could then be sold for a fat profit.

* * *

Through all this the historic relationship between product and paper has been turned upside down. Investment bankers no longer think of themselves as working *for* the corporations with which they do business. Corporations now exist for the investment bankers, who openly put them into play, buy and sell stock in them, initiate takeovers and leveraged buyouts. Whole departments of investment banks scan corporate America for businesses ripe for the plucking. It is as if doctors and auto mechanics went house to house, instructing the occupants on what they must do to aviod death or breakdown, and then ripping them and their cars apart to make the prescribed repairs.

Investment banks are replacing the publicly held industrial corporations as the largest and most powerful economic institutions in America. In 1987 Drexel Burnham Lambert, Wall Street's fastest-growing company, posted earnings of $500 million, putting it right up there with Xerox, Monsanto, and Kraft. After purchasing RJR-Nabisco, the firm of Kohlberg, Kravis, and Roberts controlled companies with total revenues of $50 billion, transforming KKR into the fifth-largest industrial company in the United States.

Twenty-five years ago the titans of American industry were chief executive officers of major industrial corporations. Today, as in the late nineteenth century, they are investment bankers. Each of the principal partners of KKR earns about $70 million a year. (One wing of the Metropolitan Museum of Art is named after its benefactor, Henry Kravis.) Michael Milken, the "junk bond king," was earning $550 million a year before his inconvenient clash with the federal government. Rarely have so few earned so much for doing so little. Never have so few exercised so much power over how the slices of the American pie are rearranged.

* * *

I do not want to suggest that all efforts directed at rearranging corporate assets are necessarily wasteful. To the extent that they allocate capital more efficiently to where it can be most productive, or smooth out what would otherwise be sudden changes in supply and demand, they make our economy perform better. But given the record of speculation and finagle, one must ask whether these benefits are worth what we're paying for them, in terms of both direct costs and future productivity.

The current obsession with asset rearranging harms productivity in four related ways:

1. Myopia Improvements in productivity often depend on investment strategies geared to the long term. Productivity gains come gradually. Research aimed at developing fundamentally new technologies is apt to go slowly, yielding little or no profit for many years. The development of the internal combustion engine, electronics, xerography, and semiconductors each depended on a quarter century or more of trial and error. Commercialization often requires the development of large production facilities, distribution and sales networks, and quality-control systems. All this demands a willingness to invest now for greater returns in a distant future.

But asset rearrangers typically require that investments pay off in the short term, at the expense of greater yields later on. General Electric's costly acquisition of RCA, for example, resulted in less research for both. In 1987 General Electric cut its research spending by 8 percent. Under new management RCA's famed David Sarnoff Research Center, for decades an incubator of television technology, slashed its staff by 25 percent. Or consider Borg-Warner, another company specializing in high technology. After a fierce takeover battle in the 1980s the firm gutted its research laboratory.

Truncated vision is due, in part, to the necessity of repaying huge loans used to finance such asset rearrangements. Nothing so focuses the corporate mind as threat of bankruptcy. Yet this is not a complete explanation. Asset rearrangers also have changed the pattern of stock ownership in ways that emphasize immediate gain. Not long ago the majority of stock on our exchanges was owned by individuals, many of whom remained with their companies for years. It was not unusual for such an investor to take a mildly proprietary interest in how his or her company was doing, and what it was planning to do. Today, 70 percent of corporate stock is bought and sold by professional portfolio managers of mutual funds, pension funds, and insurance companies. These managers must do more than invest for the future—they must also attract and keep clients. So they are under pressure to demonstrate the short-term earnings that potential clients demand. In the search for quick profits, they move in and out of large positions with little regard for the strengths of the underlying enterprise. Securities analysts and brokers likewise hope to show profits by correctly guessing the short-term fluctuation of price-earning multiples instead of the long-term potential for growth.

On the management side, the motivation is similar. The average corporate chief executive may have an even smaller stake in future growth than the average stockholder. The frenetic movement of corporate assets engenders a similar shifting of managerial talent. Top executives are fired, or they are lured to another newly rearranged corporation. They feel no loyalty to their present company, which, after all, is regarded by its directors and stockholders as little more than a collection of financial assets. Thus, the average term of office for today's chief executive officers is only four years.

Thanks to the high mobility of capital and management, those who have the strongest economic stake in the long-term health of an enterprise are apt to be its lower-level employees, whose mobility is more limited. Employees must live with the consequences of declining long-term productivity within an industry and a region; investors and managers often can bail out long before.

If you look at industries in which our competitive position continues to decline relative to that of Japan, South Korea, and West Germany— semiconductors, consumer electronics, machine tools—you will find the same pattern. The American companies have lower research and development budgets and older plants and equipment. This is the result of the precipitate balance sheet mentality, which translates into low investment in the research that may produce technological breakthroughs a decade from now, or in the modernized and expanded factories that may reduce costs and improve quality beyond the next turn in the business cycle.

2. *Wasted Talent* Asset rearranging also harms productivity by using up the energies of some of our most talented citizens. Paper entrepreneurs now embody the nation's most original economic thinking and energetic wheeling and dealing. The result is a "brain drain" from product to paper.

Today's corporate executives spend an increasing portion of their days fending off takeovers, finding companies to acquire, and responding to depositions in lawsuits instead of worrying about how their products can be made and distributed more efficiently, and with higher quality. More of our top corporate executives are trained in law and finance than in any other field—in contrast to three decades ago when most were trained in marketing, engineering, and sales.

There is a basic distortion here. The investment bankers and lawyers who helped RJR-Nabisco shift out of equities and into debt in November 1988 earned $1 billion for their efforts. This sum was double the amount devoted by the United States, in all of 1988, to the search for a cure for AIDS.

Our best minds (including my former student George) are increasingly drawn to the pie-dividing professions of law, finance, and accounting, and away from pie-enlarging professions like engineering and science. While graduate programs in law and accounting are booming, engineering and science programs are foundering—again in contrast with other industrialized nations.*

But I'm forgetting something, you might say—the recent boom in business-school attendance. Surely that reflects a shift toward hard-headed productive values? The most sought-after jobs among business-school graduates continue to be in finance and consulting, where the specialty is the shuffling of corporate assets. Out of a recent graduating class of 721 at the Harvard Business School, a grand total of 7 reported that they had gone on to start ventures of their own. "Independence" to

---

* In 1987, the majority of students graduating from American universities with doctorates in engineering were foreign nationals, most of whom would return to their home countries. Out of every ten thousand citizens in Japan, for example, only one is a lawyer and three are accountants. In the United States, twenty are lawyers and forty accountants. Out of the same group in Japan, four hundred are engineers and scientists; here, only seventy are engineers or scientists.

today's business graduate means working for the Boston Consulting Group instead of for General Motors. There, as the industrial equivalent of a lawyer, he can plot mergers and tax shelters without ever getting his hands dirty actually turning out a product.

3. Debt The money required to rearrange industrial assets—to mount hostile takeovers, to defend against hostile takeovers, to return a company to private ownership by repurchasing the publicly owned shares of stock—typically is borrowed. As has been suggested, high leverage creates extraordinary opportunities for profit. But it also creates substantial danger, should the economy sputter and interest payments be missed. This was, after all, the lesson we were supposed to have learned in the 1920s, when America last went on a speculative spree: There are few adventures more thrilling than gambling in the stock market with someone else's money, and few more dangerous to the overall economy.

Corporate debt in the 1980s has reached alarming proportions. Twenty-five years before, the average American corporation paid sixteen cents of every dollar of pretax earnings in interest on its debt. In the 1970s, it was thirty-three cents. Since 1980, the average corporation has been paying more than fifty cents of every dollar of pretax earnings in interest. The Brookings Institution, not known for its alarmist rhetoric, undertook to examine the effects on corporate America of a recession similar in severity to that which rocked the nation in 1974 and 1975. The Brookings Institution's computer simulation revealed that with the levels of debt prevailing in the late 1980s, one in ten American firms would succumb to bankruptcy.

Such fragility marks the triumph of private greed over social rationality. It may be in the self-interest of a lone paper entrepreneur to bet a giant American corporation against the odds. If he wins, he earns a fortune. If he loses, most of the loss is borne by those who lent him the money; and he can always make another bet. Eventually, he will win big. But if all paper entrepreneurs behave similarly, the entire economy is bet against the odds. This is precisely what has occurred.

4. Divisiveness An economy based on asset rearranging has a final disadvantage. It tends to invite zero-sum games, in which one group's gain is another's loss. As those engaged in rearranging the slices of the pie become more numerous and far more wealthy than those dedicated to enlarging the pie, social tranquillity is threatened. Trust declines. As trust declines, the pie may actually shrink.

There are signs that this vicious spiral has begun, as each corporate player seeks to preserve its standard of living by expropriating a portion of the declining wealth of another group. Corporate raiders expropriate the wealth of employees by forcing them to agree to lower wages and then passing the savings on to the new stockholders. Corporate borrowers using high-yield ("junk") bonds expropriate the wealth of other bondholders, and of employees, by suddenly subjecting the entire enterprise to greater risk. Executives expropriate the wealth of stockholders by paying greenmail to would-be acquirers or by undertaking a leveraged buyout and then reselling the company at a higher price. Investors expropriate other investors' wealth by trading on inside information.

The catch is that the groups seeking to grab assets from each other are often the very groups whose collaboration is necessary for real growth to occur. The clearest example is found in the field of labor-management relations. Here the portion of the pie shared by workers has been declining as inflation has outstripped wage hikes. Trying to recoup, unions demand catch-up raises, only to find that other unions do the same, which produces another round of inflation. And as corporate managers themselves become more militant in the face of declining profits, they are apt to resort to hostile counterstrategies—hiring consultants to bust the unions, moving factories to other states or countries. The result is a breakdown in cooperation between unions and management that will ensure even less product to spread around in the future. Only when an entire industry faces collapse, as in autos and steel, do labor and management begin to recognize their common interests—and by then it is usually too late to do anything other than seek protection from imports, thus expropriating the wealth of American consumers.

Blue-collar employees are still paying the heaviest price for America's competitive decline. Inner-city blacks and Hispanics have all but vanished from the productive economy. The gap between the nation's wealthiest 10 percent and poorest 10 percent has grown wider than at any time in the last fifty years. These divisions would not loom so large in an economy that was expanding rapidly. But the attempt to restore economic health will only be hobbled to the extent that citizens see themselves primarily as members of different warring factions, each seeking to exploit the other—blue-collar or white-collar, small business or big, investor or consumer, underclass or overclass.

* * *

How are we to break out of the downward spiral of asset rearranging? Defenders of free-market orthodoxy argue that nothing should be done, on the venerable principle that less government intervention is always preferable to more. What they fail to comprehend (or to admit) is that government already motivates paper entrepreneurs through tax and securities laws. The choice is not between more or less intervention but between different laws designed to motivate different behavior. When motivated by a desire to reallocate assets to their most productive uses, paper efforts can be beneficial. The goal is to reduce the incentive to speculate.

We could start with the incentives offered by our tax system. Paper entrepreneurs currently have an incentive to dedicate corporate earnings to speculative ventures—and to borrow to the hilt—because of two core features of our revenue code: First, stockholders pay income taxes on dividends they receive, but any increases in the value of their shares are taxed only when they sell their stock (and then, should George Bush get his way, at a lower tax rate). Second, the corporation can deduct from its taxable income interest payments on corporate debt but cannot deduct dividend payouts.

The bias against dividends would be less worrisome if corporations reinvested their earnings in new productive assets, rather than merely speculated on existing assets (like buying another corporation). Thus, one avenue of reform would eliminate the corporate income tax altogether and treat all corporate earnings as the direct income of stockholders—*unless* the corporation reinvested the earnings in new plants, equipment, research, or development. Corporate income thus "rolled over" into new productive investment would be taxable only to the extent that it caused share prices to rise, and then only as capital gains when the stockholder traded the stock.

A related reform would reduce the lure of debt. No longer would corporate raiders or leverage-buyout entrepreneurs be permitted to deduct interest payments on the large borrowings used to purchase corporate stock. If a prospective takeover or leveraged buyout promises new efficiencies, the deal should be sufficiently attractive to survive without the extra sweetener of a tax incentive. In addition, to deter dangerous levels of indebtedness, the Federal Reserve should establish guidelines discouraging banks from providing easy credit for such deals. (Commercial banks, still coping with precarious Latin American debtors, have been underwriting more than half of leveraged buyouts.)

A third reform would seek more *patient* capital. Stockholders who took a longer view would be rewarded; speculators, penalized. Thus, the capital-gains tax rate they paid on selling their stock would depend on how long they retained it. On assets held for a year or less, the capital-gains tax rate would be high (50 percent); on assets held for five years or more, the rate would be very low (10 percent). This scheme would result in no overall diminution of tax revenues, just a more beneficent allocation of incentives.

A fourth possibility is a national corporate stock sales tax. Pursuant to it, every sale of stock would be subjected to a small (one half of 1 percent) surcharge. This tax would be far more progressive than most sales taxes (the poor tend to gamble on things other than shares of stock). And it would actually raise $10 billion annually for the Treasury, as it reduced the speculative ardor of paper entrepreneurs.

Another set of changes would focus on the ownership of productive assets. Schemes of employee ownership and participation not only appear to improve productivity over the short term but may also improve prospects for long-run growth, since employees typically have a higher stake in the continuing viability of an enterprise than do either managers or investors. (Avis Rent-A-Car, now employee owned after fifteen years as a pawn of paper entrepreneurs, is showing record profits and productivity gains.) So why not employee-led leveraged buyouts? Employment stock option plans already offer generous tax incentives for employee ownership; these incentives might be rendered even more generous on condition that employees actually vote their own shares of stock rather than entrust them to management, as is now often the case.

Finally, the nation's securities laws would be amended to bar the more egregious forms of color-coded paper shuffling—golden parachutes and greenmail. Absent these innovations, speculation would be less attractive to all concerned.

* * *

These recommendations would help redress the balance between paper and product, but they are no cure for our nation's basic vertigo. The imbalance runs deep. A decade or more of legitimized greed has taken its toll on our collective capacity to produce high-quality goods and services. The assumption that we need only to alter tax and securities laws may be itself evidence of our paper habit. Perhaps our greatest challenge in the future is to redress the balance of paper and product within ourselves.

3

THE ANTHROPOMORPHIZATION OF WALL STREET

(Or Why the Market Crashed on October 19, 1987, and Will Do So Again)

ANTHROPOLOGISTS HAVE LONG KNOWN OF THE TENDENCY FOR PRIMI-
tive civilizations to ascribe human attributes to animals, plants, and
inanimate objects. Here in late-twentieth-century America we have gone
a step further, attributing a range of emotions to a street. In fact, we
worry incessantly about how the street is feeling. Is it confident? Hope-
ful? Despairing? Fearful? Much turns on its mood. Of late, government
policy is hostage to the street's spirits.

The street in question is, of course, Wall Street. The policy in question is no less than the budget of the United States. If Wall Street likes a
proposed budget, interest rates will fall, or so it is assumed. If interest
rates fall, the U.S. government can borrow funds more cheaply to cover
the budget deficit. Thus, the budget can be balanced sooner, and with
less pain all around. The arithmetic underlying George Bush's artful
"flexible freeze," his campaign promise to balance the budget in four
years, relies on Wall Street's cooperation in reducing interest rates by at
least two percentage points. On the other hand, if Wall Street dislikes a
proposed budget, we have hell to pay.

The anthropomorphization of Wall Street is another product of the
casual fiscal policies of the Reagan Administration. After eight years of

ever deeper indebtedness, the Street's mood swings are now enough to send our entire federal government into paroxysms of self-doubt and sycophancy. "What can we do to regain the Street's confidence?" is the question heard most often in gilded offices on the Potomac. "What does the Street *want*?"

Washington's concern for Wall Street's happiness has had one particularly unfortunate consequence. It has rendered it awkward for policy makers to propose any substantial reforms in the way Wall Street conducts its business. Any reform that might diminish the flow of profits to the Street would, quite obviously, risk severe Street demoralization. A foul mood could settle in and, with it, a decline in stock values, higher interest rates, and other awful consequences.

The Crash of 1987 provided an example of the workings of this inhibitory mechanism. After October 19, when the Dow Jones Industrial Average plummeted more than five hundred points, Congress and the White House immediately sought to understand Wall Street's view of why the crash had occurred and what needed to be done to "restore confidence." Wall Street, not surprisingly, blamed it all on Washington: on the budget deficit, on protectionist trade legislation pending before Congress, and even more importantly, on a House Ways and Means Committee proposal to remove tax deductions for interest paid on loans used to take over a company. Investment bankers demanded an end to such pernicious policies. They filled the airwaves and op-ed pages with prescriptions for how Washington should mend its ways. Typical was the statement of Donald Drapkin, vice-chairman of Revlon, Inc., and a key figure in his company's effort to take over Gillette: "If you couldn't deduct interest incurred in an acquisition, it would be a disaster for the stock market and for American companies."

Washington, in its own plodding way, tried to oblige. The President and congressional leaders sought further cuts in the federal budget. The trade bill was rendered less objectionable to free traders. And—most telling—the Ways and Means Committee tax proposal was suddenly dropped. Chairman Dan Rostenkowski sought, as he put it, to "calm some of the apprehensions of a very nervous Wall Street."

Washington's solicitude was especially ironic in light of Wall Street's central role in the debacle. That stock prices were finally back to a realistic level after more than a year of frenzied speculation should have given Washington cause for relief, as if a fevered child had awakened from its hallucinations. That the Street was finally professing concern about the health of the American economy, after a decade of reckless disregard, should have provided further assurance.

The economic "crisis" that the Street discovered on that particular October day was no different from the slowly gathering crisis that existed before October 19. Some Americans felt poorer than they had before, no doubt, but their apparent prosperity in the halcyon days of the bull market was largely illusory—a paper prosperity. The real economy had been slowly unraveling for years while America busily consumed more than it produced. In 1986 the nation had generated some $800 billion more in goods and services than it had in the recession year of 1982, but it spent about $900 billion more—Mr. Micawber's recipe for eventual misery.

America had been able to ignore its profligacy only because foreigners were more than happy to lend us money, buy our corporations, and purchase our real estate. By the time of the crash, we were $350 billion in the hole, one third of downtown Los Angeles (among other U.S. cities) was in foreign hands, and our foreign creditors were growing distinctly nervous about our ability to repay our debts.

The anomaly through it all was the Wall Street bull market, which, beginning in 1983, surged upward in seeming disregard of the underlying decline. One big reason: Stock prices were responding not to the real economy but to takeovers, and/or threats of takeovers, which prompted corporations to do whatever was necessary to raise their share prices in the short term. Often this meant purchasing their own shares and thus going deeply into debt, and jettisoning long-term projects. New corporate debt ballooned by over $700 billion between 1983 and 1987, about the same amount by which share prices tumbled on that fateful day in October. The new debt made corporate America much more vulnerable to economic downturns. Interest payments soaked up an ever larger proportion of corporate earnings.

Wall Street's reverie could not go on forever, and it did not. The balloon was sure to burst eventually. It did.

In light of this history, there is something vaguely unseemly about the demands the Street still makes on Washington to clean up its act. Of course, the budget deficit needs to be tamed. But the deeper problem is not the budget deficit per se; it is the nation's chronic unwillingness to reduce total consumption and increase total investment—both public and private. In fact, hostile takeovers are themselves responsible for part of the debt problem. Likewise, America's drift toward protectionism is a symptom of a deeper economic malaise: the scarcity of new, well-paying jobs for industrial workers whose present jobs are threatened by cheap foreign goods and the unwillingness of American corporations—obsessively concerned with their immediate bottom lines—to invest for a future that would create such jobs.

Perhaps the most brazen demand is that Washington take no action to stem takeovers. In fact, the Street's assertion that the House Ways and Means Committee proposal was somehow responsible for the crash confirmed what many had suspected all along—that the takeover threats that had pushed share prices ever higher were largely motivated by the hidden tax subsidy to begin with. When it looked as if the subsidy was about to be taken away, stocks tumbled. The great takeover binge hadn't rested on the "economic fundamentals" at all, as Wall Street had repeatedly argued. It had been part of the tax game.

* * *

In the months following the crash, there was some tentative discussion about reforming Wall Street. President Reagan appointed a commission, headed by Nicholas Brady, himself a Wall Street financier (and future Treasury secretary), to examine the matter. The commission duly reported, suggesting a number of sensible and incremental legal and regulatory changes to avoid a subsequent crash. But none of the changes was implemented. A number of investment bankers, and not a few legislators, opined that such changes might "unsettle" the Street.

In the year following, takeovers and leveraged buyouts reached levels never before achieved. Once it was clear that nothing would change, nor that Mr. Rostenkowski would advance his proposal, the game was on again, with renewed relish. Wall Street's balloon began to refill and will continue to do so, until the next big pop.

4

THE
CONVENIENCE OF BANKING

RECENTLY, MY WIFE AND I TRIED TO GET A BANK LOAN. THE SUM WE sought was somewhat large compared to the salaries we earn but still safely within five figures. We are a good credit risk; we have always paid our bills on time; we live modestly.

I shared intimate details of our family finances with the bank. The lending officer had me fill out a long questionnaire. I had to supply him with three character references and find creditors who could vouch for my solvency and reliability. I even located a former landlord, who dimly remembered that I had once paid him rent on time. My file was then shifted to the manager of the bank's "disbursement services division," who subjected me to more detailed questioning and carefully scrutinized the project in which I was intending to invest. There followed another round of forms. An assistant treasurer of the bank's documentary control unit had a problem with one of the documents I supplied, which my lawyer solved. Another account officer wanted one of the forms notarized. A deputy credit supervising officer wanted more documentation. Then, after a month of waiting, I called the vice president for credit, who said that they were still reviewing my loan application but that no decision had been reached. He suggested I come in and fill out some more forms. Finally, after another month's wait, we got the loan.

I am a small customer. During the past decade or so, American banks have also lent several hundred billion dollars to the likes of Poland, Mexico, Brazil, Texas real-estate developers, Oklahoma energy moguls, takeover entrepreneurs, and leveraged-buyout moguls. Unlike my loan, however, many of *these* loans will never be repaid. And in contrast to the picayune and prolonged review of my little loan application, decisions to lend vast sums to such risky borrowers were made quickly, without extensive information or deliberation. There is, to put it mildly, a discrepancy here.

* * *

The American banking system is fundamentally oblivious to large risk. Small risks (that someone like myself might default on a relatively small loan) are well understood; they happen often enough that their probabilities can be measured, and standard precautions can be taken in advance. More to the point, loan officers know that their superiors also know these probabilities, so that any deviation from prudent lending practice is readily apparent. But a bank has little or no institutional memory of major defaults on a grand scale. These sorts of probabilities cannot be reduced to standard operating practice. The longer the interval since the last such disaster, the more likely it is that people will behave as if it could never happen again. Under these circumstances loan officers know only one thing: If they don't approve the giant loan, some other bank will. Prudence will be rewarded by conspicuous loss of business.

Moreover, loan officers are evaluated over relatively short time periods. Their performances are rated against quarterly earnings targets and loan quotas. Small run-of-the-mill borrowers who may default quickly thus present few attractions. Large bonuses come with the largest of borrowers whose huge defaults are likely to be years away, long after the loan officer has moved on to another job.

There is, in addition, the herding instinct that obtains whenever large sums of money are involved. As groups of American banks advanced credit to Poland or Mexico, to the purchasers of oil-drilling equipment or commercial real estate, or to the promoters of leveraged buyouts and other schemes, loan officers found safety in numbers. The mounting troubles of the Bank of the Commonwealth, First Pennsylvania, Continental Illinois, and countless savings and loans confirmed this pattern. Regardless of how risky the loans, the fact that other major banks committed their funds to the same class of borrowers lent credibility to the effort. Bank officials could claim that their decisions reflected the best wisdom at the time. Others, after all, had made the same mistake.

Then there is the omnipresent assumption that larger borrowers cannot default. They are thought to be too big and too established to do what small borrowers do all the time. Walter Wriston, former chairman of Citibank, lent billions to Latin American nations during the 1970s because, he confidently asserted at the time, "countries do not fail to exist." Yet ironically it is precisely because of their sovereign status that governments cannot always be relied on to exercise self-restraint in their borrowing.

Perhaps the most important factor explaining American banks' willingness to bear enormous risk is their justifiable confidence that the U.S. government will help them out in a pinch. This is particularly true of America's largest banks, which have taken on proportionately the largest risks. The fate of a large bank is too intertwined with the fates of numerous other, smaller lending institutions; its depositors' confidence is too important to the public's confidence in the entire banking system. The directors of the Federal Deposit Insurance Corporation decided to rescue the First Pennsylvania Bank of Philadelphia in 1980 because they feared that its collapse would also bring down hundreds of smaller banks that had its uninsured funds on deposit. Four years later, they decided that the pending collapse of Continental Illinois might lead to a national banking panic, since only 10 percent of its $39 billion in deposits was insured.

Having a relatively small percentage of insured deposits is not unusual for major American banks, since they pay no insurance premiums on deposits they accept from abroad—deposits that compose a significant portion of their overall liabilities. In effect, the Federal Deposit Insurance Corporation is prepared to rescue any failing multinational institution that cannot be sold to either a foreign or domestic suitor. With such a generous rule of thumb, it is small wonder that large American banks have been emboldened to risk their shareholders' money on questionable ventures. The risk is far less than it would otherwise seem.

* * *

International banking is never simply a commercial activity. American foreign policy is implicated whenever American banks do a sizable amount of business with other sovereign governments.

A telling example is the Polish debt crisis. During the era of détente, American banks were willing to lend large sums to the Soviet Union and its Eastern European allies, whose hard-currency indebtedness climbed from $7 billion in 1970 to nearly $66 billion by the end of the decade—significantly faster than these economies were growing. By 1980 Poland, in particular, was on the brink of defaulting on $26 billion of outstanding debt. With Poland's suppression of the Solidarity movement in 1981, the Reagan Administration was placed in a difficult bind. Efforts to pressure the Polish authorities into reversing their harsh policies were compromised by worries over the Poles' indebtedness to American banks. In the end the banks won. The Administration chose to rescue Poland and the banks—to the tune of $344 million in 1982 alone—rather than countenance a formal default.

Bank rescues have also been motivated by America's security interests in debtor countries. For example, Turkey's brush with financial collapse in 1979 summoned pledges of nearly $1 billion from the United States and other Western allies mindful of Turkey's strategic importance to NATO. Turkey was not the only beneficiary of this rescue, notably; the American banks, to which Turkey owed large sums, simultaneously profited.

The story has been similar in Latin America. U.S. banks, awash with Arab oil money throughout most of the 1970s, needed customers; oil-importing nations, particularly in Latin America, needed loans. Just as détente had signaled to the banks that large sums could be lent with impunity to the Soviet bloc, so too did the U.S. government's tacit acknowledgment of the importance of recycling petrodollars signal to them that there was relatively little risk involved in lending even larger sums to Latin American countries. By 1982 Argentina, Brazil, and Mexico together owed America's nine largest banks more than 140 percent of the banks' total capital. The process of rescheduling the debts and interest arrears gradually came to resemble default in all but name: It was default by attrition. By 1984 some $35 billion was flowing from the Latin American debtors to U.S. banks—a sum equal to 10 percent of these nations' aggregate export revenues and more than twice their hard-won trade surpluses.

At first the Reagan Administration left it to the International Monetary Fund (IMF) and the banks to work out austerity plans for the debtor nations. ("Austerity" was a nice way of saying lower living standards.) The plans were intended to clamp down on these countries' consumption and investment, to free resources for debt service. But the timing was unfortunate. Much of Latin America was just beginning to experiment with democracy. Beginning in 1980, generals had allowed power to pass to elected civilian presidents in several debtor nations. These newborn democracies were delicate things. Antidemocratic forces were waiting in the wings (the military in the right wing, the communists in the left) to pick up the pieces should democracy fail. High unemployment and collapsing living standards were not the most favorable accompaniments to democratic experimentation.

Latin American indebtedness has posed problems for the United States in other ways. As these southern economies faltered, a flood of illicit and dangerous drugs was released into the United States. By 1985 the sale of cocaine represented some 10 percent of Bolivia's gross national product and twice its legal export earnings. When ambitious Latin Americans were not turning to drug production, they were trying to find work in the United States. Illegal aliens constituted another flood, the intensity of which has been directly proportional to economic hardship at home.

In the fall of 1983 the United States contributed to a substantial increase in IMF funding in order to ease the debt crisis. In October 1985 Treasury Secretary James Baker formally proposed a program for sustained growth through which the World Bank (funded largely by the United States), regional development banks (also with U.S. funds), and U.S. banks would come up with some $29 billion over three years to help fifteen hard-pressed debtor nations. But by 1988 Latin American debtors were in even worse shape than before. U.S. banks hadn't fulfilled their part of the deal. Yet U.S. policy still placed the banks' interests over those of hemispheric peace and prosperity.

*   *   *

The Latin American debt crisis is not an entirely new phenomenon. U.S. bankers who claim they could not have foreseen the problems when they made the loans had only to examine history. In the late 1880s London's Baring Brothers Bank extended substantial loans to Argentina. When Argentina's pending default threatened to bring down the bank and undermine confidence in the entire British banking system, a rescue was organized by the Bank of England and the British Treasury, including a special commission to oversee a restructuring of the Argentina debt.

Government involvement was not always so mild. When Venezuela repudiated its debts in 1902, the Royal Navy blockaded Venezuela's harbors (giving rise to the term "gunboat diplomacy"). Concerned about the increased meddling of European powers in the hemisphere, Theodore Roosevelt pledged that the United States would henceforth assume responsibility for ensuring that the Latin American states fulfilled their financial obligations—thus committing the United States to subsequent interventions in the Dominican Republic, Haiti, Honduras, and Nicaragua, among others. The U.S. government became, in effect, a collection agency for the world's major banks. In the 1930s Britain's Royal Institute of International Affairs noted that "the history of investment in South America throughout the last century has been one of confidence followed by disillusionment, of borrowing cycles followed by widespread defaults."

*　　*　　*

What should be done to avoid more of the same in the future? If our biggest banks are prone to make large and dubious loans because of certain bureaucratic and political incentives built into the practice of large-scale banking, then no number of bank examinations or meetings between bank officers and government officials is likely to make much of a difference.

Most bank rescues are invisible. Decisions are highly technical, rendered by bureaucrats in the Federal Deposit Insurance Corporation, the Federal Savings and Loan Insurance Corporation, or the IMF and the World Bank. The avowed purpose is never to rescue a bank but to ensure the credibility of the banking system, protect unwary depositors, guard America's security interests, or stabilize debtor nations and improve the world economy. We seem to take for granted that achievement of these proximate goals necessarily entails saving a big bank—and the bank's shareholders—along the way. But so long as this assumption remains unquestioned, the internal incentives operating on bank officers will continue to lead them toward making big, risky loans. Why not, when the government will pick up the pieces?

A more lasting solution would seek to detach these other goals from saving the banks' shareholders. Many of our largest banks are still carrying mammoth loans on their balance sheets at face value, even though a significant portion of these loans are effectively in default. No one is prepared to blow the whistle and force the banks to write down the loans. Why not? Because this would impose enormous losses on the banks. Many would not have sufficient capital to meet the minimums required by law. It seems far safer to wait it out, to accept the charade of rescheduling the loans, all the while hoping that a government rescue will eventually put matters right.

But how disastrous would it really be to require that all loans be carried on the banks' books at market value? At worst, the banks would have to cut their dividends to build their capital back up to where it should be. Share prices would drop as a result. Perhaps shareholders would demand more prudence in the future; they might even vote out the old management, or tender their shares to somebody capable of doing a better job. Operating incentives would shift toward more care in lending large sums of money. As an added advantage, banks would be encouraged to sell the loans on the open market at a price reflecting their true, lower values. (That is something the banks dare not do now, for fear that the loans would then have to be entered on their books at the lower sale price.) This in turn would create a secondary market in such loans, allowing purchasers of the loans to swap them for equity in troubled debtor companies or in healthy companies within troubled debtor nations. Thus, the debts would be rescheduled in a way that would give debtors the freedom and incentive to restructure themselves. At the same time, bank shareholders would be deprived of their windfall.

American capitalism is premised on the comforting notion that public and private sectors are, and forever will remain, safely distinct. This prevailing view leads us to all sorts of policy prescriptions for tidying up the less desirable side effects of business activity. Occasionally, however, the veil is lifted and we are allowed to gaze in wonderment at a private sector whose largest institutions are guaranteed peace, safety, and profits by a public sector ever anxious to please them.

There are few callings more comfortable than commercial banking. Thus it has been for over a century, as the modern nation-state has quietly bailed out its bankers. But this tradition may be on the wane. After the binge of Third World lending in the 1970s, the thrift crisis of the 1980s, and what is likely to be the leveraged-buyout crisis of the 1990s, taxpayers may start resenting the fact that their tax dollars are used to cover the mistakes of these determinedly risky individuals.

5

THE
ORIGINS OF RED TAPE

ASK ANY BUSINESS EXECUTIVE ABOUT GOVERNMENT REGULATIONS, AND he will tell you a horror story of bureaucratic excess. But the executive will not, most likely, object to the *goal* of regulation. Most executives agree that the public deserves protection from toxic wastes, nuclear accidents, air and water pollutants, unsafe products, fraudulent claims, and monopoly. Even in such eras as the present, when business is ascendant and government suspect, the public supports these broad objectives. The complaints of American business center not on the purposes of regulation but on the ways they are designed and implemented: Statutes are overly complicated, and the rules devised to fulfill them are excruciatingly detailed, comprising voluminous rulings and interpretations, interpretations of interpretations, opinions and dissenting opinions of interpretations.

Even the simplest public goal spawns an imposing herd of rules requiring exhaustive filings, reports, nit-picking inspections, and picayune compliance with every jot and tittle of the law. And they are subject to constant alteration, elaboration, and ever-more-detailed explication. Under the spell of congressional committees, regulatory-agency officials, hearing examiners, administrative-law judges, appellate judges, and scores of zealous government lawyers, inspectors, and bureaucrats, regulations grow more complicated by the hour. They multiply in the *Federal Register*; they engorge the *Code of Federal Regulations*; they inundate companies with their petty requirements.

Tales of bureaucratic atrocities abound. The chairman of one large pharmaceutical firm complains that his company spends more hours filling out government forms and reports than it does on research for cancer and heart disease combined. Others tell of trivial, often silly requirements, such as giving loan applicants pages of detailed information that nobody ever reads or putting a toilet within one hundred yards of each employee. The laws are impenetrable: The Employee Retirement Income Security Act, which regulates private pension plans, runs to more than two hundred pages. It has been estimated that federal agencies require American business to fill out forty-four hundred different forms each year, together consuming 143 million hours of executive and clerical time, and costing $25 billion.

Nit-picking regulation has been blamed for slowing America's productivity and impairing the nation's competitiveness. But other advanced industrial nations require that their companies achieve similar regulatory goals. Environmental, health, and safety requirements in Japan and most of Western Europe are no less stringent than in the United States. There is one significant difference, however. Although the results of regulation are about the same among all advanced nations, the *means* of regulating are quite distinct. In other nations regulations are far less detailed than they are in the United States. They involve fewer rules and interpretations, impose less paperwork, entail only informal inspections and reports, and generate significantly lower compliance costs. If American business is conspicuously burdened by government regulation, it is not due to the ends that regulation seeks but to the means employed. Among advanced industrial nations, the regulation of American business is uniquely picayune.

* * *

Many who speak from or for American business attribute the trouble to the attitudes and values of the people who inhabit government regulatory agencies: These people want to be nettlesome. They compose a "new class" of college-educated social planners and public-policy professionals who disdain economic growth and abhor private enterprise. According to Irving Kristol, a principal exponent of such views, regulators "find it convenient to believe the worst about business because they have certain adverse intentions toward business to begin with." They seek "the power to shape our civilization—a power which, in the capitalist system, is supposed to reside in the free market." Their ambition is "to see much of this power redistributed to government, where *they* will then have a say in how it is exercised."

Kristol and his fellow travelers believe that denizens of the new class populate the staffs of regulatory agencies, surviving administration after administration. These individuals relish any chance to harass American business with endless, trivial commands, to clog the channels of commerce with their piddling requirements and endless forms. They take delight in transforming commonsensical regulatory goals into reams of nettlesome detail. According to Kristol and others who share his views, the new class is waging a war of attrition against capitalism. Paul H. Weaver, who wrote an article for *The Public Interest* entitled "Regulation, Social Policy, and Class Conflict," put it this way:

> The New Regulation [to protect the environment, safety, and health] is the social policy of the new class. . . . They have merely transferred power from those who produce material goods to those who produce ideological ones—to the intellectuals, policy professionals, journalists, and "reformers," who are arguably much less representative of the American people as a whole than those whose influence has been curtailed. . . . With each passing year it becomes clearer that the real animus of the new class is not so much against business or technology as against the liberal values served by corporate capitalism and the benefits these institutions provide to the broad mass of the American people.

This conspiracy has proved to be an oddly comforting phantom for American business. First, it provides a ready explanation for why business has felt so besieged. It is not any serious failing or erosion of legitimacy on the part of industry but rather the machinations of a group bent on undermining free enterprise. It is an enemy within that seeks to substitute centralized planning for free markets. Second, the story suggests a plan of action. All we need do is to expel from government these ideological traitors and put in their place teams of levelheaded and unbiased civil servants.

Finally, the story promises a happy ending. Once the saboteurs have been ejected, the present regulatory miasma will be transformed into simple, sensible rules. The public will continue to be protected—as it should be—from the irresponsible acts of a few misguided managers. The rest of American business will be freed of the nit-picking, the technicalities, and the meticulous excesses of the present system.

* * *

Unfortunately for those who find the story satisfying, it wilts in the face of the facts. To begin with, the "new class" of interventionist zealots who are supposedly responsible for the picayune character of so much modern regulation have been far harder to track down than expected. Both the Carter and Reagan Administrations were committed to reducing the burden of government regulation. Indeed, the latter installed its own counterzealots at the controlling levels of government agencies to track down the guilty parties. The Reagan Administration did succeed in abandoning some regulatory efforts. None other than George Bush himself was in charge of the effort. But—and here is the important point —it did nothing to change the *way* in which the remaining regulations were administered. The Administration's concerted efforts notwithstanding, the *Code of Federal Regulations* continued to swell with detail, the *Federal Register* bulged with new interpretations and elaborations, and American business continued to writhe under the burden of pettifogging directives from Washington.

The underlying problem had nothing to do with nefarious forces hidden within regulatory agencies; it was inherent in the American regulatory process itself. A probusiness administration might succeed in rescinding particular regulations but not in reducing the amount of niggling minutiae surrounding any regulatory goal.

In addition, it turns out that the vast majority of regulatory-agency lawyers and middle-level managers aspire not to undermine American capitalism but to live off it. After gaining experience in government, they move on to the private sector. They gain jobs in law firms, representing companies before regulatory agencies. They join consulting firms, accounting firms, research institutes, and public-relations firms. They move into government-affairs offices of large corporations and into trade associations. Some have even been known to join university faculties, from which they sell extracurricular insights to corporations. Their experience in government makes them valuable to the private sector, and they are not reluctant to trade on that value.

If America's regulatory miasma is not due to a covert war against capitalism waged within government agencies, then what is the real cause?

* * *

Unlike such capital cities as London, Paris, and Tokyo, which serve as national centers of trade, finance, education, and the arts, Washington, D.C., has only the federal government to give it prominence. Major business, intellectual, and creative enterprises are, for the most part, located elsewhere. Thus, although in other capitals government leaders meet frequently and informally with the leaders of other influential communities, no such easy communication takes place in Washington. (We owe this unique allocation of urban responsibility to Alexander Hamilton, who agreed to a plan to move the nation's capital city from New York to a swamp on the banks of the Potomac River in exchange for Thomas Jefferson's agreement that the federal government would absorb the Revolutionary War debt.) This fact, especially when coupled with the relatively short tenure of most U.S. regulatory officials, prevents federal policy makers and business executives from enjoying the same casual give-and-take, comfortable candor, and long-term familiarity that often characterize business–government relationships elsewhere.

Whatever dangers such frequent and informal contact may pose to the democratic control of the policy-making process, it does at least facilitate efficient communication between public and private sectors. Advanced industrial societies—with their complex technologies, intricate trading and financial arrangements, and labyrinthine government bureaucracies—require extensive internal coordination if they are to run smoothly, and such coordination requires, in turn, efficient communication. In Washington communication has come to depend on specialized professionals who act as intermediaries between government policy makers and business executives.

Who are these intermediaries? They are the approximately twelve thousand Washington-based lawyers who represent business before regulatory agencies and the federal courts, the nine thousand lobbyists who represent business before Congress, the forty-two thousand trade-association personnel who keep close watch on pending regulations and legislation, the eight thousand public-relations specialists who advise business executives about regulatory issues, the twelve hundred specialized journalists who report to particular industries on government developments that might affect them, the thirteen hundred public-affairs consultants who help business organize to deal with regulation, and the thirty-five hundred business-affairs consultants who provide regulatory officials with specialized information about particular industries.

Together with the 15,500 lawyers, lobbyists, and public-relations specialists within regulatory agencies and large corporations, these intermediaries comprise a virtual industry of their own.

Members of the industry usually work in Washington for several years in a variety of related positions—first, say, on a congressional staff, then on a regulatory-agency staff or a trade association, then in a Washington law firm or public-relations firm, then perhaps again in a senior congressional agency position, and then in a senior trade-association position. They circulate freely among the points of the Washington compass and change jobs frequently.

Their skills are for the most part strategic, not substantive. They know how to "position" a client to reduce unfavorable exposure, minimize risk, gain a positive image, fend off threats to its autonomy, enlarge its domain, reduce its vulnerability, or generally thwart its rivals. And though they may on occasion consult with economists or scientists, they are not so much interested in the truth or falsity of what these specialists have to say as in the tactical value of what they say—the extent to which it can bolster a client's argument or discredit the argument of a specialist on the other side.

Tension between business and government is necessary if intermediaries are to sustain or enlarge their economic base. This is not to suggest that intermediaries seek to foment business–government confrontation or that they do not often provide valuable help and information. Confrontation is, however, an unstated principle of their calling. It is their professional frame of reference, and it is within this frame that they measure their own success.

Several principles, therefore, can be observed to guide their actions:

1. SEEK TO ACHIEVE CLEAR CONTROVERSIES IN WHICH A CLIENT'S POSITION CAN BE SHARPLY DIFFERENTIATED FROM THAT OF ITS REGULATORY OPPONENT.

A sharply drawn regulatory dispute can be used to justify the services provided a client and perhaps even convince the client that still more resources are needed to carry on the battle. It can also be used to demonstrate to other potential clients the intermediary's virtuosity in mounting an aggressive campaign of legal maneuver, media management, and political pressure tactics. A dispute provides a standard by which an intermediary's services can be evaluated: A victory in the dispute strengthens the intermediary's reputation and thus provides a vehicle for self-promotion in the future.

This principle manifests itself in several ways. First, it encourages intermediaries to take extreme positions that tend to exaggerate the differences between the two sides. More important, it actively discourages intermediaries from heading off regulatory disputes—by engaging in informal problem solving at an early point, by seeking voluntary solutions that would prevent the necessity for regulation, by taking steps to avoid problems before they occur, or by seeking out areas of agreement on which compromise might be based.

Not long ago the National Highway Transportation Safety Administration (NHTSA) conducted tests of the crashworthiness of various automobiles. Afterwards, in an effort to obtain voluntary agreement about how the models could be made safer, NHTSA officials sought meetings with the manufacturers of cars, both domestic and foreign, that had failed the tests.

The U.S. manufacturers, represented at the meetings by their lawyers and government-relations staffs, refused to discuss possible improvements. They argued instead that the tests were flawed. The Japanese manufacturers, represented at the meetings by the engineers who had designed the cars in question, wanted to know precisely why their cars had failed. They brainstormed with NHTSA staff about the best means of increasing safety and, largely on the basis of those discussions, eventually devised low-cost improvements that enabled their automobiles to pass the test.

Several years ago, while serving as a Washington bureaucrat, I invited several corporate executives to a meeting to discuss a consumer problem that had arisen within their industry. The Federal Trade Commission (FTC) had been inundated with complaints for months, and it seemed clear that if the complaints were well founded, some sort of regulatory action would be necessary unless the industry took steps to mend its ways.

Each of the executives agreed to the meeting. Some expressed surprise and even gratitude that the agency was willing to talk informally about the problem and seek voluntary solutions to it before taking formal action. Within ten days of my invitation, however, each of the executives called back with a similar message: Each had been advised against attending such a meeting by legal counsel, a government-affairs vice president, or a trade-association representative.

A few of the executives were particularly candid about the advice they had received. It was not in their interest, so they were told, to "stick their necks out" by attending such a meeting at this early stage. The visibility could be dangerous. Moreover, it would, by lending credence to the agency's concerns, almost certainly encourage the agency to take some sort of regulatory action. Far better to wait until the issue became crystallized—that is, until they could get a clearer idea of what the agency was planning to do and how seriously the agency was taking the problem. I received a similar message from the FTC staff members responsible for regulating the industry. They were also opposed to such a meeting because, they argued, it might "tip our hand." The industry might learn what information we at the agency had about the problem, how far we were prepared to go in fighting it, and what strategies we might use in attempting to regulate against it. It would be preferable, they warned, to wait until we had more information about the problem —that is, until we had a much better idea of what we wanted from the industry—and until we could readily threaten the industry with a specific set of regulatory initiatives.

Both sets of advice came from people who believed they were acting in the best interests of their clients. Given the frame of reference in which these intermediaries work, their advice was probably correct. Regulatory battle could not be waged successfully if both sides talked candidly at an early stage about how to remedy the problem at issue. But their frame of reference was, of course, inappropriate. The proper goal was not to wage battle successfully but to remedy the problem quickly and efficiently.

2. WHEN INFORMING A CLIENT ABOUT ITS REGULATORY OPPONENT, EXAGGERATE THE DANGERS THAT THE OPPONENT'S ACTIVITIES AND DESIGNS IMPLY.

Providing the worst possible interpretation of an opponent's activities and motives often alarms a client and stiffens its resolve to fight. Such an extreme characterization may also elicit additional resources from the client and may even enable the intermediary to convince several other clients to join in the fray.

This principle is most evident in trade-association newsletters, bulletins, and conferences, which regularly excoriate regulatory agencies and caricature their activities.

Once, while still in Washington, I met with the editor of a trade-association newsletter who wanted a "background briefing" about the sorts of initiatives the FTC might undertake in the next few years. After explaining to him that my list of possibilities was extremely tentative (the five commissioners had not as yet approved any of them and comparatively few of them had any likelihood of reaching fruition), I let loose.

Three weeks later I was aghast, to put it mildly, to see the entire list printed in the trade-association newsletter under the headline FTC MAPS FUTURE POLICY. The article described the list as "what we can expect from FTC activists" and cautioned association members about the FTC's "ambitious designs" on their industry. The article ended with an ominous warning that "unless we take effective action now, these initiatives will be undertaken within the next two years."

Dire warnings are also sounded by legal counsel. Lawyers are, after all, trained to foresee the worst possible consequences stemming from any given situation and to prepare a client for them. This skill, when finely honed, necessitates not only a skeptical and somewhat pessimistic attitude toward all undertakings but also a degree of suspicion (occasionally bordering on paranoia) concerning the plans and motives of any potential opponents.

This kind of advice can be of enormous value, but it can also become dysfunctional when business executives and regulatory officials lose sight of the fact that legal counsel naturally conjures up worst-case scenarios. Their job is primarily to avoid such eventualities rather than to accomplish some positive goal.

Warnings of possible legal problems can intimidate all but the most fearless executive. Too often, the worst possible implications to be drawn from an opponent's actions or intentions are accepted as fact, and confrontation strategies are perceived to be the only rational means of dealing with them.

3.   ONCE CONFLICT HAS BEGUN, PROLONG AND INTENSIFY IT.

A regulatory skirmish is by no means as useful a vehicle for advancing an intermediary's career as is an intense and protracted battle. Reputations of lawyers, lobbyists, and public-relations specialists have been established on the basis of such major conflicts as whether automobiles must be equipped with airbags, the requisite number of peanuts in an ounce of peanut butter, and the disclosure of health risks in certain foods and drugs.

Prolonged hostilities provide a continuing showcase for tactical acumen and warlike aggressiveness. They usually involve many parties—industries, corporations, trade associations, law firms, congressional committees, and regulatory agencies. Intermediaries who follow a typical career path often wish to demonstrate their political savvy and adversarial skill to as wide a range of potential employers as possible. I know of some successful intermediaries who, rising to ever more responsible positions as the original conflict grew and spread into new battles and second-order skirmishes, have worked on various sides of the same major issue for fifteen years in a half dozen different organizations.

Besides facilitating career advancement, these regulatory marathons can also provide intermediaries with a secure source of income for many years. Lawyers may spend a large portion of their working lives on a few such controversies, and public-relations specialists who represent clients in a protracted battle may gain semipermanent employment. For example, when in 1959 the Food and Drug Administration proposed a standard for the content of peanut butter, it launched a regulatory battle that kept a goodly number of intermediaries gainfully employed for twelve years.

Of course, their motives are not solely pecuniary. Pride in their work, a concern for punctiliousness, a desire to win for the sake of winning, and a limited understanding of the broad goals of business–government cooperation all play a part.

4. KEEP BUSINESS EXECUTIVES AND REGULATORY OFFICIALS APART.

Direct contact between business executives and regulatory officials, under any but the most formal circumstances, can jeopardize the intermediary's efforts to create and maintain regulatory conflict. Since these leaders, given a chance, are liable to discover their mutual interest in avoiding conflict and solving problems, they may also discover that they have little need for the elaborate infrastructure of intermediaries they support.

Intermediaries, therefore, usually seek to maintain a monopoly over the channels of communication between business executives and regulatory officials. They must be kept at a safe distance from each other, and on the few occasions when they do meet, intermediaries must be in attendance to ensure that tensions are sustained.

Washington lawyers, trade-association officials, and public-relations specialists usually advise business executives against meeting directly with regulators to discuss mutual problems. Their reasoning is that the executives are not sufficiently knowledgeable about issues that could arise and may, as a result, inadvertently say something prejudicial to their own interests. Not surprisingly, staff members of regulatory agencies proffer much the same advice to regulatory officials.

When one small Midwestern trade association asked me to set up a meeting between a dozen of its member executives and several FTC officials to discuss issues affecting the region's industry, a national trade association and its Washington counsel, which also represented several of the businesses, objected violently. They argued that such a meeting would jeopardize the delicate relationship they had established with the regulatory agency. The agency staff also objected on similar grounds.

A compromise of sorts was reached: A predictably useless meeting took place with 150 people in attendance, including all the Washington lawyers, trade-association staff, and regulatory staff whose "delicate relationship" could not risk a less formal setting.

5. ENGAGE IN ENDLESS ROUNDS OF DISCOVERING AND CLOSING LOOPHOLES.

This fifth and last rule is perhaps the most pervasive. It explains from whence regulatory "red tape" derives. So important is this principle, and so ubiquitous, that it deserves special attention.

Let us consider the case of an inventor named Henry and his turbocharged automatic vacuum cleaner. You just place Henry's vacuum on a shelf for five minutes, and—presto!—the room is spanking clean. Imagine that the product proves enormously popular and that Henry forms a major manufacturing company around his wonder vacuum. But Henry's brainchild suffers from one small flaw: It emits a roar something like a jet engine at full throttle, only louder. Every time the machine is switched on, the noise loosens tooth fillings and induces deep neurosis in dogs within a radius of two hundred yards. This flaw does not deter consumers from using the vacuum, however; following operating instructions, they simply set the timer, sedate the dog, and go off to the movies while the machine cuts loose. Soon, in neighborhoods all over America the vacuum's roar issues from empty houses, causing flocks of passing birds to fall stunned from the sky and neighbors at table to drop plates and fling drinks into the air. Henry would like to make a quieter version of the product, but adding an adequate muffler would triple the cost.

Now suppose that several years before all this, Congress had instructed the Environmental Protection Agency (EPA) to take steps to "ensure that no household appliance emits excessive noise." That was all the legislation said. Congress decided to leave it to the EPA to devise and enforce regulations concerning neighborhood noise pollution. Since then, the agency has issued only one broad rule: "No consumer product shall generate noise in excess of 110 decibels." That's it—nothing more specific than this, no reporting requirements, no interpretations, no elaborations. The EPA publishes the rule and considers the problem settled.

Henry has hired a Washington lawyer named Seymour, who informs him of the regulation. Worried about the threat to his company, Henry asks Seymour whether he can think of some legal way to continue selling the turbocharged vacuum cleaner. Seymour is a smart lawyer who specializes in federal regulations. "Not to worry," Seymour assures Henry. "I can think of two hundred ways to dodge this regulation."

Two months later, the EPA inquires about the vacuum. It seems they have been getting complaints about its noise. Seymour meets with the agency's attorney. "The regulation doesn't apply to the turbocharged automatic vacuum," says Seymour. "It says that no *consumer product* should emit a sound in excess of one hundred ten decibels, but this isn't a consumer product. It's designed for industrial applications, although consumers happen to use it. And it's not a product but a service, since under our unique payment plan it is leased rather than purchased outright." The attorneys silently take off their hats to Seymour and go back to their law books and word processors.

Two months after that, the agency announces a more detailed set of rulings, which define "consumer product" as "any product or service sold or leased to industrial or consumer users." They then return to Seymour's office. "Still doesn't apply," says Seymour calmly. "The regulation prohibits sounds in excess of one hundred ten decibels. But our automatic vacuum records only ninety-five decibels when we've tested it outside in the middle of a field during a hailstorm. Here's the proof." He hands the attorneys computerized results of the experiment. They take off their hats again, shake his hand, and drag back to the office.

Two months later, the agency announces precise specifications for how such products are to be tested to determine decibel levels—the kind of sound chamber in which testing is to occur, the type of testing equipment, scientific definitions for "decibel," and detailed requirements for when testing must be done and under whose auspices. The agency also announces that hereafter all manufacturers of a new product "designed for or adaptable to household use" must file a report with the agency stating its decibel level according to the prescribed test. All over America, developers of new cat beds, corn poppers, and sock matchers fume as they pay for the premarketing decibel tests Washington demands.

Over the next several years Seymour meets with the agency's attorneys innumerable times. Each time he claims that the burgeoning regulations, rules, and interpretations still do not apply. Each time thereafter, they become more detailed. Seymour disputes their applicability before administrative-law judges, and he appeals their rulings to the federal courts. He argues, as the occasion warrants and the spirit moves him, that the agency has exceeded its mandate from Congress, or that it has acted arbitrarily in singling out the turbocharged automatic vacuum, or that the company's constitutional rights have been violated. The administrative judges and appellate courts issue opinions that further elaborate on the agency's regulations and interpretations and its authority to regulate in this area. Meanwhile, the original statute has been amended by Congress to avoid the loopholes and ambiguities that Seymour (and others like him) have discovered. The new law is far more detailed and complex, spelling out in excruciating specificity what is required.

Five years later, Henry meets with Seymour. "I'm afraid," says Seymour, "we've reached the end of the line." Seymour points to a bookshelf sagging under the weight of statutes, regulations, rulings, advisory opinions, interpretations, court opinions, and appellate decisions, all concerning noise pollution. "But at least I got you more than five years of delay." Henry is downcast nonetheless. "Does this mean we have to stop selling the turbocharged automatic vacuum, or else install the muffler?" he asks. "Either that," Seymour warns, "or you'll have to pay the fine every year you violate the regulation." "How much?" Henry asks, trembling. "A full twenty-five hundred American dollars," Seymour says as he grins and takes off his hat to himself. Henry jubilantly goes back to his company, where he asks his secretary to organize a bake sale to cover the fine.

* * *

This example exaggerates, but not by much, the typical fate of a regulatory effort. It describes a familiar dynamic between American business and government. American corporations are not reluctant to test the limits of the law. They pay lawyers handsome sums to discover loopholes, technicalities, and elegant circumventions. In many instances the investment is worth it to the corporation. At least it buys temporary relief from a regulation, enabling the company to continue profitably doing what it was doing before. Each such maneuver generates a countermaneuver from within the regulatory bureaucracy and Congress; every feint and dodge, a more complicated prophylactic for the next encounter. The result, over time, is a profusion of regulatory detail that confounds and strangles American business.

There are no plotting villains in this tale. Seymour and lawyers like him have no intention of confounding American capitalism. Seymour does his job as he understands it and is good at what he does. Henry and other chief executives are not revolutionaries, either. Henry is trying to protect his company's interests. Indeed, Henry has a responsibility to his shareholders to do whatever he can, within the limits of the law, to maximize the firm's profits. If he did not hire good lawyers to maneuver around statutes and regulations that were open to such circumnavigation, Henry might be found liable for breach of fiduciary duty to his shareholders, or he might be taken over by someone with fewer scruples about exploiting every possible route to higher profits. Every actor in this sad and silly tale is simply carrying out the responsibilities assigned him within a set of rules that we all have accepted.

The story, exasperatingly, suggests no obvious plan of action. Any fundamental improvement would require a broader definition of responsibility by which businesses would not simply yield to the letter of the law but endorse its spirit, or else openly challenge the goals underlying the laws. And the story promises no happy ending, because such a change in attitude and practice will be difficult to achieve. Business executives like Henry, lawyers like Seymour, shareholders, and regulatory officials alike act on the expectation that American business will try to outmaneuver government. As thrust meets parry, the miasma of red tape thickens.

II

THE
REAL
ECONOMY

6

THE ECONOMICS OF ILLUSION AND THE ILLUSION OF ECONOMICS

SOCIETIES, LIKE INDIVIDUALS, OFTEN WANT TO AVOID FACING THEIR most pressing problems. Recognizing reality can be painful; addressing it can be even more painful—requiring sacrifice and change. Thus, societies, like individuals, often deny that their problems exist. Or they erect "straw men," which are not the real problems at all, and try to confront them instead. Or they deny responsibility for problems, blaming others. America has been using all these ploys to avoid coping with its economic mess.

Some still deny a problem exists. Those who call themselves "supply-siders" claim, notwithstanding the nation's mounting indebtedness to the rest of the world (estimated at more than $400 billion by the close of 1988), that the economy is still buoyant, and we have only to keep taxes down in order to reap the eventual rewards. Monetarists are somewhat less optimistic, but their solution is no less simple: The Federal Reserve Board must exercise a steadier hand in controlling the money supply. As reality has steadily intruded upon orthodoxy, however, these two schools of denial have claimed fewer and fewer adherents. Both supply-side economics and monetarism share a rare but unfortunate distinction among economic theories: They have been tried in practice, and they have failed.

* * *

If none of the other standard methods of denial work, there is always the possibility of blaming others for our economic problems—in this case, foreigners. Foreigners are the perfect foil. American politicians can talk tough without committing public money; foreigners cannot vote.

Consider, for example, America's recent "dollar diplomacy." In 1987 and 1988 the Reagan Administration insisted that it wanted to "coordinate" its economic policies with other advanced industrial nations but found the others resistant. The Louvre accord of February 1987, in which the major trading nations agreed to stabilize currencies and simultaneously reduce America's budget deficit while expanding their own economies, seemed a step in the right direction. But in the late summer and early fall West Germany had the temerity to raise its interest rates—prompting Treasury Secretary James Baker to announce on October 18, 1987, (the day before the Dow Jones Industrial Average dropped over five hundred points) that the United States would allow the dollar to fall in response to their uncooperativeness. In other words, the economic strain was *their* fault, and they were to be punished for it.

Left out of the Administration's calculation was Japan's and West Germany's understandable skepticism that the United States would fulfill *its* side of the bargain. Not even the flurry of postcrash negotiations between the White House and Capitol Hill produced much more than the already mandated Gramm–Rudman deficit reductions. The Japanese worried about their own large budget deficit and about the future needs of their rapidly aging population; the West Germans were, as usual, afraid of inflation and suspicious of Americans' spendthrift habits. From the viewpoint of these countries, the Reagan Administration was unreasonable, even hypocritical, in blaming them for the deteriorating economic situation. It was as if the town drunk were criticizing everyone else for excessive sobriety.

By the start of 1989 American officials were quietly predicting that the dollar would have to fall by another 20 percent or so to cure the U.S. trade imbalance. Yet a falling dollar would impose significant penalties on the likes of Japan and West Germany, whose exports to the United States would become correspondingly more expensive and thus fewer. Germany was already experiencing high unemployment; a further decline in exports would push unemployment perilously higher. Were the United States to balance its trade account by importing less or exporting more, four million additional Americans would be put to work, but approximately the same number of foreigners would become jobless— two thirds of them Japanese and Europeans. This was hardly a recipe for future coordination or cooperation.

*　*　*

A second means of blaming foreigners has also gained a certain cachet in recent years: our mounting economic problems attributable, at least in part, to our allies' insistence that we defend them from communists and terrorists, despite their unwillingness to pay a fair share of the cost of such defense. Were our trading partners to pay their due, our budget and trade deficits would shrink markedly, or so the argument goes.

It is true that the defense burden is unequally allocated. In 1983, for example, Americans produced a little over 40 percent of the combined gross national product of the United States, Japan, France, Great Britain, and West Germany yet provided almost 57 percent of the group's defense spending. By contrast, Japan's share of advanced-nation GNP was 14 percent, but its defense share was only 3.3 percent. But here again, the blame is not without a touch of hypocrisy. Our trading partners have never insisted that we bear this disproportionate share. It is, rather, a price we have been willing—even eager—to pay, in order to contain what we have perceived to be the spread of world communism (a concern shared by our allies, but rarely to quite the same degree) and to ensure our continued leadership in the defense of the free world. The Reagan Administration showed little reluctance in raising American defense spending from its low of 4.6 percent of GNP in 1979 to almost 7 percent in the 1980s—an explosion that partly accounts for America's mounting indebtedness—while simultaneously reducing foreign aid and support for international institutions.

Of course, it may be necessary in future years for all allies and trading partners to foot a larger part of the combined cost of defending us all. But such a move would not be without political consequence: America would no longer be in the same position of leadership; our allies would be more independent of us, able and perhaps willing to seek different accommodations with the Soviets and other perceived threats. In addition, a militarized Japan and more militarized West Germany would represent a substantial change in how we and they, and others, understand their power in the world. Amid growing fears of American abandonment in the face of Soviet conventional forces, West European leaders are already talking of defense cooperation among themselves and of a greater European role in NATO decision making. However the issue may be resolved, there is no basis at this juncture for arguing that our economic predicament is wholly or even mostly attributable to our allies' unwillingness to bear a fair burden of the common defense.

* * *

Congress, meanwhile, has been devising a third means of blaming foreigners for our economic problems and of deflecting costs on them. A mammoth new trade bill emerged from the House of Representatives in 1988 and was reluctantly signed into law as one of Ronald Reagan's last official acts. The trade law was designed, according to its progenitors, to ensure that American exporters competed on a "level playing field." Most of the law's provisions reduced presidential discretion over what to do about foreign nations found to have kept American goods out of their home markets, subsidized their exporters, or "dumped" their goods on American soil. Missouri Congressman Richard Gephardt, a Democratic presidential candidate, championed a provision that would have penalized imports from nations that maintained trade imbalances with the United States. He argued that his innovation was designed not to protect the American market but to open foreign markets. Even without the provision (which was left out of the final version), the trade law's focus was indisputably on the transgressions of foreigners.

In its waning months the Reagan Administration, not to be outdone, and perhaps to forestall even more extreme measures by Congress, vowed to "get tough on unfair foreign trade." First came a stiff duty on Canadian softwood shakes and shingles in response to alleged unfair subsidies, followed by 100-percent tariffs on $300 million worth of Japanese electronics products in retaliation for Japan's apparent dumping of semiconductors in Third World markets, a brief war with the European Economic Community over citrus and pasta, threatened tariffs on $100 million worth of Brazilian imports in response to Brazilian curbs on American computers and software products, talk of additional tariffs on $100 million worth of food imports from Europe in retaliation for bans on meat from animals treated with growth hormones, and a movement to withdraw special duty-free preferences for products from developing nations that have maintained substantial trade imbalances with the United States. Summarizing these and related developments, Special U.S. Trade Representative (soon to be Bush's secretary of agriculture) Clayton Yeutter touted what he terms the Administration's "extremely aggressive" approach to foreign trade. "Some of our trading partners have complained loudly about what they see as high-handed American practices," he said, proudly. "But that won't dissuade us from protecting our interests."

Here again, the responsibility for America's economic problems has been safely externalized. It is true, of course, that some nations subsidize their exports to us and hobble our exports to them. But absent international agreement on what sorts of subsidies and nontariff protections are unfair, America's responses merely reflect what the United States unilaterally deems to be unfair. The dominant metaphors create the impression of unsportsmanlike, if not indecent, behavior—"tilting the playing field," "dumping"—when in reality the playing field has always been as hilly as the Ozarks, and dumped goods are often known to American consumers by the less pejorative term "bargains."

* * *

Our trading partners may sense hypocrisy here as well. All told, by the start of 1989 fully 35 percent (by value) of the goods produced in the United States was protected by some form of nontariff barrier—including countervailing duties, antidumping levies, and so-called voluntary restraint agreements ("voluntary" only to the extent that our trading partner willingly accepted American demands to hold back exports under threat of more severe quotas should no agreement be reached). The comparable figure in 1980 had been 20 percent. Moreover, the U.S. government continues to subsidize American industry to a degree that makes most other nations seem like laissez-faire purists by comparison. Federally subsidized loans and loan guarantees, state and local tax abatements, and generous grants of "eminent domain" authority are routinely available to American businesses. Over one third of all the research and development costs of American corporations are now funded by the federal government.

The Defense Department and its sister agencies—the Department of Energy and the National Security Agency—have emerged as the most magnanimous and determined developers of American technology. The year 1988 marked something of a record. For example, in January the Administration formally approved a $4.4 billion plan for building a "superconducting supercollider," a fifty-two-mile underground racetrack for subatomic particles deemed by the Energy Department to be "critical" for America's international competitiveness in related technologies. Then in July the President announced that the Pentagon would lead a $150 million effort aimed at developing practical applications for "superconducting" materials—special alloys that when cooled lose all resistance to the flow of electric current. The National Security Agency, meanwhile, has been pouring $20 million a year into its Supercomputer Research Center, which is seeking to build the world's fastest computers. In October the Pentagon agreed to fund "Sematech," a research joint venture comprising America's leading semiconductor manufacturers, designed to improve their manufacturing competitiveness. And at the end of the year the National Aeronautics and Space Administration, whose mission has drifted steadily toward Defense Department needs, awarded $5 billion in contracts to design and build components for a space station —a project justified by NASA as having "potentially vital consequences for the nation's defense and its competitiveness."

In short, the Pentagon and its sister agencies have become the source of America's high-technology industrial policy—a policy that is more costly, complex, and intrusive upon the private sector than any ever imagined by our trading partners. The problem is not that they do it and we don't. The real problem for us is that we do it under the aegis of national defense—which is an exceedingly awkward and inefficient way to promote high technology—while they do it more openly and directly.

Blaming others for our economic problems may be reassuring but has two unfortunate consequences. It makes others angry and resentful and thus less inclined to cooperate over the longer term. And it makes us less inclined to take responsibility for what needs to be remedied in ourselves—the issue to which I now turn.

* * *

Our nation's growing economic problem is due neither to the federal budget deficit per se, nor to foreigners' unwillingness to treat us fairly. It is due to our overwhelming failure to invest in our collective productivity and the consequent decline in our capacity to add value to the world economy.

Indebtedness would be no cause for great alarm if the proceeds were invested in our future productivity. America's foreign debt is still small relative to its gross national product; Mexico has borrowed twice the amount as a proportion of its GNP. In the nineteenth century we borrowed far more, relatively speaking. But a century ago the loans were invested in factories, railroads, oil wells, inventions, and an array of other assets that produced future wealth. Not this time around. We are consuming our way into economic oblivion. Even Wall Street's reverie before Black Monday was based not on productivity gains but on threats of takeovers, which prompted corporations to do whatever was necessary to raise their share prices in the short term—often cutting back on long-term investment while purchasing their own shares and going deeply into debt.

Without a surge in productivity, the present debt cannot be repaid unless we drastically reduce our standard of living. Our predicament is analogous to that of any person living beyond his means, who must grow poorer unless he generates more wealth. The plot is familiar: As creditors realize that he is unlikely to be able to repay, his IOUs begin to decline in value, and new loans—if available at all—come only at exorbitant rates. To maintain present consumption, he begins selling off the contents of his house, including family heirlooms, and finally the house itself—which he thereupon rents from the new owners until he has no money left with which to pay the rent. So too with America; our failure to invest in future productivity is now reflected in a declining dollar, rising interest rates, and the steady sale to foreigners of shares in our companies and of our prime real estate. Trying to offset our trade imbalance by selling off our assets makes as much sense as selling the house to help pay future rent.

Most of the panaceas now being offered by politicians and economists provide alternative means of growing poorer—by, for example, allowing the dollar to continue to fall, cutting wages, reducing environmental and safety regulations, slashing public spending, even engineering a recession. While these strategies impose the burden of becoming poorer on different groups of citizens over slightly different periods of time, their overall effects are much the same. There is no secret to becoming poorer. Even if we did nothing, the becoming-poorer strategy would occur automatically as the dollar continued to slide. To repeat, the only becoming-richer strategy is to invest in our future productivity.

*   *   *

The current obsession with the federal budget deficit obscures an important point about the nature and purpose of productive investments. Popular wisdom holds that government expenditure "crowds out" private investment. But the reverse may now be closer to the truth. A significant portion of the investments undertaken by American corporations in recent years has been unrelated to the task of improving American competitiveness, while many of the most important types of productive investment can be undertaken only by the public sector.

Even as America's trade deficit has widened, American-owned corporations have continued to maintain their competitiveness by going overseas. Recent studies reveal that, while the percentage of world markets held by American corporations exporting from the United States has steadily declined during the last quarter century, such declines have been offset by the gains of American corporations exporting from other nations. As the dollar declines, some American corporations are coming back to America, and some foreign-owned corporations are joining them. Toshiba soon will be exporting to Japan microwave ovens and television sets made in its Tennessee plant, for example. But to the extent such corporations are being drawn to the United States by the relatively low costs of production here associated with a low dollar, their new investments in America are unlikely to be of a sort that will greatly enhance the value of what Americans contribute to the world economy. They are more likely to be in plant and equipment tailored to relatively low-skilled labor. Should the dollar hit sufficiently low depths, the United States may eventually become an attractive place to make things now produced in Southeast Asia and Latin America. But under these circumstances the real incomes of Americans—adding no more value to globally available plant and equipment than is added by any other low-skilled workers around the globe—would be very low indeed.

* * *

The only factors of production that are relatively immobile internationally, and thus on which depends uniquely the value that the nation adds to world commerce, are the skills of our citizens and their capacities to work together. To a significant extent, such assets represent returns on public investments—in education, training and retraining, research and development, and in all the systems for transporting our citizens and communicating among them—which comprise the nation's infrastructure. We do not commonly think of these sorts of expenditures as investments—the federal budget fails to distinguish capital expenditures, and the national income accounts treat all government expenditures as consumption—but they dramatically affect our future capacity to produce.

These public investments have either declined during the 1980s or, at best, remained at about the same level. Government spending on commercial research and development has declined 95 percent from its level two decades ago. (Even when added to private-sector research and development, the total is still less than 2 percent of GNP, lower than comparable research and development expenditures in any other advanced industrial nation.) Government spending to upgrade and expand the nation's infrastructure dropped from 2.3 percent of GNP two decades ago to 0.4 percent in the 1980s. Per-pupil expenditures on public elementary and secondary education have shown no gain in real terms; as a percent of GNP, they have declined—and this during an era in which demands on public education have significantly increased, due to the growing phenomena of broken homes, unwed mothers, and a rising population of poor. The federal government has retreated from the field of public education, leaving states and localities—many of them severely handicapped by low tax bases—with almost the entire job. Not surprisingly, an estimated 20 percent of American eighteen-year-olds are now functionally illiterate; one quarter of today's high school students drop out before graduation. This is not the sort of population likely to generate high productivity in future years.

We must do several things to reverse the trend. First, we must gradually scale back aggregate consumption by, for example, spurring the growth of personal savings through expanded Individual Retirement Accounts and Keogh plans, hobbling hostile takeovers and leveraged buyouts, and taxing more of Social Security benefits. Consumption might also be limited by reducing farm supports, jettisoning weapons projects that are of low priority or fail to perform as planned, and taxing consumption directly—through, for example, a progressive tax on a family's net spending.

But this is only half the agenda. We must *simultaneously* attend to the investment side of the ledger by, for example, inducing more private-sector spending on plant and equipment in the United States (restoring the investment tax credit and accelerated depreciation on investments made in the United States) and increasing government spending for education, retraining, child nutrition, prenatal and postnatal care, research and development, and infrastructure. These investment strategies may make it more difficult to reduce the federal budget deficit in the short term, but they are more important to our long-term economic health than any immediate fix. To focus singularly on reducing the federal budget deficit distracts us from this more fundamental agenda.

An additional aspect of our investment strategy should be to take the nation's research and development efforts out from under the Pentagon and its sister agencies and turn them over to civilian agencies whose explicit goal is to spur the nation's commercial competitiveness. As has been noted, we already have a bold industrial policy for high technology, but it is run out of the Defense Department. There are commercial spin-offs of course, but because the Pentagon's needs are quite different from what consumers need at a price they are willing to pay, the spin-offs are relatively few and far between. And defense projects are so enshrouded in secrecy that commercial entrepreneurs often cannot take advantage of the discoveries even if they want to. It is time we acknowledged our high-technology industrial policy—and, by implication, the legitimacy of other nations' similar programs—but undertook ours in a far more efficient and direct manner.

Reality can be painful. Denial, escapism, and self-righteous indignation toward others are common defenses against such pain, no less for a nation than an individual. But reality can become progressively more painful the longer it is avoided. Our immediate responsibilities are to accept the truth about ourselves—that we are falling behind in our collective capacities to add value to the world economy and that we must invest in one another to regain our stride—and to do something about it.

7

THE EXECUTIVE'S
NEW CLOTHES (I)

SINCE THE MID-1970S, AMERICA'S FIVE HUNDRED LARGEST INDUSTRIAL corporations together have failed to generate a single new job. In fact, their portion of the civilian labor force declined from 17 percent in 1975 to less than 11 percent in 1988. And their share of the nation's product has declined as well: from 55 percent of GNP in the mid-1970s to just over 40 percent in 1988.

True, not all of the problems were of their own making. During the 1970s, they had to contend with two oil shocks and a spate of new regulations—all of which, in turn, required extensive new investments. And the onslaught of foreign competition—much of it based on low-wage labor—posed an unprecedented challenge. Still, large American corporations proved themselves remarkably inept in responding to these demands. After all, Japanese companies faced the same oil shocks, similar regulatory requirements, and an even more intensely competitive environment, and did so without the American corporations' home-player advantage of a huge and sophisticated domestic market.

Not even the current recovery has changed the picture dramatically. America's biggest corporations continue their long downward slide, like prehistoric beasts quietly expiring. Few have come even close to matching their 1960s performance. The Dow Jones Industrial Average began its spurt in August 1982. But when adjusted for inflation, the peak reached in August 1987 was still below the old peak of January 1966.

The poor performance is all the more remarkable in light of the privileged position enjoyed by large corporations in Ronald Reagan's and George Bush's America. Not since the 1920s has big business been so unconstrained. Consider the extraordinary cut in corporate taxes that began with the Economic Recovery Tax Act of 1981. In 1965 corporate tax payments accounted for 26 percent of federal revenues; by 1986 the portion was down to 8 percent. "Safe-harbor leasing" and other similar devices built into the tax code allowed the biggest corporations to enjoy their lowest effective tax rates in fifty years. General Electric, for example, paid no taxes at all between 1981 and 1983, on profits of $6.5 billion. Since then, in the wake of the tax reforms of 1986, the corporate burden has inched upward, but only by inches, reaching 13 percent in 1988.

John Kenneth Galbraith once wrote reassuringly of the "counter-vailing power" within the American system, which offsets the influence of large corporations. But in the America of the 1980s, these counter-weights were all but removed. Health, safety, and environmental regulations were deferred or cut back; consumers and environmentalists no longer claimed the media attention they once did. Organized labor was cowed; union membership was down to 17 percent of the private-sector work force, and wage concessions became the order of the day. Few voices any longer broached the subject of corporate responsibility to the poor or to the communities and nations in which they do business. In fact, the dominant issues on the public agenda in the 1980s were those over which American business itself is divided—how to simplify taxes, reduce the budget deficit, and get foreign nations to open up their markets to our goods and services. At the same time, and with increasing boldness, state and local officials—anxious to lure or keep major businesses—promised corporate leaders all sorts of special subsidies and tax breaks. Not even foreign competitors imposed an enduring constraint, as protectionism waxed.

* * *

Nothing so exemplifies the unfettered position of today's large corporations as the autonomous power enjoyed by their chief executive officers—"CEOs" in business-speak—notwithstanding the continuing poor performance of the companies they run. One measure is found in their salaries and bonuses, which have increased much faster than inflation, and twice as fast as the earnings of hourly workers. In 1988 CEOs of the one hundred largest publicly owned industrial corporations received raises averaging almost 12 percent, while the wages of hourly workers increased by less than 6 percent. Between 1977 and 1987 hourly wages barely kept up with inflation; but the salaries and bonuses of America's top CEOs rose three times faster than inflation. (Most top executives are less defensive about their remuneration than John Nevin, CEO and chairman of Firestone Tire and Rubber Company, who claimed, at Firestone's 1987 stockholder meeting, that his $5.6 million bonus that year had not "caused me to have any feelings of embarrassment and is not . . . a payment for which I believe I owe anyone any apologies." Nevin's stockholders were not convinced. The company had lost money and jobs. It employed half the people it had employed a decade before. Within months of Nevin's appearance, most of the company was sold to Japan's Bridgestone Corporation.)

We are faced with a paradox. Our major corporations are stewards for a sizable chunk of our national wealth. The long-term performance of these corporations is less than sterling and continues to worsen. But at the same time American citizens seem willing to grant these companies, and their CEOs, ever greater wealth and privilege. The only constraint is the possibility of an unfriendly takeover; but even this, as we have seen, leads only to a new round of musical chairs. The tune remains the same.

What will come of this? One possibility is that these divergent trends eventually will clash. At some point we can expect a resurgence of the sort of economic populism that periodically captures the American imagination. The large corporation and its leaders will be vilified in the media. This will be accompanied by a new round of regulatory restraints on corporate action. We may even get serious about proposals for economic democracy.

But a more likely possibility, at least in the short run, is that the United States will consider the twin problems of poor corporate performance and the privileged position of the CEO as challenges to managerial attitudes and techniques. (As a culture, we tend to prefer pep talks to social criticism—stories about what works to exposés about what doesn't—at least until the underlying problems loom so large that they can no longer be ignored.) Indeed, there is evidence that we have already embarked on this Panglossian path. It comes in the form of a new literary genre that has emerged during the last few years: the CEO success story.

* * *

The new genre has been enormously popular. *In Search of Excellence: Lessons from America's Best Run Companies* by Thomas J. Peters and Robert H. Waterman, Jr., first published in 1983, has sold six million copies to date. The celebrated book tells the stories of the best American companies and their leaders—Walt Disney Productions, Ray Kroc and McDonald's, Caterpillar Tractor, Texas Instruments, and so on—and suggests lessons to be learned from them. Not far behind in total sales is *The One Minute Manager* by Kenneth Blanchard and Spencer Johnson. This book is written as a fairy tale about a young man whose search for the perfect manager leads him to a guru—the One Minute Manager—who shares his great wisdom with the young man in a mere 106 pages of large-type text. Then come the autobiographies, among them *Iacocca,* the story of the irrepressible CEO of Chrysler, which held first place on *The New York Times* best-seller list for months, and *Managing* by Harold Geneen and Alvin Moscow, the tale of the erstwhile CEO of ITT. All of these CEO success stories have spawned imitations and variations. Bookstores are now bulging with new volumes of stories and anecdotes about creating, achieving, or becoming impassioned about "excellence"—preferably within one minute—and about tales of tough-minded CEOs who have overcome adversity to make millions.

I do not mean to tar with an overly broad brush. The books in this new genre vary substantially in quality and sophistication. *Iacocca,* for example, is a delight to read; the story he relates is charming, funny, in places quite poignant. On the other hand, Harold Geneen's attempt at self-revelation is ponderous and pedantic. Iacocca doesn't take himself too seriously; Geneen seems desperate to secure for himself a place in history. *In Search of Excellence* offers rare insights into motivating employees and satisfying customers; the authors skillfully weave their stories into memorable lessons. *The One Minute Manager,* by contrast, is a fatuous exercise in manipulative managerial techniques. But these important differences notwithstanding, the books share some features that help explain the popularity of the genre as a whole and shed some light on its significance in this era of repressed criticism.

The heroes of these stories are mavericks. They are crusty, strong-willed characters who have no patience for fools or slackers. They buck the system. They take no crap. They win. Iacocca's story really begins when Henry Ford fires him. The reason? "Sometimes you just don't like somebody," Ford explains. Iacocca then takes over Chrysler when the firm is at rock bottom. The rest of the take is about Iacocca's and Chrysler's joint comeback, and ultimate victory. The victory permits a bittersweet revenge on Henry Ford—and on all other autocrats and naysayers. Indeed, it is the American saga of the underdog who eventually makes it big—whose hard work, perseverance, and cunning finally prevail over the powerful elites that try to keep him down. The same story inspired Horatio Alger's novellas. It powers Rocky. It runs through *In Search of Excellence*—from Ray Kroc's hamburgers to the product champions at 3M.

Even Harold Geneen comes off as a maverick. As financial vice president of Raytheon in the 1950s, he refuses to report to the president through the president's staff. He tells the president: "Either I am running this company or they are. I want to get my orders directly from you and not from them. So, you think it over. And let me know Monday morning." When it looks like he won't be president, Geneen quits Raytheon to become CEO of ITT. At the time ITT is little more than a lackluster collection of overseas telephone companies that the Bell System has discarded. Over the next eighteen years Geneen builds it into a massive conglomerate with annual sales of $17 billion and profits of $550 million —the thirteenth largest company in the United States. He is tough as nails, True Grit.

*   *   *

Second, these CEOs are colorful and outspoken. They are the antithesis of the gray-flanneled professional manager of yore whose very blankness was his more distinguishing quality. Although many of them share a background in finance, they are contemptuous of the "bean counters" and the superanalytic MBAs, who in Iacocca's words "seem to think that every business decision can be structured and reduced to a case study." They eschew memorandums and elaborate procedures. They detest office politics. Geneen describes political maneuvering as "a form of unfair self-aggrandizement which, if not curbed, will destroy the morale and forward thrust of any company." In short, these heroes hate bureaucracy in all its many forms.

Third, they believe in "hands-on" management. They want to confront people directly, touch them, challenge them, and motivate them through the sheer force of personality. Geneen spends countless hours grilling his managers—demanding that they think through what they're proposing, that they get the facts exactly right, that they tell the truth.

Iacocca is a whirlwind of handshakes and inspirational talks—to employees, middle managers, shareholders, bankers, members of Congress, customers, anyone who will listen. General Electric's Reg Jones, portrayed in another of these tomes, personally meets all the company's new young managers, visits ailing employees in the hospital, asks that company technicians explain to him precisely what they are working on, in ways that he can understand. All the heroes of *In Search of Excellence* manage by walking around their offices and factories, talking to employees and customers, getting directly involved. Even the One Minute Manager puts his hands on employees' shoulders and gives them one minute of praise.

Finally, these CEOs are missionaries. Their stories take on an evangelical tone because these men have been inspired. They have found meaning and value in the services they provide. They manage their enterprises by ensuring that employees share those same meanings and values. The atmosphere in these companies is part religious revival, part pep rally. Personnel at Disney theme parks are trained to be "hosts," to think of visitors as personal guests. IBM is fanatical about customer service. Iacocca is a zealot, inspiring his followers with the Belief in Chrysler. Reg Jones effuses about "the distinctive spirit of G.E. . . . that intangible but ever-so-real amalgam of enterprise and loyalty and honor." These CEOs stage contests, award ceremonies, and celebrations; they foster myths, rituals, and legends. They love excitement and hoopla; they downplay cool rationality. In fact, their contempt for the abstractions of professional managers can be understood, in part, as a rejection of intellectualism—of the notion that knowledge and meaning derive from access to special expertise.

The evangelical message is that with enough guts, tenacity, and charisma you too—gentle reader—can be a great manager, a captain of industry. Geneen says, "Managers must manage!" Iacocca says, "You have to be a motivator!" The heroes of *In Search of Excellence* say, "Make the average Joe a winner and a hero!" *The One Minute Manager* says, "Invest in People!"

* * *

Considered together, these characteristics make popular heroes. In their contempt for bureaucracy, formal process, and intellectual abstraction—and their passion for outspoken independence, direct dealing, and charismatic leadership—these CEOs seem perfectly in tune with the antiestablishment tendencies now found on both the right and left of the political spectrum. They are cowboy capitalists.

These stories thus give comfort to Americans who harbor vague misgivings about the place of the large, sluggish corporation in American life—and about the faceless oligarchs who run them. The cumulative message of these books is that we are entering upon a new populist era in which the mavericks are in charge. They are shaking up torpid corporate bureaucracies, bringing forth a new sense of team spirit and entrepreneurship. The Henry Fords of the old world are being replaced by the Lee Iacoccas of the new. The imperious bean counters are on the run. There is no reason to question the fundamental legitimacy of big business in the United States, or to flirt with economic populism, because the populists already have taken over—from the inside. And they are wildly successful.

Surely the heroes of these books deserve our applause. They have brought a new dynamism to American enterprise and generated an aura of team spirit and collective commitment that is new to big business. They have properly shaken up encrusted bureaucracies—substituting charisma and zeal for standard operating procedures. But we should not be too quick to accept the comforting message these stories imply. The populism that these heroes evince may be relatively superficial. Beyond the new atmospherics, it remains unclear precisely what our heroes have accomplished. These books are strangely silent, for example, on precisely how corporate success should be defined or measured. The authors talk incessantly about "excellence," "top performance," and "winning"— and occasionally profitability. But for the most part the genre assumes away the central questions. How should we define corporate success? Have these mavericks really made a difference? Are the fundamental problems of big business susceptible to managerial solutions?

Consider the record. Harold Geneen writes that when he was CEO, he defined success as a 10-percent growth in earnings per year. He insisted that every one of ITT's far-flung divisions and subsidiaries attain at least this level of performance. "I used to say ITT was a 'lockbox' stock. That meant that shareholders, large and small, could put our stock on the bottom of the safe-deposit box and not have to look at it again. It would take care of itself." But ITT's actual performance during these years raises some doubts about Geneen's claims. Between 1959 and 1977 —Geneen's years at the helm—the firm's per-share earnings increased 117 percent. This just about matched the rise in the consumer price index. In fact, investors who took Geneen up on his "lockbox" notion —purchasing ITT stock when Geneen took over the company and selling it when he resigned—did less well than they would have done had they invested in a portfolio of all stocks on the New York Stock Exchange.

Geneen also asserts that in order to make money, you have to make a "contribution to society"—you must "create value." Geneen took this admonition seriously; during his tenure as CEO, he played an active role in politics. But one could question what sort of "contribution" this involvement represented. When the Brazilian government threatened to seize ITT's assets without adequate compensation, Geneen was instrumental in getting passage of the 1962 Hickenlooper Amendment, which barred U.S. economic aid to any government that seized American assets without adequate compensation; soon thereafter, Brazil improved its offer. Geneen and his corporation also sought to prevent the election of Salvador Allende to the presidency of Chile. During this same year, ITT paid millions of dollars in bribes to public officials in a number of countries. And according to an internal memo from ITT lobbyist Dita Beard, the company agreed to help finance the 1972 Republican National Convention in the expectation that Nixon's Justice Department would drop an antitrust suit against it.

Lee Iacocca's goal was less ambitious—to save Chrysler. He seems to have succeeded splendidly. But it remains unclear to what extent Chrysler's resurgence has been attributable to its management. In 1979 and 1980, when Chrysler plummeted into the red, Ford and General Motors were not far behind. In 1980 Ford lost about $1.5 billion— almost as much as Chrysler—and GM lost about $1 billion. Then, beginning in 1981, all three automakers rode the same wave upward, ultimately to new record profits.

What accounts for this almost identical pattern? In 1979 Paul Volcker and the Federal Reserve Board he chaired decided to "break the back of inflation" by squeezing the money supply. Interest rates skyrocketed, and Americans stopped buying cars. In 1981 the Reagan Administration got the Japanese to limit the number of cars they shipped to the United States, and in 1982 the Federal Reserve Board loosened the money supply. At that point Americans started buying American cars again. It seems likely that Chrysler—flush with a federal loan guarantee —would have bobbed back to the surface again even without the charismatic leadership of Chairman Lee.

In fact, one might ask whether the goal of "saving Chrysler" was all that important—to anyone other than Chrysler's beleaguered stockholders, that is. During 1979, when Congress debated whether to guarantee $1.2 billion of new loans to the ailing firm, there was a great deal of talk about the importance of Chrysler to the American economy. But by 1985 Chrysler employed one-third fewer people than it did six years before. And more and more of the components that go into the cars that

Chrysler assembles—indeed, more and more of the cars that Chrysler sells—are manufactured outside the United States. Some commentators have suggested that in a few years the firm will be more appropriately called Chrysler Imports. In short, while Lee Iacocca seems to be a man of extraordinary talents, it's difficult to gauge exactly how much credit is due him, and for what.

The same ambiguities about the meaning of "success" plague many of the other success stories. During the 1970s, when Reg Jones was CEO of GE, the firm's growth in sales and net income just about held even with the growth of the American economy. This was hardly a stellar performance. Other companies that were doing well a few years ago when these stories were being gathered are now foundering; their leaders evidently did not position them for sustained profitability. By 1985 Walt Disney Productions was plagued by takeover battles, management shake-ups, and strikes. Texas Instruments was fighting for its life. Apple Computer was losing key personnel. Caterpillar Tractor was sustaining losses and moving its production abroad. ITT was on the verge of being broken up.

If our maverick heroes have had little practical effect on the performance of their firms—if their actions have merely perpetuated corporate privilege, notwithstanding their fiery rhetoric—then these CEOs cannot be the agents of economic populism. If the lessons they preach come down to mere atmospherics—making employees feel like winners, but not fundamentally altering the structure of ownership and control; creating a team spirit, but reserving the option of moving production abroad—then their populism is a sham. If their "successes" are defined so narrowly as to be meaningless in an era when economic change often entails large social costs and benefits, then it is only a matter of time before the sham is discovered. When this happens, our CEOs will be roundly condemned.

There is an overwhelming tendency in American life either to lionize or pillory the people who stand at the helms of our large institutions— to offer praise or level blame for outcomes over which they may have little control. This tendency is particularly apparent in regard to the performance of large corporations, whose legitimacy in our political and economic system continues to be an open question. The current infatuation with successful CEOs offers an illustration. The unfortunate result is that we are distracted from deeper questions about the organization of our economic system. In personalizing these exciting tales, we overlook much bigger stories.

8

THE EXECUTIVE'S
NEW CLOTHES (II)

IN AMERICA BUSINESS MANAGEMENT IS A PROFESSION. IT HAS ITS OWN graduate schools and advanced degrees; its own professional associations, conferences, and conventions; its own books, magazines, and professional newsletters; and a professional culture that distinguishes it from the general culture by language, clothing, income, and style of work.

The professional manager in America exists above the industrial din, away from the dirt, noise, and irrationality of people and products. He (he is almost always a he) dresses well. His secretary is alert and helpful. His office is as clean, quiet, and subdued as that of any other professional. He plans, organizes, and controls large enterprises in a calm, logical, dispassionate, and decisive manner. He surveys computer printouts, calculates profits and losses, sells and acquires subsidiaries, and imposes systems for monitoring and motivating employees, applying a general body of rules to each special circumstance. Because the professional manager deals in abstractions, he can move from company to company with relative ease, manipulating people and capital as he goes.

This may be why American productivity gains have declined over the past fifteen years, while those of Japan—a country of the approximate size and topography of Montana, without any physical resources to speak of, and more dependent on imported oil than we are; a country with over half our population, aging more quickly than ours, whose workers now receive a slightly higher average wage than we do—continue to rise. The Japanese do not have professional managers. Nor, for that matter, do the West Germans, whose productivity also has burgeoned over the decade. They have managers, all right, but their managers get their hands dirty. They work directly with people and machines. They come up through the ranks after spending most of their working lives with the same company and are considered part of the production team. In America, by contrast, it is rare for a manager to spend his working life with the same company and even rarer for him to have started out on the shop floor.

* * *

Professional management is relatively new as professions go. The first graduate school of business administration was established in America in 1908. It came in the wake of a vast thirty-year wave of mergers creating the first large vertically integrated manufacturing corporations —controlled by a centralized cadre of administrators. The Administrative Management Association was founded eleven years later. Efficiency experts like Frederick Winslow Taylor, Henry L. Gantt, Frank Gilbreth, and Harrington Emerson were soon espousing progressivist notions of scientific management through which the workplace was to become a well-oiled machine and work was to be designed systematically to fit the aptitudes of workers. "Under scientific management," wrote Taylor, "arbitrary power, arbitrary dictation ceases. . . . [T]he man at the head of business . . . is governed by rules and laws which have been developed through hundreds of experiments."

Through scientific management each step of production was to be reduced to its simplest components and arranged in sequence to ensure the highest level of productivity consistent with reasonable levels of quality and fatigue. Jobs were to be uniform and specialized. Discretion and skill were to be minimized. Thus, the very process of production was to be removed from the province of workers. The first step of scientific management, according to Taylor, was "the gathering on the part of [management] of all knowledge which in the past has been kept in the heads of the workmen." The solution to quality control, for example, was to be mechanical—a system of inspectors, and inspectors over inspectors, combined with random sampling. It was no longer necessary for workers to think.

By the late 1920s the American business leader had been transformed from a person whose success was ensured by the Protestant virtues of prudence, punctuality, and perseverance to one whose rise depended on his ability to motivate and manipulate others. And the American worker was transformed into an object to be motivated and manipulated. The new bureaucratic enterprise required businessmen who could apply management techniques to large numbers of employees. Business leaders flocked to management courses in human engineering. Dale Carnegie's first book, *Public Speaking and Influencing Men in Business* (1926), became an instant best-seller. Researchers like Elton Mayo and F. J. Ruethlisberger instructed managers about human relations. A new branch of the profession appeared called "personnel management," replete with studies of industrial physiology and psychology to aid business leaders in getting the most out of their employees.

It was not until after World War II, however, that professional management came into its own. The spectacular performance of American industry during the war drew worldwide attention to American management techniques. Sir Stafford Cripps, chancellor of the exchequer in Britain's postwar Labour government, sent teams of British businessmen to America to learn our secrets. The Marshall Plan further exported American management ideas. But only in Britain did they take firm root, perhaps because the British class structure had already drawn a sharp distinction between white-collar and blue-collar, and the ideal of professional management fit neatly into this hierarchical scheme.

* * *

Even today no single word in French, German, Swedish, or Japanese conveys the general meaning of management as we know it. Indeed, the role of professional business manager is viewed with suspicion abroad, where most business administrators are trained instead in engineering or applied economics. To be sure, there are institutes of management training in Western Europe and Japan, but they exist outside the traditional educational system and are designed for mid-career executives who want specific training in particular aspects of management. They don't give degrees. Nor do they confer professional status. In continental Europe and in Japan business administration is a vocation rather than a profession.

The founding fathers of Japanese and continental European industry —the Yataros, Zenjiros, and Krupps of the late nineteenth century— were succeeded by a generation of business leaders who ascended to management from the factory floor. They intuitively understood the importance of worker participation and job security to productivity. By and large, they supported trade unionism. They accommodated a variety of schemes to ensure that workers were given responsibility for their work—codetermination on boards of directors, workers' councils, elaborate systems of consultation. And they built job security into their productive processes.

Moreover, by the time large, multidivisional corporations first appeared in these countries, government bureaucracies responsible for social welfare were already well established. Thus, business leaders tended to accept the legitimacy of welfare programs and to acknowledge the responsibility of the corporation to contribute to social welfare through the provision of some modicum of employment security. Full employment remains a national goal to which business leaders in these countries subscribe.

By contrast, our professional managers have been less than enthusiastic about social welfare. Perhaps this is because the rise of professional management here preceded the development of our welfare state or because few of our managers have had direct shop-floor experience. Whatever the reason, American managerial elites have fought unionization and opposed job security and worker participation and to this day view the welfare state as sharply antithetical to productivity.

Because the ideal of professional management never took firm root in continental Europe or in Japan, there was not the sharp division of labor between the planning and execution of work, which has characterized Anglo-Saxon enterprise. In recent years this bifurcated way of viewing production—separating thinkers from doers, corporate mind from corporate body, white-collar from blue-collar—has had unsuccessful results in America and Britain. It has spawned two distinct corporate cultures that communicate primarily through formal channels of management directives and union complaints. While U.S. and British companies typically are deeply concerned about the career advancement and job enrichment of their managers, they exhibit no such passion for their workers. The gap between the average blue-collar wage and top executive compensation is larger in America than in any other developed country. And blue-collar workers in America and Britain have little access to company data. They are kept in the dark about company plans and profits.

* * *

The costs of this artificial distinction between corporate thinkers and doers are by now obvious. White-collar strategists and planners often don't comprehend life on the production line, and in consequence their schemes are either impractical or irrelevant, either sabotaged or ignored by the work force. Meanwhile, workers who understand production and could improve it in countless ways don't give a damn. They have no institutional voice. Moreover, the insensitivity of professional managers to the everyday needs of employees has taken a toll. Many of our businesses are plagued by chronic absenteeism and work stoppages. In the mid-1980s the average number of days per year lost to industrial disputes for every one thousand employees was over 1,000 in the United States and over 800 in Britain, compared to 45 in Sweden, 250 in Japan, and 85 in West Germany. The quality of products made in America or Britain is widely considered to be inferior to those of West Germany or Japan. American and British employees are notoriously suspicious of automation, mechanization, or other innovations to improve productivity—and for good reason, since their jobs may be jeopardized as a result. For all these reasons American and British productivity has been increasing at a slower pace than elsewhere.

This is not to suggest that companies in continental Europe and Japan are models of labor-management harmony. On the contrary, Japanese labor unions annually mount a rhetorically threatening "spring offensive" against management. Swedish workers are proud of their militancy. Many French workers espouse socialist ideals. And West German labor unions periodically fulminate against their companies. The difference is that these adversarial contests take place within an institutional and political framework based on the premise of near-full employment and worker participation. Workers in these countries understand that their fates are tied to the profitability and competitiveness of their industries. They are the ultimate beneficiaries of productivity improvements. Adversarial contests are a means of reasserting this central fact. Militancy is thus highly symbolic—a periodic ritual through which all elements of the work force reestablish their social compact. Indeed, in many of these countries white-collar employees are themselves union members who duly participate in these rites. Nothing could be further from the bitter and continuous conflicts that have long separated professional managers from workers in America and Britain.

The first step toward revitalizing Anglo-Saxon economies will be to break down this artificial wall separating thinkers from doers and to render the workplace truly collaborative. This will happen eventually because we have no choice but to make it happen if we are to sustain our economic base. The transformation will not be couched in ideological terms but will be viewed simply as a means of increasing productivity. Our workplaces will become more equitable, secure, and democratic— notwithstanding the individualistic, social-Darwinist rhetoric of the Reagan, Bush, and Thatcher Administrations—because international competition will require that they be so.

The danger is that this transformation will occur later rather than sooner, by which time the road to economic renewal in America and Britain will be straight uphill. The ideology of professional management is by now so deeply embedded in Anglo-Saxon culture that our business leaders at first may seek to emulate the social reality of the Japanese or German workplace through the mere implementation of new management techniques. The sharp distinction between thinkers and doers will remain intact but will be camouflaged by cosmetic devices—quality circles, work groups, collaborative teams, encounter groups, meetings of all sorts and sizes—which serve to soften or blur the underlying structure of management control. Organization-development specialists and consultants will swarm over the workplace advising professional managers about how to improve the "quality of working life" without fundamentally altering the organization of production.

* * *

This silliness has already begun. America is awash with new managerial theories promising to transform miraculously the American workplace into its Japanese counterpart. *Theory Z: How American Business Can Meet the Japanese Challenge,* by William G. Ouchi, and *The Art of Japanese Management: Applications for American Executives,* by Richard T. Pascale and Anthony G. Athos, to take two notable examples, are both how-to books in the best tradition of professional management. Both exhort American business leaders to use management techniques that will, they allege, make American workers as dedicated as their Japanese counterparts. These techniques include giving workers more job security, developing nonspecialized career paths for them, providing them with gradual and standardized promotions that minimize competition among workers, undertaking collective decision making, and displaying a "holistic" concern for the welfare of workers. *Theory Z* provides managers with a step-by-step guide to implementing these techniques and includes several case histories of American firms that seem to have succeeded with them. *The Art of Japanese Management* contrasts the management style of ITT's Harold Geneen with that of Konosuke Matsushita, head of the Matsushita Electric Company (maker of Panasonic, Quasar, and Technics products). Where Geneen was tough and confrontational—driving his employees relentlessly, firing them if they didn't perform, and wielding almost despotic authority over ITT's vast organization—Matsushita used his authority in far more subtle and supportive ways. ITT's profitability dropped precipitously after Geneen's retirement, but Matsushita continues to prosper. To the authors, the moral is clear: American managers must strive to create an atmosphere of intimacy and trust in the workplace. Rather than terrorize their employees by using techniques of fear and control, managers should obtain their loyalty and devotion by tending to their needs.

These are worthy goals. If fully implemented, they surely would enhance American productivity. But they will not be fully implemented so long as the American corporation continues to be dominated by professional managers. Because the authors in no way challenge the dominance of professional managers, their prescriptions are mere management techniques to achieve short-term profitability. There will be no real job security because managers cannot justify the high short-term costs of keeping workers employed during economic downturns. There will be no genuine career paths or real prospects of promotion for most blue-collar workers, because it is cheaper for managers to hire mid-level employees who are already trained than to train blue-collar workers for mid-level jobs. And there will be no real collective decision making, because managers cannot afford to lose control. Moreover, collective decision making is extraordinarily time-consuming and costly in the short term. Thus, while it may be profitable in the short term to make employees *feel* as though they have job security, career prospects, and direct input into company decisions, it is not immediately profitable to restructure the corporation along these lines.

Since the authors studiously ignore the possibility of a reorientation of the American corporation and the financial institutions on which it relies, the issue becomes one of how business managers can create the impression of a collaborative workplace. Accordingly, when they get down to specifics, the authors of both books dwell on atmospherics and attitudes. They urge managers to give their employees "meaning," to transform the workplace from a setting in which work is merely performed to one in which employees are spiritually uplifted. Indeed, they go so far as to blame our economic problems in part on our historic insistence on separating church, state, and corporation—distinctions that have, they argue, led to a highly mechanistic view of production in which employees are viewed as interchangeable units. By way of contrast they offer Matsushita, who merged these separate institutions into one. His was the first company in Japan to have a song and a code of values. Each morning eighty-seven thousand Matsushita employees together sing the song and recite the code. By these and other devices they are inspired to be zealous.

* * *

This emphasis on the atmospherics of intimacy and trust at the workplace is hardly new to professional management in America. In their attempt to stem the rising tide of trade unionism during the first decades of the century, American managers adopted "workplace cooperation" as their slogan and devised an elaborate system of committees to represent worker interest. By 1922 there were 385 different companies maintaining 725 plans of employee representation, which together involved 690,000 workers. Frederick Winslow Taylor, the founder of scientific management, declared that his whole object was to create a trusting relationship between worker and manager and thereby to "remove the cause for antagonism." By the mid-1930s the preeminent business journal, *Management Review,* was urging business leaders to give their employees "what every human being asks for in life: respect for his personality, his human dignity, an environment that he comprehends, and an assurance that he is progressing." The *Review* was adamant about the importance of collaboration: Workers want to be treated "not as servants, but as cooperators."

Such trust and collaboration was of course nothing more than a means of motivating and manipulating the work force while maintaining professional control. The new management theorists merely extend these devices by offering techniques designed to create spiritual togetherness. One is reminded of the Amana and Oneida utopian communities of nineteenth-century America that succeeded so well as commercial enterprises (making iceboxes and tableware, respectively) precisely because they had so thoroughly socialized their workers to share a single vision. Or the modern Amway and Shaklee soap and vitamin distributors, which periodically rev up their door-to-door sales forces through evangelical pep rallies. The logical ending point for psychological manipulation at the workplace is old-time religion, with professional managers as its priests. Management continues to be the applied science of short-term manipulation.

America's new management gurus' emphasis on the spiritual side of the Japanese company is misplaced. The religiouslike devotion of Japanese workers to their companies is the least appealing and least transferable feature of Japanese production. Do we want American workers to behave like the sales officer of a large Japanese company who in 1979 committed suicide after being caught in a scandal over aircraft imports from the United States? Does anyone believe that American workers would subscribe to the sentiments he expressed in his suicide note: "[T]he company is eternal. . . . I must be brave and act as a man to protect that eternal life"?

* * *

Potentially far more important and relevant to the American workplace is the Japanese organization of production, and the political and social context in which it exists—issues on which the new management theorists barely touch. Japanese workers enjoy a far higher degree of equity, job security, and responsibility than their American counterparts —and these features are real, not cosmetic. In Japan, unlike in the United States, the risk of severe economic downturns is borne by stockholders rather than by employees. Employees are not laid off when sales decline, because the company's major stockholders—banks and other companies with whom it does business—come to its aid. And its most senior managers take substantial cuts in pay rather than allow lower-level workers to bear a financial burden. One has only to compare how Mazda handled its huge deficit in the early 1970s—cutting the pay of senior managers by 20 percent, freezing the pay of middle-level managers, but maintaining cost-of-living increases for its low-level workers and keeping them all employed—with Chrysler's decision, when it faced a similar crisis, to lay off 28 percent of its blue-collar work force but fire only 7 percent of its middle-level managers and cut its white-collar salaries by an average of only 5 percent. Is it any wonder that Mazda's work force was committed to restoring the company to competitive health? Could we expect the same enthusiasm from Chrysler's workers?

Japanese managers ascend the same company ladder as do all other employees; their training begins on the factory floor. A Japanese worker can look forward to becoming a subsection head or a section head in a few years, and with enough diligence may one day become a company director. Indeed, the directors of most Japanese companies come from the ranks of employees, after having worked their way up through the company for twenty or thirty years. Such directors are naturally more likely to identify with the interests of the employees with whom they've worked for decades than with stockholders. They are apt to encourage consultation with employees and to minimize distinctions between labor and management. They are likely to take the long view—investing in their employees' training, career advancement, and long-term welfare.

Perhaps most significantly, Japanese corporate executives draw substantially lower salaries than their American counterparts do: While it is rare for a top manager in Japan to earn more than six times the salary and benefits of the lowest-level workers in the company, it is hardly unusual for top American executives to earn fifteen times that of their company's lowest-level employees.

To an extent unprecedented in the United States, Japanese unions are company unions. Bargaining occurs almost exclusively at the company level; the unions are part of the company. In the largest firms employees are guaranteed employment until the age of fifty-five. Most employees of smaller subcontractors are also protected by the larger companies they serve. Job dismissals are rare. These relationships are codified in Japanese labor law: Japanese courts generally will not uphold a dismissal unless the employer can show that there was no less onerous alternative. Because unions are company unions and because workers expect to stay on forever, the interests of the company and those of the union tend to converge.

American labor law, by contrast, presumes fundamental conflict between managers and employees, as exemplified by the National Labor Relations Act. Supervisors are excluded from the act's protections because they represent management; union membership, it is assumed, would involve supervisors in a conflict of interest. Section 8(a)(2) of the act even makes it an unfair labor practice for employers to "dominate or interfere with the formation or administration of any labor organization or contribute financial or other support to it." It thus bars many management-initiated measures designed to increase union participation in the firm.

This assumed conflict of interest has influenced other areas of American labor-management relations. Under American labor law, employers have no obligation to reveal company finances to employees unless the employers claim an inability to pay the specific wages and benefits that the union demands. Nor do employers have a duty to bargain about decisions to scale back their operations. Nor, in general, must they bargain about investment, production, or site locations. The express logic of these and other related rules is that the National Labor Relations Act did not contemplate perfect equality between labor and management and that in fact managerial prerogatives must be preserved so that companies can maximize shareholders' return on investment. The act requires only that labor and management negotiate toward an agreement in good faith, not that they share the same goals. Indeed, the statute permits parties to employ sometimes debilitating economic weapons to induce the other side to come to terms.

*   *   *

In sum, the Japanese company exists primarily for its employees rather than for its senior managers or stockholders. It seeks to adapt itself to employee needs. In Japan one repeatedly hears the phrase "the enterprise and its employees share a common destiny." Japanese firms do not rely substantially on equity held by individual stockholders, institutions, or companies existing outside the industrial group to which the firm belongs. For the most part, their profit margins are small. Japanese companies aim instead to enlarge their market shares, influence, and dominance—and thereby to enhance the prestige and economic security of all the people associated with them. The network of economic relationships that define the enterprise gives it its value and social meaning. Instead of serving merely as a *means* through which various parties—including investors—make money, the enterprise has independent value as a system of relationships.

The law and ideology underlying American enterprise is fundamentally different. Companies compete for both consumers' dollars and investors' dollars. It is assumed that capital flows to where it can get the highest return and that the primary function of enterprise is to maximize that return. The enterprise is little more than a network of financial relationships within which managers must act on behalf of the investors of capital. Thus, in principle, there is an inherent clash of interests between managers and investors on the one side and employees on the other. Each group will inevitably seek to increase its own share of the firm's revenues.

Without such fundamental conflict, enterprise harmony is possible; with it, harmony is merely an armistice during the intervals between rounds of negotiation, a temporary cessation of reciprocal threat. Not withstanding the quality circles and teams that are now all the rage in American factories, the basic reality of corporate life is not lost on American workers.

This is ironic, of course, because American workers are coming to own more and more of American industry. The growth in employee pension plans over the past twenty years has been no less extraordinary, now reaching over 50 percent of corporate equity. Indeed, pension funds are now America's largest single source of investment. Add to this the group health and life insurance funds of which American workers are the beneficiaries and you have a sizable chunk of all investment in American enterprise. Accordingly, it is becoming technically accurate to say that American companies do *in fact* exist primarily for their employees. But because the lines of responsibility from company to employee are so attenuated—through a maze of plans, trustees, institutional investors, and stock portfolios—most employees don't feel as if their companies exist for them, and American companies don't act as if they do.

* * *

Those who say that the Japanese form of enterprise capitalism cannot take root here because our culture is so different should consider how comparatively new this Japanese ideal is even in Japan. Industrial harmony is largely a postwar phenomenon. The prewar years were marked by bitter struggles between factions within the Army and Navy, between the military and the industrial groups, between tenant farmers and landlords. There were few large enterprises to confer benefits on those who worked for them. Company unions scarcely existed. Trade unions were suppressed by the authorities. Lifetime employment had little meaning in an industrial system in which nearly half the population consisted of impoverished peasants. Economic growth was elusive in the wake of the financial panic of 1927, the invasion of Manchuria in 1931, the fascist attacks on capitalism during the 1930s, the war with China from 1937 to 1941, World War II, the economic collapse of 1946, and the post–Korean War recession of 1954. In the decades ahead, as the Japanese economy and society become further integrated into a global capitalist system in which neither social harmony nor enterprise benefit is a central tenet, these premises may further evolve—or wither.

At the same time, the liberal individualism that infuses America's contractual approach to matters of economic organization is not the only tradition on these shores. There is also a deep strain of civic republicanism, of local political organizations, economic cooperatives, religious groups, and community associations, that has been as concerned with the moral quality of civic life and the relationships on which it is based as with the protection of individual liberties. It is to this tradition, which confers intrinsic value on economic and social relationships, rather than to the direct emulation of the Japanese, that we probably will owe our most enduring experiments with worker participation in management, employee profit sharing, and employee and community ownership of industry.

Of course, there is much about Japanese capitalism that one would not wish the United States to emulate. The job security enjoyed by employees of the largest firms and most of their suppliers is to some extent made possible by the *insecurity* of temporary workers—the vast majority of whom are women—who constitute about 20 percent of the labor force. Although unions comprise a larger percentage of the eligible workers in Japan than in the United States, union coverage does not extend to such temporaries or to the employees of small subcontractors, who typically absorb most of the unemployment during the slack periods. Moreover, several groups continue to be rejected from the Japanese economy. Social barriers have blocked the advancement of Japan's 1.2 million *burakumin* ("ghetto people"), descendants of the lowest social order in feudal Japan. The vast majority of them remain trapped in urban ghettos, working in menial jobs. Japan's seven hundred thousand Koreans and fifteen thousand Ainu—descendants of the country's earliest inhabitants—are also excluded. In addition, women in Japan face social barriers that effectively bar them from responsible positions in industry.

Another unattractive feature of Japanese enterprise is the belief that it is not *possible* for employees' interests to conflict with managers, because managers are working for the benefit of the employees. Employees may make suggestions, of course; they may even, on occasion, express anger over managers' actions. But ultimate responsibility for their well-being rests with those at the top of the management hierarchies. Such paternalism delegitimates employees' independent conclusions about their own needs and interests. Disputes are akin to family squabbles between children and parents; they are to be taken seriously, but everyone realizes that the parents really know best.

*   *   *

Moral exhortation, evangelical pep rallies, and quality circles are no substitutes for the identity of interest between labor and management that occurs within an organization existing primarily and directly for its employees. American managers who try techniques of psychological manipulation may be successful in the short run. But manipulation has no staying power. Workers are not stupid, nor are managers omnipotent. Psychological manipulation invariably breaks down over the long term, resulting in more distrust and higher levels of adversarial combat.

We need fewer managerial lessons in how to better manipulate employees that seek to make professional managers into better manipulators. Perhaps we need fewer professional managers. Instead, we need men and women who understand intimately the nature of work and the processes of production, and who thus can provide practical and effective leadership. And we need productive organizations that unequivocally exist for the benefit of those who work within them.

There is no art to Japanese management. There is no mystery about how to meet the Japanese challenge. While there is much about the Japanese company that we would find abhorrent if transplanted here, there is also much that we can learn from the Japanese about the effective organization of production. Put most simply, we can learn that people are motivated to be productive not because they are well manipulated but because they have a direct stake in future productivity.

9

THE TEAM AS HERO

"Wake up there, youngster," said a rough voice.
Ragged Dick opened his eyes slowly and stared stupidly in
the face of the speaker, but did not offer to get up.
"Wake up, you young vagabond!" said the man a little
impatiently; "I suppose you'd lay there all day, if I hadn't called
you."

So begins the story of *Ragged Dick, or Street Life in New York*,
Horatio Alger's first book—the first of 135 tales written in the late 1800s
that together sold close to twenty million copies. Like all the books that
followed, *Ragged Dick* told the story of a young man who, by pluck and
luck, rises from his lowly station to earn a respectable job and the promise of a better life.

Nearly a century later, another best-selling American business story
offered a different concept of heroism and a different description of the
route to success. This story begins:

All the way to the horizon in the last light, the sea was just
degrees of gray, rolling and frothy on the surface. From the
cockpit of a small white sloop—she was 35 feet long—the
waves looked like hills coming up from behind, and most of the

crew preferred not to glance at them. . . . Running under
shortened sails in front of the northeaster, the boat rocked one
way, gave a thump, and then it rolled the other. The pots and
pans in the galley clanged. A six-pack of beer, which someone
had forgotten to stow away, slid back and forth across the
cabin floor, over and over again. Sometime late that night, one
of the crew raised a voice against the wind and asked, "What
are we trying to prove?"

The book is Tracy Kidder's *The Soul of a New Machine,* a 1981
tale of how a team—a crew—of hardworking inventors built a computer
by pooling their efforts. The opening scene is a metaphor for the team's
efforts and treacherous journey.

Separated by one hundred years, totally different in their explanations of what propels the American economy, these two stories symbolize
the choice that America will face in the 1990s; each celebrates a fundamentally different version of American entrepreneurialism. Which version we choose to embrace will help determine how quickly and how
well the United States adapts to the challenge of global competition.

Horatio Alger's notion of success is the traditional one: the familiar
tale of triumphant individuals, of enterprising heroes who win riches and
rewards through the combination of Dale Carnegie–esque self-improvement, Norman Vincent Peale–esque faith, Sylvester Stallone–esque
assertiveness, and plain, old-fashioned good luck. Tracy Kidder's story,
by contrast, teaches that economic success comes through the talent,
energy, and commitment of a team—through *collective* entrepreneurship.

Stories like these do more than merely entertain or divert us. Like
ancient myths that captured and contained an essential truth, they shape
how we see and understand our lives, how we make sense of our experience. Stories can mobilize us to action and affect our behavior—more
powerfully than simple and straightforward information ever can.

To the extent that we continue to celebrate the traditional myth of
the entrepreneurial hero, we will slow the progress of change and adaptation that is essential to our economic success. If we are to compete
effectively in today's world, we must begin to celebrate collective entrepreneurship, endeavors in which the whole of the effort is greater than
the sum of individual contributions. We need to honor our teams more,
our aggressive leaders and maverick geniuses less.

* * *

The older and still dominant American myth involves two kinds of actors: entrepreneurial heroes and industrial drones—the inspired and the perspired.

In this myth entrepreneurial heroes personify freedom and creativity. They come up with the Big Ideas and build the organizations—the Big Machines—that turn them into reality. They take the initiative, devise technological and organizational innovations, discover new solutions to old problems. They are the men and women who start vibrant new companies, turn around failing companies, and shake up staid ones. To all endeavors, they apply daring and imagination.

The myth of the entrepreneurial hero is as old as America and has served us well in a number of ways. We like to see ourselves as born mavericks and fixers. Our entrepreneurial drive has long been our distinguishing trait. Generations of inventors and investors have kept us on the technological frontier. In a world of naysayers and traditionalists, the American character has always stood out—cheerfully optimistic, willing to run risks, ready to try anything. During World War II, it was the rough-and-ready American GI who could fix the stalled jeep in Normandy while the French regiment only looked on.

Horatio Alger captured this spirit in hundreds of stories. With titles like *Bound to Rise, Luck and Pluck,* and *Sink or Swim,* they inspired millions of readers with a gloriously simple message: In America you can go from rags to riches. The plots were essentially the same; like any successful entrepreneur, Alger knew when he was on to a good thing. A fatherless, penniless boy—possessed of great determination, faith, and courage—seeks his fortune. All manner of villain tries to tempt him, divert him, or separate him from his small savings. But in the end, our hero prevails—not just through pluck; luck plays a part too—and by the end of the story he is launched on his way to fame and fortune.

At the turn of the century Americans saw fiction and reality sometimes converging. Edward Harriman began as a $5-a-week office boy and came to head a mighty railroad empire. John D. Rockefeller rose from a clerk in a commission merchant's house to become one of the world's richest men. Andrew Carnegie started as a $1.20-a-week bobbin boy in a Pittsburgh cotton mill and became the nation's foremost steel magnate. In the early 1900s, when boys were still reading the Alger tales, Henry Ford made his fortune mass-producing the Model T and in the process became both a national folk hero and a potential presidential candidate.

Alger's stories gave the country a noble ideal—a society in which imagination and effort summoned their just reward. The key virtue was self-reliance; the admirable man was the self-made man; the goal was to be your own boss. Andrew Carnegie articulated the prevailing view: "Is any would-be businessman . . . content in forecasting his future, to figure himself as labouring all his life for a fixed salary? Not one, I am sure. In this you have the dividing line between business and nonbusiness; the one is master and depends on profits, the other is servant and depends on salary."

The entrepreneurial hero still captures the American imagination. Inspired by the words of his immigrant father, who told him, "You could be anything you want to be, if you wanted it bad enough and were willing to work for it," Lido Iacocca worked his way up to the presidency of Ford Motor Company, from which he was abruptly fired by Henry Ford II, only to go on to rescue Chrysler from bankruptcy, thumb his nose at Ford in a best-selling autobiography, renovate the Statue of Liberty, and gain mention as a possible presidential candidate. Could Horatio Alger's heroes have done any better?

Peter Ueberroth, son of a traveling aluminum salesman, worked his way through college, single-handedly built a $300 million business, went on to organize the 1984 Olympics, became *Time* magazine's Man of the Year and the commissioner of baseball. Steven Jobs built his own computer company from scratch and became a multimillionaire before his thirtieth birthday. Stories of entrepreneurial heroism come from across the economy and across the country: professors who create whole new industries and become instant millionaires when their inventions go from the laboratory to the marketplace; youthful engineers who quit their jobs, strike out on their own, and strike it rich.

In the American economic mythology these heroes occupy center stage: "Fighters, fanatics, men with a lust for contest, a gleam of creation, and a drive to justify their break from the mother company," says George Gilder. Prosperity for all depends on the entrepreneurial vision of a few rugged individuals.

* * *

If the entrepreneurial heroes hold center stage in this drama, the rest of the vast work force plays a supporting role—supporting and unheralded. Average workers in this myth are drones—cogs in the Big Machines, so many interchangeable parts, unable to perform without direction from above. They are put to work for their hands, not for their minds or imaginations. Their jobs typically appear by the dozens in the help-wanted sections of daily newspapers. Their routines are unvaried. They have little opportunity to use judgment or creativity. To the entrepreneurial hero belongs all the inspiration; the drones are governed by the rules and valued for their reliability and pliability.

These average workers are no villains—but they are certainly no heroes. Uninteresting and uninterested, goes the myth, they lack creative spark and entrepreneurial vision. These are, for example, the nameless and faceless workers who lined up for work in response to Henry Ford's visionary offer of a $5-per-day paycheck. At best, they put in a decent effort in executing the entrepreneurial hero's grand design. At worst, they demand more wages and benefits for less work, do the minimum expected of them, or function as blank bureaucrats mired in standard operating procedure.

The entrepreneurial hero and the worker drone together personify the mythic version of how the American economic system works. The system needs both types, it is assumed. But rewards and treatment for the two are as different as the roles themselves: The entrepreneurs should be disciplined through clear rules and punishments. Considering the overwhelming importance attached to the entrepreneur in this paradigm, the difference seems appropriate. For, as George Gilder has written, "All of us are dependent for our livelihood and progress not on a vast and predictable machine, but on the creativity and courage of the particular men who accept the risks which generate our riches."

* * *

There is just one fatal problem with this dominant myth: It is obsolete. The economy that it describes no longer exists. By clinging to the myth, we subscribe to an outmoded view of how to win economic success—a view that on a number of counts endangers our economic future.

In today's global economy the Big Ideas pioneered by American entrepreneurs travel quickly to foreign lands. In the hands of global competitors, these ideas can undergo continuous adaptation and improvement and reemerge as new Big Ideas or as a series of incrementally improved small ideas.

The machines that American entrepreneurs have always set up so efficiently to execute their Big Ideas are equally footloose. Process technology moves around the globe to find the cheapest labor and the friendliest markets. As ideas migrate overseas, the economic and technological resources needed to implement the ideas migrate too. Workers in other parts of the world are apt to be cheaper or more productive—or both—

than workers in the United States. Around the globe, millions of potential workers are ready to underbid American labor.

Some competitor nations—Japan, in particular—have created relationships among engineers, managers, production workers, and marketing and sales people that do away with the old distinction between entrepreneurs and drones. The dynamic result is yet another basis for challenging American assumptions about what leads to competitive success.

Because of these global changes, the United States is now susceptible to competitive challenge from two directions. First, from developing nations: By borrowing the Big Ideas and process technology that come from the United States and providing the hardworking, low-paid workers, developing nations can achieve competitive advantage. Second, from the Japanese: By embracing collective entrepreneurship, the Japanese especially have found a different way to achieve competitive advantage while maintaining high real wages.

Americans continue to lead the world in breakthroughs and cutting-edge scientific discoveries. But the Big Ideas that start in this country now quickly travel abroad, where they not only get produced at high speed, at low cost, and with great efficiency but also undergo continuous development and improvement. And all too often, American companies get bogged down somewhere between invention and production.

Several product histories make the point. Americans invented the solid-state transistor in 1947. Then in 1953 Western Electric licensed the technology to Sony for $25,000—and the rest is history. A few years later, RCA licensed several Japanese companies to make color televisions —and that was the beginning of the end of color television production in the United States. Routine assembly of color televisions eventually shifted to Taiwan and Mexico. At the same time Sony and other Japanese companies pushed the technology in new directions, continuously refining it into a stream of consumer products.

In 1968 Unimation licensed Kawasaki Heavy Industries to make industrial robots. The Japanese took the initial technology and keep moving it forward. The pattern has been the same for one Big Idea after another. Americans came up with the Big Ideas for videocassette recorders, basic oxygen furnaces, microwave ovens, automobile stamping machines, computerized machine tools, integrated circuits. But these Big Ideas and many, many others quickly found their way into production in foreign countries: routine, standardized production in developing nations or continuous refinement and complex applications in Japan. Either way, the United States has lost ground.

Older industrial economies, like our own, have two options: They can try to match the low wages and discipline under which workers elsewhere in the world are willing to labor, or they can compete on the basis of how quickly and how well they transform ideas into incrementally better products. The second option is, in fact, the only one that offers the possibility of high real incomes in America. But here's the catch: A handful of lone entrepreneurs producing a few industry-making Big Ideas can't execute this second option. Innovation must become both continuous and collective. And that requires embracing a new ideal: collective entrepreneurship.

*　*　*

If America is to win the new global competition, we need to begin telling one another a new story in which companies compete by drawing on the talent and creativity of all their employees, not just a few maverick inventors and dynamic CEOs. Competitive advantage today comes from continuous, incremental innovation and refinement of a variety of ideas that spread throughout the organization. The entrepreneurial organization is both experience based and decentralized so that every advance builds on every previous advance and everyone in the company has the opportunity and capacity to participate.

Although this story represents a departure from tradition, it already exists, in fact, to a greater or lesser extent in every well-run American and Japanese corporation. The difference is that we don't recognize and celebrate this story—and the Japanese do.

Consider just a few of the evolutionary paths that collective entrepreneurship can take: Vacuum-tube radios became transistorized radios, then stereo pocket radios audible through earphones, then compact discs and compact-disc players, and then optical-disc computer memories. Color televisions evolve into digital televisions capable of showing several pictures simultaneously; videocassette recorders, into camcorders. A single strand of technological evolution connects electronic sewing machines, electronic typewriters, and flexible electronic workstations. Basic steels give way to high-strength and corrosion-resistant steels, then to new materials composed of steel mixed with silicon and custom-made polymers. Basic chemicals evolve into high-performance ceramics, to single-crystal silicon and high-grade crystal glass. Copper wire gives way to copper cables, then to fiber-optic cables.

These patterns reveal no clear life cycles with beginnings, middles, and ends. Unlike Big Ideas that beget standardized commodities, these products undergo a continuous process of incremental change and adaptation. Workers at all levels add value not solely or even mostly by tending machines and carrying out routines, but by continuously discovering opportunities for improvement in product and process.

In this context it makes no sense to speak of an "industry," like steel or automobiles or televisions or even banking. There are no clear borders around any of these clusters of goods or services. When products and processes are so protean, companies grow or decline not with the market for some specific good but with the creative and adaptive capacity of their workers.

Workers in such organizations constantly reinvent the company; one idea leads to another. Producing the latest generation of automobiles involves making electronic circuits that govern fuel consumption and monitor engine performance; developments in these devices lead to improved sensing equipment and software for monitoring heartbeats and moisture in the air. Producing cars also involves making flexible robots for assembling parts and linking them by computer; steady improvements in these technologies, in turn, lead to expert production systems that can be applied anywhere. What is considered the "automobile industry" thus becomes a wide variety of technologies evolving toward all sorts of applications that flow from the same strand of technological development toward different markets.

In this paradigm entrepreneurship isn't the sole province of the company's founder or its top managers. Rather, it is a capability and attitude that is diffused throughout the company. Experimentation and development go on all the time as the company searches for new ways to capture and build on the knowledge already accumulated by its workers.

Distinctions between innovation and production, between top managers and production workers, blur. Because production is a continuous process of reinvention, entrepreneurial efforts are focused on many thousands of small ideas rather than on just a few big ones. And because valuable information and expertise are dispersed throughout the organization, top management does not solve problems; it creates an environment in which people can identify and solve problems themselves.

Most of the training for working in this fashion takes place on the job. Formal education may prepare people to absorb and integrate experience, but it does not supply the experience. (See "Dick and Jane Meet the Next Economy," which follows.) No one can anticipate the precise skills that workers will need to succeed on the job when information processing, know-how, and creativity are the value added. Any job that could be fully prepared for in advance is, by definition, a job that could be exported to a low-wage country or programmed into robots and computers; a routine job is a job destined to disappear.

* * *

In collective entrepreneurship individual skills are integrated into a group; this collective capacity to innovate becomes something greater than the sum of its parts. Over time, as group members work through various problems and approaches, they learn about each other's abilities. They learn how they can help one another perform better, what each can contribute to a particular project, how they can best take advantage of one another's experience. Each participant is constantly on the lookout for small adjustments that will speed and smooth the evolution of the whole. The net result of many such small-scale adaptations, effected throughout the organization, is to propel the enterprise forward.

Collective entrepreneurship thus entails close working relationships among people at all stages of the process. If customers' needs are to be recognized and met, designers and engineers must be familiar with sales and marketing. Salespeople must also have a complete understanding of the enterprise's capacity to design and deliver specialized products. The company's ability to adapt to new opportunities and capitalize on them depends on its capacity to share information and involve everyone in the organization in a systemwide search for ways to improve, adjust, adapt, and upgrade.

Collective entrepreneurship also entails a different organizational structure. Under the old paradigm companies are organized into a series of hierarchical tiers so that supervisors at each level can make sure that subordinates act according to plan. It is a structure designed to control. But enterprises designed for continuous innovation and incremental improvement use a structure designed to spur innovation at all levels. Gaining insight into improvement of products and processes is more important than rigidly following rules. Coordination and communication replace command and control. Consequently, there are few middle-level managers and only modest differences in the status and income of senior managers and junior employees.

Simple accounting systems are no longer adequate or appropriate for monitoring and evaluating job performance: Tasks are intertwined and interdependent, and the quality of work is often more important than the quantity of work. In a system where each worker depends on many others—and where the success of the company depends on all— the only appropriate measurement of accomplishment is a collective one. At the same time the reward system reflects this new approach: Profit sharing, gain sharing, and performance bonuses all demonstrate that the success of the company comes from the broadest contribution of all the company's employees, not just those at the top.

Finally, under collective entrepreneurship workers do not fear technology and automation as a threat to their jobs. When workers add value through judgment and knowledge, computers become tools that expand their discretion. Computer-generated information can give workers rich feedback about their own efforts, how they affect others in the production process, and how the entire process can be improved. One of the key lessons to come out of the General Motors–Toyota joint venture in California is that the Japanese automaker does not rely on automation and technology to replace workers in the plant. In fact, human workers still occupy the most critical jobs—those where judgment and evaluation are essential. Instead, Toyota uses technology to allow workers to focus on those important tasks where choices have to be made. Under this approach, technology gives workers the chance to use their imagination and their insight on behalf of the company.

* * *

In 1986 one of America's largest and oldest enterprises announced that it was changing the way it assigned its personnel: The U.S. Army discarded a system that assigned soldiers to their units individually in favor of a system that keeps teams of soldiers together for their entire tours of duty. An Army spokesperson explained: "We discovered that individuals perform better when they are part of a stable group. They are more reliable. They also take responsibility for the success of the overall operation."

In one of its recent advertisements BellSouth captured the new story. "BellSouth is not a bunch of individuals out for themselves," the ad proclaimed. "We're a team."

Collective entrepreneurship is already here. It shows up in the way our best-run companies now organize their work, regard their workers, design their enterprises. Yet the old myth of the entrepreneurial hero remains powerful.

Bookstores bulge with new volumes paying homage to American CEOs. It is a familiar story; it is an engaging story. And no doubt, when seen through the eyes of the CEO, it accurately portrays how that individual experienced the company's success. But what gets left out time after time are the experiences of the rest of the team—the men and women at every level of the company whose contributions to the company created the success that the CEO so eagerly claims. Where are the books that celebrate their stories?

If the United States is to compete effectively in the world in a way designed to enhance the real incomes of Americans, we must bring collective entrepreneurship to the forefront of the economy. That will require us to change our attitudes, to downplay the myth of the entrepreneurial hero, and to celebrate our creative teams.

First, we will need to look for and promote new kinds of stories. In modern-day America, stories of collective entrepreneurship typically appear in the sports pages of the daily newspaper; time after time, in accounts of winning efforts we learn that the team with the best blend of talent won—the team that emphasized teamwork—not the team with the best individual athlete. The cultural challenge is to move these stories from the sports page to the business page. We need to shift the limelight from maverick founders and shake-'em-up CEOs to groups of engineers, production workers, and marketers who successfully innovate new products and services. We need to look for opportunities to tell stories about American business from the perspective of all the workers who make up the team, rather than solely from the perspective of top managers. The stories are there—we need only change our focus, alter our frame of reference, in order to find them.

Second, we will need to understand that the most powerful stories get told, not in books and newspapers, but in the everyday world of work. Whether managers know it or not, every decision they make suggests a story to the rest of the enterprise. Decisions to award generous executive bonuses or to provide plush executive dining rooms and executive parking places tell the old story of entrepreneurial heroism. A decision to lay off 10 percent of the work force tells the old story of the drone worker. Several years ago, when General Motors reached agreement on a contract with the United Auto Workers that called for a new relationship based on cooperation and shared sacrifice and then, on the same day, announced a new formula for generous executive bonuses, long-time union members simply nodded to themselves. The actions told the whole story. It is not enough to acknowledge the importance of collective entrepreneurship; clear and consistent signals must reinforce the new story.

Under collective entrepreneurship all those associated with the company become partners in its future. The distinction between entrepreneurs and drones breaks down. Each member of the enterprise participates in its evolution. All have a commitment to the company's continued success. It is the one approach that can maintain and improve America's competitive performance—and America's standard of living —over the long haul.

10

DICK AND JANE
MEET THE NEXT ECONOMY

WHAT KIND OF EDUCATION WILL THE NEXT GENERATION OF AMERICANS need? The conventional view is that they will need *more* and *better* education, but there is surprisingly little agreement about what *more* and *better* actually mean.

Education is one of those issues about which many people have strong opinions. This is because almost everyone has been educated. Or more accurately, almost everyone has been *subjected* to education. Those with the strongest views on the matter tend to be those on whom the experience has had the least lasting effect. The truly educated person understands how ambiguous are the goals of education, and how complex the means.

By focusing on the relationship between education and the next economy, I do not mean to suggest that education's only, or most important, purpose is economic. To the contrary: A truly educated person is motivated by, and can find satisfaction in, a wide array of things that are not traded in markets or that cost very little. A just and democratic society depends on a citizenry educated in civic responsibility rather than economic aggrandizement.

* * *

In the early postwar years most young people could look forward to jobs requiring only that they be able to learn some relatively simple task that could be repeated, over and over. That's because the American economy was organized around economies of scale. The overarching goal was high-volume standardized production in which large numbers of identical items could be produced over long runs, allowing fixed costs to be spread as widely as possible. Whether it was wheat, steel, or even insurance, the same overarching rule prevailed: Every step along the production process was to be simple and predictable so that it could be synchronized with every other step. Productivity was a function of high volume and low cost.

There was little room or need for innovation. Once in a while someone came up with a major invention—for example, continuous casters for making steel, automobile stamping machines, plastics—but these big breakthroughs were relatively rare. In fact, innovation often was seen as a problem rather than as a solution. Innovation meant changes in products and production processes, and such changes cost money. If the changes happened too often, it was difficult to achieve the economies of scale necessary to pay for them and still make a profit.

In fact, competitors quietly agreed not to innovate very much for fear of rocking this profitable boat. These were the days when most industries were dominated by a few large companies—the Big Three automakers, a handful of steel producers, three or four major food processors—who quietly, but efficiently, coordinated prices and investments in order to achieve the stability and predictability necessary for vast economies of scale. The tail fins on our cars grew longer, but underneath the hoods the autos remained about the same year after year, and it did not matter very much which brand one bought.

Under high-volume standardized production, as has been noted in a previous chapter, a few people at the top made all the decisions. They designed the system and planned all the standard operating procedures by which it would run. Most people followed orders. Indeed, for the production system to be stable and predictable, the majority had to follow orders exactly. Rigid work rules and job classifications posed no challenge to this hierarchical system, because every job was rigid to begin with—like cogs in a giant wheel.

A primary goal of public education within this stable system was to prepare most young people for such "cog" jobs. They had to be trained to comprehend and accept instructions, and then to implement them conscientiously. Discipline and reliability were core virtues.

A much smaller number of young people had to be prepared to act as decision makers at the top. They needed to be trained to gather information, translate the information into abstract symbols, manipulate the symbols to find answers, turn the answers into operating instructions, and then communicate the instructions downward. Here, abstract logic, clarity, and firmness were the core virtues.

Our schools were reasonably effective at preparing Americans for these two kinds of jobs. Most children graduated from high school or vocational school ready to accept cog jobs. A few were set on an advanced track through high school and into colleges that prepared them either for careers as professional managers or for the related professions of law, banking, engineering, and consulting. Productivity soared.

* * *

Unfortunately, high-volume standardized production can no longer provide the productivity gains needed to maintain our standard of living. In a world where routine production is footloose and millions of potential workers are eager to work for wages far lower than Americans are willing to work for, we can no longer expect to be competitive simply by producing more of the same thing we produced before, at lower cost. As the production of commodities shifts to other nations, America's competitive advantage correspondingly must shift toward work the value of which is based more on quality, flexibility, precision, and specialization than on its low cost. For example, only a small fraction of the American work force is still employed on the farm. But the food industry nevertheless accounts for close to one quarter of the jobs in the United States. That's because most of what Americans and consumers in other advanced nations now spend for food goes to the people who process, package, market, and retail it, and to the agricultural epidemiologists, geneticists, international bankers, commodity traders, chemists, and process engineers who supply the technology and money for producing it, rather than to those who actually grow and harvest it. Similarly, most of what is spent on appliances, clothing, cars, computers, air travel, or a host of other things is for designing, engineering, fabricating, and advertising, rather than for standardized, routine work. In fact, much of the growth in what has been termed services within the American economy is attributable to just such businesses.

The older industrial economies like America thus have two options: (1) They can try to match the wages for which workers elsewhere are willing to labor, or (2) they can compete on the basis of how quickly and how well they can transform ideas into incrementally better goods and services. Both paths can boost profits and improve competitiveness in the short run, but only the second can maintain and improve the standard of living of most Americans over time.

The first path—toward stable mass production—relies on cutting labor costs and leaping into wholly new product lines as old ones are played out. For managers this path has meant undertaking (or threatening) massive layoffs, moving (or threatening to move) to lower-wage states and countries, parceling out work to lower-cost suppliers, automating to cut total employment, and diversifying into radically different goods and services. For workers this path has meant defending existing jobs and pay scales, grudgingly conceding lower wages and benefits, shifting burdens by accepting lower-pay scales for newly hired workers, seeking protection from foreign competition, and occasionally striking.

The second path involves increasing labor's *value*. For managers this path means continuously retraining employees for more complex tasks, automating in ways that cut routine tasks and enhance worker flexibility and creativity, diffusing responsibility for innovation, taking seriously labor's concern for job security and giving workers a stake in improved productivity via profit-linked bonuses and stock plans. For workers this second path means accepting flexible job classifications and work rules, agreeing to wage rates linked to profits and productivity improvements, and generally taking greater responsibility for the soundness and efficiency of the enterprise. The second path also involves a closer and more permanent relationship with other parties that have a stake in the firm—suppliers, dealers, creditors, even the towns and cities in which the firm resides. On this second path, all those associated with the firm become partners in its future, sharing downside risks and upside benefits. Each member of the enterprise participates in its evolution. All have a commitment to its continued success.

The second path to the next economy relies, above all, on a work force capable of rapid learning. Many important skills will be transferred informally among workers as they gain experience on the job, rather than gleaned through formal education and training. But the ability to learn on the job will depend on learning skills and attitudes developed long before.

*   *   *

In some respects, the training of young people in the old economy resembled the system of high-volume standardized production in which they were to take part when their training was complete: Responsibility was exercised by a very few, at the top. The majority of students were pushed, as if on an assembly line, through a preestablished sequence of steps. Each step involved particular routines and practices. Teachers— the production workers—had little discretion over what they had to do to each batch that passed through; students passively received whatever was doled out. Inspectors tried to weed out the defects, sometimes returning them to an earlier step for reworking. Most students got to the end of the assembly line, more or less ready to take their places along real assembly lines somewhere in the economy.

The premises of education in the next economy must be quite different. Just as productivity can no longer be a matter of making more of what we already make at less cost per unit, productivity in education cannot be solely a function of the numbers of children who pass standardized examinations at a lower cost per unit. Because our future economy will depend to an ever greater extent on thinking, rather than repeating learned information, future reforms must motivate teachers and students alike to engage in the *process* of learning. Rather than prescribe exactly what should be learned and how and when the information should be doled out, reformers should aim at improving students' capacities to learn. Just as in the enterprise of the future, responsibility for education must be pushed downward, to students and teachers. They must be allowed and encouraged to take more initiative in deciding what is learned, and when and how it is learned. Education modeled around long lists of facts that "every adult should know" and standardized tests will produce robots adept at Trivial Pursuit but unable to think for themselves or to innovate for the future.

How can teachers better help students learn how to learn? First, instead of giving students information along a preestablished sequence of steps and then asking them to "play back" the information on tests, the emphasis in teaching should be on educating young people to formulate problems and questions for themselves. Thus, rather than teach students to assume that problems and solutions are generated by others (as they were under high-volume standardized production), students should be led to understand that problems and questions are created, that students can have an active role in creating them, and that such critical and creative approaches can guide them through their careers.

Second, instead of teaching through repetition and drill, the emphasis should be on allowing students to experiment for themselves with solving the problems they help define. Thus, rather than conveying particular pieces of information or imposing established routines—a type of teaching and learning relevant to high-volume standardized production —teachers must help students gain the experience of working through problems and thus discovering underlying principles that help define and solve related problems.

The difference between absorbing information and gaining understanding depends on how much responsibility students are taught to accept for their own continuing learning. It is like the difference between learning how to get from one location to another in a city by having someone drive you or by driving yourself with a guide sitting beside you. In the first instance you may eventually learn the way, but you probably will learn sooner by being in the driver's seat. Indeed, if your guide also allows you to experiment a bit, warning you only when you're going down blind alleys or heading in the wrong direction, you may gain even more understanding of the terrain and thus learn how to find other places as well.

An understanding of underlying principles and patterns allows discovery of other information and gives that new information added context and meaning. The new information, in turn, permits deeper insight into the principles and patterns. As Michael Polanyi has written, "[w]e cannot comprehend the whole without seeing its parts, but we cannot see the parts without comprehending the whole." *

The habits and techniques of experimentation—of iterative discovery of parts and wholes—will be critical in the next economy, where technologies, tastes, and markets are likely to be in constant flux. Informal, on-the-job education will be a central aspect of work. Formal education and training will no longer be limited to young people but will be available on a continuing basis to workers throughout their working lives—an accepted and expected aspect of one's career. A work force capable of taking responsibility for its own continuous learning will prove a more precious national asset than countless new factories and equipment.

* * *

In the old economy, a relatively few people at the top could analyze and plan the production process by themselves and then issue operating instructions to everyone else. So long as professional managers and their professional aides—bankers, lawyers, accountants, and engineers—got it "right" on paper, it was assumed that the rest would follow automat-

* *The Study of Man* (Chicago: University of Chicago Press, 1958), pg. 29.

ically. But paper professionals are far less relevant to the future economy. As has been noted, the weakest link in the American economy is between ideas and implementation, between paper and product. Thus, if our business enterprises are to be as flexible and innovative at all levels as they need to be, our youngsters must be prepared to work with and through other people. While there will always be a need for a certain number of solo practitioners, the more usual requirement will be that combinations of individual skills are greater than their sums. Most of the important work will be done by groups, rather than by individual experts.

Learning to collaborate suggests a different kind of education than one designed to prepare a relatively few talented young people to become professional experts. Instead of emphasizing the quiet and solitary performance of specialized tasks, a greater emphasis should be placed on interactive communications linked to group problem-definitions and solutions. Students should learn to articulate, clarify, and then restate for one another how they determine questions and find answers. Rather than be trained to communicate specialized instructions and requests— skills relevant to high-volume standardized production—students should learn how to share their understandings and build on each other's insights.

Communication skills are only one aspect of collaboration. Young people also must be taught how to work constructively together. Instead of emphasizing individual achievement and competition, the emphasis in the classroom should be on group performance. Students need to learn how to seek and accept criticism from their peers, to solicit help, and to give credit to others, where appropriate. They must also learn to negotiate—to articulate their own needs, to discern what others need and see things from others' perspectives, and to discover mutually beneficial outcomes.

The "tracking" system, by which students are grouped in the classroom according to the speed of their learning, is another vestige of high-volume standardized production—the deluxe models moving along a different conveyor belt from the economy cars. This may be an efficient way to cram information into young minds with differing capacities to absorb it; but tracking or grouping can also reduce young people's capacities to learn from and collaborate with one another. Rather than separate fast learners from slow learners in the classroom, all children (with only the most obvious exceptions) should remain together so that class unity and cooperation are the norm. Faster learners would thus learn how to help the slower ones, while the slower ones would be pushed harder to make their best effort.

In sum, it is not enough to produce a cadre of young people with specialized skills. If our enterprises are to be the scenes of collective entrepreneurship—as they must be—experts must have the ability to share their skills broadly and transform them into organizational achievement; and others must be prepared to learn from them.

III

OF COLD
AND
TEPID
WARS

11

THE RISE
OF TECHNO-NATIONALISM

ON OCTOBER 23, 1986, FUJITSU, LTD., THE LARGE JAPANESE ELECTRON-
ics company, announced that it would buy Fairchild Semiconductor Corporation, a Silicon Valley firm. (Fairchild had needed cash in order to
stay competitive; its executives had approached Fujitsu, which had been
seeking to acquire an American technology company.) The announce-
ment of the proposed sale was greeted with dismay in Washington.
Fairchild produces high-speed electronic circuits on tiny chips of silicon,
which instruct all sorts of weapons systems in how they should operate.
Between a third and a half of Fairchild's production is sold to American
defense contractors. Pentagon officials worried that the proposed sale
would put critical technology into the hands of the Japanese. Officials in
the Commerce Department were concerned that the deal would give
Fujitsu control over related chip technologies that are used in many
American products, from automobiles to telecommunications equipment
—at a time when American competitiveness is thought to be in jeopardy.

The Reagan Administration never decided whether to ban the sale.
It didn't have to. Citing the "rising political controversy" in the United
States, Fujitsu finally decided to drop the deal on its own. But the concern
that the proposed deal aroused is itself noteworthy. Fairchild is not the

only American company producing such specialized chips. Technically, it is not even an American company; it was bought in 1979 by Schlumberger, the French oil-field-services firm. The proposed sale to Fujitsu would violate no American law. Nevertheless, the deal touched a raw nerve. All over America there is growing worry that the Japanese are running off with our technology.

This new concern is, I believe, misplaced. Americans are correct to worry about national technological prowess but not about Japanese access to our technology. The emerging debate over how to restore America's technological preeminence misconstrues the problem and thus advances the wrong solutions. The underlying predicament is not that the Japanese are exploiting our discoveries but that we can't turn basic inventions into new products nearly as fast or as well as they can. Rather than guard our technological breakthroughs, we should learn how better to make use of breakthroughs wherever they occur around the globe. In this, the Japanese may have much to teach us.

* * *

With the important exceptions of restrictions on the transfer of "sensitive" technologies to the Soviets and their allies, on the sale of major weapons systems, and on the pursuit of classified research by Eastern-bloc nationals, techno-globalism has been the norm in America. From the techno-globalist's point of view, it is meaningless to speak of America's discoveries and technological breakthroughs relative to those of Japan, West Germany, or any other friendly nation, because there is no way to separate "our" technological advances from "theirs." Technological development is a joint product of multinational institutions— universities, research laboratories, corporations, even defense programs —that link talented people from all corners of the globe through computers, satellite communications, and jet airplanes.

This organizing principle has taken deep root in America. Basic research is now a worldwide undertaking. The scientists and engineers who populate American universities and laboratories typically think of themselves as members of a global community of researchers who work jointly on projects, meet periodically at international conferences, exchange papers, and publish their findings worldwide. Their graduate students come from every nation on earth. Even the funding of American university research is now global. A substantial portion is sponsored by foreign companies, especially Japanese.

Foreign companies, meanwhile, are setting up research laboratories in the United States and staffing them with American scientists and engineers. American companies are doing much the same abroad—especially in Japan. More than 180 Japanese scientists and technicians now populate DuPont's Yokohama laboratory, where they develop new materials technologies. IBM is investing heavily in Japanese research: At IBM's Tokyo Research Laboratory, tucked away behind the far side of the Imperial Palace in downtown Tokyo, a small army of Japanese engineers is busy perfecting image-processing technology. At IBM's Kanagawa lab, in Yamato City, Japan, fifteen hundred researchers are developing hardware and software for the next generation of computers.

In 1988 Japanese companies placed more than $500 million in U.S. venture-capital funds. Rather than high financial returns, the Japanese want licensing, marketing, and joint-venture agreements with the companies they back. American companies likewise are buying some of their most complex technologies from foreign firms. West Germany's Siemens and Canada's Northern Telecom have become key suppliers of electronic components used by American makers of telecommunications equipment. West German and Italian companies are supplying other American manufacturers with precision castings, forgings, and ball bearings.

Even the Defense Department, which is responsible for funding about one third of all the research and development undertaken by U.S. corporations, has for the most part adopted an ecumenical attitude toward the advancement of new technologies. In 1983 it got Tokyo's agreement to allow Japanese companies to sell or license technology to American corporations working under contract to the Pentagon (marking the first time that the Japanese government had allowed Japanese companies to work even indirectly on American defense contracts). In 1986 the Pentagon secured West Germany's and Japan's cooperation on research for the Strategic Defense Initiative (unceremoniously dubbed "Star Wars"). Our allies remain skeptical that Star Wars will ever work as advertised. But they were seduced into joining the effort by the prospect of picking up expertise in the technologies involved—technologies that they believed would be important to their future economic competitiveness.

Techno-globalism, in sum, has come to be America's central, albeit tacit, organizing principle for developing new technologies. The notion of "American" technology has thus become a meaningless concept. Across a broad expanse of the globe (excluding little but the Soviet Union and its allies) national boundaries have in this respect become less and less relevant.

* * *

The principle of techno-globalism has helped American universities, corporations, and the Pentagon accomplish what each of these institutions has understood to be its primary goal: generating, respectively, new knowledge, high profits, and state-of-the-art weaponry. But other interests are at stake as well, and they appear to be in fundamental conflict with these more proximate goals. Increasingly, techno-globalism is being challenged by a different organizing principle, which looks to America's relative prowess—both military and economic—in the world of sovereign nations.

There is a new concern that as America becomes ever more dependent on "them" for advanced technologies, our economic leadership will be threatened and our national defense imperiled. Two related phenomena lie behind this anxiety. The first is America's trade balance in high-technology goods, like computers, communications equipment, and scientific instruments, which in 1986 turned negative for the first time ever. This negative balance is owing in part to the insatiable appetite of American consumers and government officials for all sorts of imports (of which high-tech products are a mere subset), and in part to the sluggishness of overall foreign demand. But the loss of competitiveness in high-technology products within our domestic markets is troublesome nonetheless. As our indebtedness to the rest of the world—particularly to Japan—steadily mounts, the loss of high-tech competitiveness threatens our standard of living. The only way to pay off the debt without dramatically lowering our standard of living sometime in the future is to achieve equally dramatic increases in productivity. To become that much more productive, we would need to perfect and apply the very technologies in which Japan is gaining dominance. The knowledge gleaned by perfecting each new generation of technology spills over into other areas of the economy, creating a national pool of talent and technological experience that can improve productivity overall. Because each new generation of technology builds on that which came before, once off the technological escalator it's difficult to get back on. At best, our standard of living would continue to fall relative to that of the Japanese.

The second phenomenon is our new commercial and military vulnerability to the Japanese, should they choose to hold back their high-tech gadgets from us. Japanese microelectronics, in particular, now lie at the heart of many American products—from telecommunications equipment to automobiles. They are also vital to our advanced weapons systems. Most primary defense contractors on advanced weapons systems are American firms, but more and more, their subcontractors supplying the most advanced electronic components are Japanese. On the basis of data supplied by the Board of Army Science and Technology and the International Trade Commission, I estimate that 40 percent, by value, of the advanced electronics finding their way into American weapons systems are now coming from Japan. If the present trend continues, the proportion will rise to 55 percent by 1992. A substantial portion of the advanced electronics for the Strategic Defense Initiative will be produced in Japan.

In many cases American companies that were on the leading edge of microelectronics several years ago have simply dropped out of the running. With the costs of perfecting each new generation of technology escalating rapidly, and the time interval during which the investment can be recouped growing shorter, the price of staying in the race has often become too high relative to the return. A world-class factory for fabricating semiconductors now costs around $200 million. By 1995, when X-ray lithography will be used to fabricate semiconductors, the cost will be $1 billion. Few firms will be able to afford to stay in the race. Monsanto used to produce "float-zone" silicon, a material used in fabricating high-power electronic switching devices, indispensable to space-based weaponry. But since Monsanto abandoned the market, in 1983, the Pentagon has been totally dependent on Japanese companies for it. In 1987 Intel announced that it would cease production of "bubble" memories, used primarily in fighter planes and communications satellites. This left the Pentagon dependent on Hitachi and Fujitsu. The National Security Agency, charged with electronic eavesdropping and communications security, buys almost all its ceramic packages (used to house and protect the chip circuits) from one Japanese company, Kyocera. Richard Reynolds, director of the Defense Sciences Office at the Defense Advanced Research Projects Agency, summed up the situation: "In some cases you either buy from Japan or you don't get it."

Most of the world's memory chips—the fingernail-size circuits that drive just about every electronic gadget you can name, including almost all of the electronics necessary for Star Wars—are now made in Japan, which is also their largest market. Japanese companies are on the way to dominating world production of gallium-arsenide computer chips (capable of processing data much faster than conventional silicon chips), on which Star Wars is particularly dependent. The innards of supercomputers, also vital to Star Wars, increasingly come from Japan as well. Cray

—the largest American manufacturer of supercomputers—must get its advanced memory chips from either Fujitsu or Hitachi. Japanese companies are even taking over the technologies needed to make advanced memory chips—everything from the microlithography that prints tiny circuits on slivers of silicon to the manufacture of the ceramic casings surrounding the circuits. Japanese companies are now the dominant producers of equipment for scrubbing and baking silicon wafers, for insulating the circuits, inspecting and testing them, and assembling and packaging them. The Japanese dominate world production of the materials of which chips are made, such as high-quality silicon and quartz glass. Japanese dominance extends even to the construction companies that produce "clean rooms," in which advanced chips are made.

In 1980 fifteen American companies, all of them profitable, were producing most of the world's memory chips, and American companies produced most of the components and equipment for making chips. By now, most American producers of chip-making equipment have closed up shop. Erich Bloch, the director of the National Science Foundation, said, "The [American chip] industry is going downhill at a faster rate than anybody ever thought possible."

* * *

The Pentagon's new vulnerability in microelectronics is now a subject of heated debate in Washington, particularly at the highest reaches of the Pentagon and the National Security Council (NSC). In 1987 the NSC circulated a draft report on the extent of American dependence on Japanese microelectronics. The report is notable not only for linking the two kinds of vulnerability—military and economic—but also for portraying America's interests in terms quite different from the prevailing globalism:

> Leadership in research and development in advanced (non-silicon) semiconductor materials and devices seems to already be passing to Japan, especially in the optical electronic fields which may be the basis of the highest performance end products of the future. . . . With some significant exceptions computer software R&D is still clearly an American strength, but the Japanese are becoming expert in the architecture of mainframes and supercomputers, and obviously in the manufacturing and engineering of personal computers. Telecommunications component research is becoming dominated by the Japanese, and while their strengths in downstream system and network

industries are more limited, the trend is toward Japanese leadership in some communication systems based on their advantages in semiconductor components. Industrial automation is a field where the Japanese not only already dominate the present market, but also research and development in most subdisciplines. Clearly the conventional model of U.S. technological leadership in basic research followed by more successful Japanese commercial exploitation is no longer accurate in many of the critical technologies targeted by the Japanese.

According to the NSC report, this trend threatens not only America's defense capabilities but also its standard of living:

> By the turn of the century, microelectronics will certainly have major direct effects upon the performance of industries which will directly account for perhaps a quarter of GNP, and which have powerful effects upon military capabilities, economy-wide productivity, and living standards. These include automobiles, industrial automation, computer systems, defense and aerospace products, telecommunications, and many consumer goods. . . . If the United States loses competitive advantage in these industries, its productivity, living standards, and growth will suffer severely. Moreover, these industries are dominated by a few nations and firms so that competitive advantage brings significant economic profits and political influence. Thus if the United States becomes a net importer and a technically inferior producer, it would also become a less independent, less influential, and less secure nation.

The immediate danger, according to the NSC report, is that Japanese high-tech firms could withhold their advanced chips and related technologies from American firms that have become dependent on them and could thus "impede the ability of the United States to compete in almost any area of manufacturing."

The report speaks of America's declining technological strength and of Japan's coming technological lead. The adjectives alone convey the critical difference between this view and that of techno-globalism.

* * *

New policies are being proposed to help America pursue advanced technologies. The policies take many forms and are being advocated, piecemeal, in many quarters. Their unifying characteristic is the unambiguously *national* orientation they would give to the development of new technologies. The goal is to keep technological knowledge *here*. In contrast to the prevailing principle of techno-globalism, this one might be called techno-nationalism.

Listen to the new voice of techno-nationalism: When asked whether he would support a proposal to boost federal research funds for American universities on the condition that the research be restricted to American citizens, Richard Cyert, the president of Pittsburgh's prestigious Carnegie-Mellon University (one of America's centers of research on advanced industrial processes), responded affirmatively. "I'm sure it would be unpopular, in the sense that we like to think of ourselves as world citizens. . . . But we want to have America get some temporary advantage from the research that we can do."

Watch Congress turn toward techno-nationalism: The Federal Technology and Transfer Act of 1986, quietly passed by the Ninety-ninth Congress, authorizes America's national laboratories to license their inventions to private firms—but not just to any company willing to pay the highest price. The legislation requires that preference be given to American firms. Watch American companies seek government's help in furthering techno-nationalism: The Semiconductor Industry Association, a trade group of American chip makers, has joined forces with a congeries of giant American computer firms to create an ultramodern chip-production facility. Known as Sematech, the plant is to be a proving ground for state-of-the-art equipment necessary for making the next generation of chips. "This is our last chance," the president of the trade group told me in late 1987. "If we lose the ability to make this equipment in America, we might as well fold up the tent." Every major American chip producer and computer manufacturer has signed up to participate in the project, the cost of which will exceed $1 billion over the next five years. The Pentagon has agreed to pay a substantial portion of the cost. But here's the condition: Whatever state-of-the-art devices emerge from this ambitious project must go only to American companies.

One of the strongest recommendations to emerge from all the policy panels, industry groups, and think tanks is to increase federal spending for American research and development. In a report to the secretary of defense, for example, the Defense Science Board recommended that the U.S. government spend roughly $2 billion over the next five years for semiconductor research and development. About half that sum would go to the above-mentioned project, from which foreign companies would be banned. The remainder would establish university "centers for excellence" in scientific and engineering research (open to American researchers) and directly fund semiconductor research by American firms.

We can expect more of the same in the future. Democrats in Congress are busily devising plans for spurring American technology by spending more on research and development by American companies. The White House, meanwhile, has been exploring ways to tap Star Wars research for American commercial technology and to ward off further Japanese takeovers of American companies in "strategic" industries. The Bush Administration wants to enlarge the budget of the National Science Foundation, sponsor science and technology centers in American universities, and fund giant research projects, such as a $6 billion particle accelerator.

The overriding goal of these initiatives is to protect future American technological breakthroughs from exploitation at the hands of foreigners, especially the Japanese. In contrast to techno-globalism, this new principle presumes the possibility—indeed, the necessity—of viewing American technology as a body of knowledge separate and distinct from that possessed by other nations. Technology is viewed as something that can be uniquely American—developed here, contained within the nation's borders, applied in America by Americans. It is like a precious commodity that we should save for ourselves rather than allow foreigners to carry off.

* * *

Techno-nationalism faces three formidable difficulties. First and most obvious is the logistical challenge of confining new knowledge within national borders. Modern technology typically doesn't leak out in boxcars or briefcases. Instead, blueprints and designs flow out over the airwaves, by satellite, from one computer to another.

The second challenge is more paradoxical. As we have seen, American universities, corporations, and even the Defense Department are now international endeavors. Their technological advances come by way of global projects that draw upon talented people the world over. To graft techno-nationalism onto these techno-global systems leads to absurd results.

The paradox becomes clear when considering how any of these initiatives might actually work in practice. How, for example, might an American university go about the task of excluding foreigners from major research projects? The first problem would be how to define who was foreign. A good many American university professors and graduate students are of foreign origin and only later become American citizens. Some are permanent resident aliens; some, here on temporary visas, hope and expect to remain in the United States. Some are American citizens who plan to teach and live abroad for long periods of time after they finish their research, and who will thus carry off whatever they learn. What about an American citizen employed by a Japanese company? Should he be excluded as well? Beyond the problem of deciding who should be excluded, there is the issue of what such people should be barred from doing. Should foreigners be permitted to talk with American researchers about what's being learned? May they assist the American researchers—as research assistants or as administrative, clerical, or maintenance workers?

The questions grow even more tangled when it comes to distinguishing between American and foreign companies. Only American firms will be allowed to participate in the Sematech project; American firms will get first crack at inventions coming from national laboratories; the Defense Department doesn't want foreigners owning American high-tech companies. But what's an "American" firm?

Suppose that most of the shareholders and directors of a company are foreign, but its headquarters is in the United States and most of its employees are American. (This describes Fairchild before Fujitsu sought to take it over.) Does this firm qualify? Or suppose that a large and growing portion of the firm's shareholders are foreign, and 40 percent of its employees live and work abroad. Does this firm qualify? (It's IBM.)

Or consider an American-owned and -managed firm that has factories and research laboratories around the globe. This firm continuously applies what it discovers in one country to new products and processes being developed in another and regularly shifts its scientists and engineers around the world. Should it be given special access to American technology? And what about an American-based firm that shares its technology with a Japanese firm and markets the Japanese-made products in the United States? In both instances American firms are apt to be exploiting American technology but using it elsewhere. Do these firms pass muster?

Most American high-tech companies are well along in the process of losing their uniquely American identities. Faced with Japanese competitors that have more money to spend on research and development, and better-trained employees, even the largest and most well-endowed American firms have concluded that joining them is a wiser strategy than trying to beat them. Motorola—one of America's leading electronics companies—is linking up with Toshiba to build a new chip-making factory in Sendai, Japan. Toshiba is supplying the technology needed for the next generation of memory chips, and Motorola the technology for the next generation of logic chips (Motorola still has an edge in this category of chip technology, which instructs computers in how to solve problems). AT&T has joined with Fujitsu to challenge IBM's dominance in computer systems. In both deals the American firms are sharing their latest technology with their Japanese partners, and vice versa. If the underlying purpose of techno-nationalism is to keep American technology here, then presumably Motorola, AT&T, and all the other American electronics firms now sharing technology with their Japanese counterparts should be excluded—lest the Japanese gain instant access to our technology. But by this criterion few "American" firms—if any—would remain eligible.

These paradoxes suggest an inconvenient truth: Techno-nationalism cannot be superimposed on institutions organized on the basis of techno-globalism. Even if it were clearly in the national interest to try to keep America's technological learning at home, this goal is too sharply at odds with the premises on which our universities and corporations are based for it to provide a meaningful guide for public policy.

* * *

The third challenge that the principle of techno-nationalism faces goes even deeper: It is not in America's interest to bar foreigners from the fruits of our research and development. Technology is not like a scarce commodity, to be hoarded up. Its real value to us is only indirectly related to the gadgets it spawns at any given time. Nor does its value lie in information that can be conveyed through data, blueprints, or instructions. The value of technological learning is a certain kind of knowledge, founded in shared experience. It exists in people's heads. Thus, the real worry is not that we are becoming dependent on Japan's high-tech gadgets but that we are losing the ability to transform new discoveries into gadgets nearly as efficiently as they can.

Most advances in technology build on what has come before—on prior technological experience. A dramatic discovery or ground-breaking invention may win a prize and bring fame to its progenitor. But such breakthroughs generally mean less to a nation's economic or military might than the speed and success with which they are absorbed, improved upon, and incorporated into new products and processes.

Scientists, engineers, and tinkerers of all sorts progress mostly by applying their understanding of technologies to new problems. They rearrange solutions in new ways, make incremental improvements in previous methods of doing things, and try out new variations on themes.

Experience—the breadth and depth of familiarity with technology—is what determines the technological fecundity of a society. Mere information, such as specific data about the latest discovery or blueprints of a new invention, is relatively useless for designing future generations of technology. It may solve an immediate technological problem, but it does not provide experience for solving the next one. It supplies answers but it does not teach. (Indeed, access to information may actually inhibit learning. As anyone knows who has tried to solve a puzzle with the answer book open, the ready availability of help can substitute for direct experience and thus make it more difficult to do it yourself the next time.)

What does it mean, then, to speak of America's (or any nation's) technological prowess? Basic inventions do of course yield improvements, but these are easily disseminated as information, in blueprints, codes, and instructions—which reach Seoul almost as soon as they reach St. Louis. What's crucial is the extent of American engineers' and production workers' technological experience—their cumulative insights into how technologies work and how they can be adapted and improved —for only prior experience enables one to absorb the new technological learning and translate it into new experience.

The warnings now issuing from Washington that Japan might hold back certain high-tech gadgets mistakenly assumes that high-tech gadgets are like strategic raw materials—the kind of thing that one shouldn't have to depend on a foreign power to supply. But the analogy is inapt. These days our security depends less on ready access to blueprints or materials than on our collective ability to apply knowledge quickly to solving new problems. What needs to be stockpiled is not gadgets or things but experience and competence. As long as our engineers and production workers have accumulated experience in the technologies on which the Japanese gadgets are based, they can easily contrive replacements. Indeed, because high technologies evolve so quickly, both our military security and our commercial competitiveness turn on how quickly we can transform emerging technologies into the *next* generation of gadgets.

Here we come to the nub of our problem. Americans continue to lead the world in scientific discoveries and Nobel laureates. But we have had difficulty turning our basic inventions into streams of commercial products. As I have emphasized before, we tend to get bogged down somewhere between the big breakthrough and its application.

Why have the Japanese been so much more successful than we have in turning basic inventions into new products? Because Japanese engineers and production workers have been getting more technological experience than Americans. Given a choice between buying a particular high-tech component off the shelf from the Japanese or spending more money to build it from scratch, most American executives opt for the former. Building the component would enable American engineers and production workers to learn the technology from the inside and thus to improve on it in the future. But American executives, it seems, cannot guarantee themselves any harvest from investing in the experience of their engineers and production workers. American engineers change jobs, on average, every two years. Their restlessness creates geographic centers of technology like Route 128 around Boston, and Silicon Valley. This is good for the engineers but bad for the firms that have invested in them. Why go to the expense of giving them valuable experience when they'll just walk off with it? Japanese engineers and production workers, in contrast, tend to stay put for life. Investments in their technological competence are more certain to reap returns to the corporation that makes them.

* * *

Investments in experience cannot be protected like investments in real estate or machinery. Investors can claim and defend their stake in tangible assets but not in value that resides in people's minds. American executives cannot force their workers to stay with the firm. Patents are no answer when the learning is cumulative, taking the form of increased intuition and judgment, and yielding a stream of innovations over a number of years. As global competition has intensified and profits have been squeezed, more and more American firms have chosen to buy from the Japanese or otherwise link up with Japanese firms rather than build for themselves. Accordingly, investments in Americans' technological experience have declined. Even Route 128 and Silicon Valley are showing signs of faltering.

The answer is not to hold back our basic inventions from the Japanese. It is to help corporations profit from investments in the technological competence of Americans and thus give American engineers and production workers experience in quickly turning basic inventions into first-class products. The nationality of the corporation's shareholders and directors—and whether the corporation goes by a Japanese or an American name—is irrelevant to the task. Today's corporations engage in research, fabrication, and production all over the globe. Their retained earnings are invested wherever they can get the highest return. Which nation's engineers and production workers will gain technological experience? Our national interest lies in ensuring that Americans get at least a fair share.

Applying this logic to Fujitsu's proposed purchase of Fairchild suggests a response quite the opposite of that evinced by Washington. Fujitsu is one of the world's leaders in the production of complex memory chips. Making advanced memory chips is a skill that Americans need. Rather than trying to prevent Fujitsu from buying Fairchild, we should have invited Fujitsu into America to design and produce its most complex chips here. If Fujitsu needed to be coaxed to do so, we should have subsidized it.

Japanese companies like Fujitsu can help American workers discover how to transform research findings into practical innovations of all kinds. Our national policy goal should be to ensure that they do indeed teach us and that we do in fact learn.

12

HIGH-TECH WARFARE

THE UNITED STATES IS ENGAGED IN TWO GLOBAL CONTESTS. THE FIRST IS a political contest with the Soviet Union. The second is an economic contest with Japan. The first began shortly after World War II; it requires complex weapons systems and rests on a delicate set of alliances and spheres of influence. The second began about a dozen years ago; it requires complex technologies and depends on an intricate set of trading relationships. Both contests are critical to the future of America—the second quite as much as the first. But Washington seems incapable of viewing international relations in any terms other than cold war diplomacy.

* * *

The fiasco over the Soviet gas pipeline in October 1981 illustrates the problem. After six years of negotiation, the Western European nations agreed to supply the Soviets with equipment to build a pipeline that would carry natural gas thirty-six hundred miles from the Siberian fields to Western Europe. The equipment was to include compressors, which would work like giant fans to push the gas along the pipeline, and some 125 turbines, which would supply the power to operate the compressors. The most intricate part of a turbine is the rotor—a collection of carefully shaped blades, arranged along a shaft. Their manufacture requires sophisticated casting techniques and exotic metals. The rotors were to be designed and supplied by America's General Electric Company; equipment for the compressors was to come from other American companies, such as Dresser, Caterpillar, and Cooper Industries. But citing the Soviet Union's "heavy and direct responsibility for the repression in Poland," the Reagan Administration abruptly barred American export of any high technologies to the Soviets, forcing the cancellation of these subcontracts, which were worth some $250 million.

The ban did not have much effect on the timetable for the pipeline, however, since several European companies, which hold licenses from the U.S. firms to manufacture American-designed equipment on their own, stepped in to fill the gap. Even this inconvenience appeared to be short-lived when, at the Versailles economic summit the following June, then Secretary of State Alexander Haig suggested to Western European leaders that the President would ease the pipeline restrictions if the Europeans would limit their practice of extending favorable credit terms to the Soviets. The Europeans accepted the bargain, agreeing to raise their interest rates on Soviet loans. But then the other shoe dropped: On June 18 President Reagan, apparently irked at statements by some Europeans that the limits on export credits were meaningless, extended the original pipeline ban to cover sale to the Soviets by foreign subsidiaries of American companies (technically, any firm in which an American company has a controlling interest, even if that means ownership of a comparatively small percentage of the foreign company's outstanding shares) and also to include sales by foreign firms of American-licensed technology. The reason given for this sweeping ban was that the Soviets had simply failed to respond to the earlier sanctions.

European reaction was swift. The French and Italian governments promptly instructed their companies to defy the American ban and fulfill the Soviet contracts. West German Chancellor Helmut Schmidt urged German companies also to flout the U.S. sanctions. Even Margaret Thatcher, Reagan's ideological soul mate, invoked Britain's 1980 law on trade, which limits the extraterritoriality of U.S. laws. On August 25 the French subsidiary of Dallas-based Dresser Industries began loading three large compressors onto a cargo ship bound for the Soviet Union. Other European companies followed suit.

The pipeline simply meant too much to the Europeans to bow to American pressure. It promised jobs for several thousand European workers (a weighty consideration with over ten million Europeans unemployed), orders worth at least $11 billion, and a source of energy from somewhere other than the Persian Gulf.

Even if the pipeline ban could have been enforced, it would not have seriously hurt the Soviets. At most, it would have postponed the building of the pipeline for one or two years while European companies redesigned the turbines and the Soviets produced substitute rotors. In the meantime, the Soviets would have collected sizable penalties and performance bonds from the European companies in default. Ironically, the only internationally traded items that the Soviets really needed, and on which a widely observed trade embargo might therefore have had a noticeable effect on Soviet policy, had nothing to do with the pipeline. It was grain. For every $160 million in grain the Soviets buy abroad, they save enough resources to produce $700 million worth of oil. And yet, eager to placate hard-hit Midwestern farmers, the Reagan Administration—at the height of the pipeline controversy—extended for another year the U.S. agreement to sell the Soviet Union up to twenty-three million tons of wheat and corn. In light of the grain agreement, Reagan's insistence that the nations of Western Europe must bear the cost of whipping the Soviets into line seemed churlish, if not duplicitous. The Administration's main argument, that Soviet gas sales would earn the Soviets hard currency while American grain sales to the Soviets would cost them currency, would have been stronger was not the currency earned by the Soviets on the gas sales merely passed on to American farmers in exchange for grain.

Even less convincing was the Administration's concern that the pipeline would make the Europeans overly dependent on the Soviets and therefore render them more vulnerable to Soviet power politics. By the most optimistic forecast, Soviet gas exports to Western Europe would account for less than one fourth of Europe's gas consumption by 1990 —with much of the rest still coming from the Middle East. And that fraction of Europe's gas needs would amount to a much smaller fraction —no more than 8 percent—of Western Europe's total energy bill. From the standpoint of Europe's vulnerability, it seemed wiser to diversify energy supplies than to continue to gamble on a steady supply from the Middle East. More to the point, with its missiles poised at Europe's major cities and its tanks amassed along Europe's borders, the Soviet Union had more effective means for twisting Europe's collective arm than sacrificing revenues on its sales of natural gas. The leaders of Western Europe may not wear Adam Smith ties, but they do understand that because trade generates benefits for both traders, it inevitably creates mutual dependencies, and this mutuality deters either side from doing anything that may displease the other. The Europeans saw the pipeline as a bulwark against Soviet power politics in the region.

Europe's open and noisy defiance of the pipeline ban was a blow to American credibility and a setback for the Atlantic alliance as a whole. But there was no serious danger that this break signaled the beginning of a gradual dissolution of NATO. Europe and America simply had too much at stake in their mutual security to let a pipeline come between them. The real damage of the imbroglio was to the American economy, and the real beneficiaries were the Japanese. To understand why this was so, it is necessary to look at the new global environment in which Japanese and American companies are now competing.

* * *

High-technology components are the fastest growing and most competitive segments of international trade. They are coming to be the building blocks for countless manufactured products. Precision gadgetry like semiconductors, microprocessors, lasers, fiber-optic cables, robots, turbines, and rotors are finding their way into all sorts of complex machines, from automobiles to guided missiles. Because semiconductors can store huge amounts of information on the miniature circuits that are etched onto them, for example, they are key elements in new computer, telecommunication, and aerospace technology. Dominance in technological building blocks like these will provide the same economic strength that steel production gave the United States in the first half of this century. The nation that can produce them cheaper and better than any other will have a huge advantage in producing and selling the advanced technologies of the future.

As noted, success in selling such components as miniature circuits and fiber-optic cable depends on experience and technological innovation. With experience in reducing the cost of material and overhead and in fabrication, the cost can drop while quantity improves. Even the production of precision products like rotors benefits substantially from know-how and experience.

The racecourse is worldwide. Japanese and American companies are competing to obtain experience by selling around the globe to manufacturers that use the technologies in their final products. These Japanese or American companies sometimes can gain more ground by licensing a foreign company to manufacture the equipment on its own, on the basis of Japanese or American designs; this is typically done when there are substantial costs to transporting the equipment or where a foreign country—anxious to preserve employment and gain technological know-how—has erected import barriers. The American or Japanese company that licenses the technology earns royalty fees that help it pay for further research and development and also gains potential customers for additional technology that complements the licensees' equipment. In this way, licensing often provides a foot in the door to obtaining experience and volume in a whole range of related components.

Viewed in this light, the pipeline ban was ominous. The real losers were American companies that supplied or licensed European manufacturers with high-technology components. These European manufacturers would think twice before again contracting with an American company. Who knows when another ban—tenuously related to American defense interests—would be invoked by the White House? Whenever possible, these European manufacturers would look to Japan for their high-technology needs. They have learned their lesson, and American companies—not just General Electric, Dresser, Caterpillar, and Cooper, but the whole array of American high-technology manufacturers—would suffer for it.

* * *

The same sort of economic myopia can be seen in Washington's policies toward Latin America. The Reagan and Bush Administrations have piously decried the use of foreign aid and export credits to bolster the economies of our southern neighbors, preferring to rely instead, in Ronald Reagan's memorable phrase, on "the magic of the marketplace." It was to be through trade, not aid, that Latin Americans would come to embrace the wonders of capitalism. In retrospect it is clear that this talk was aimed more at shoring up America's political and military influence south of the border than at bolstering the region's economies. While American arms sales to Latin America increased dramatically through the 1980s, the door to the promised U.S. market was slammed shut. The United States imposed quotas on sugar imports, costing Latin American and Caribbean exporters some $180 million annually—to say nothing of the extra $3 billion that American consumers would now be paying each year. The beneficiaries were fourteen thousand American sugar producers and processors—notably Gulf and Western Industries, the Hunt brothers' Great Western Sugar Company, and the Monitor Sugar Company, owned by Barlow Rand, Ltd., of South Africa.

Other Latin American industries were also denied access to the U.S. market. In what was ultimately a futile effort at protecting U.S. textile manufacturers from foreign competition, the United States signed bilateral deals with Mexico and Brazil designed to limit their textile exports to America to the same low levels as were permitted under the old Multifiber Agreement. And Brazilian steel makers came under fire for allegedly unfairly subsidizing its steel industry, resulting in duties against Brazilian steel makers.

Meanwhile, the Japanese have been busy building markets in Latin America for their high technologies. The Japanese understand that the demand for many products that incorporate high technologies is growing faster there than in industrialized countries. Sales of automobiles, television sets, and home appliances have been relatively sluggish in the United States and Western Europe because most Americans and Europeans already own these products. But in Latin America sales have mushroomed in recent years. By selling in these expanding markets, building manufacturing facilities there, licensing Latin American producers to manufacture Japanese-designed components, and providing Latin Americans with entire plants of their own, the Japanese have participated directly in that growth. Japanese companies thereby have gained the sales volume and experience they need to set a very low price for their high technologies, enabling them to undercut American competitors even in the U.S. market. At the same time, the Japanese are setting up channels to market their older technologies.

Meanwhile, Latin Americans are gaining the resources and skills necessary to make use of the new technologies. All this is made possible by the continual forward movement of Japanese industry. Collaborating with the government, Japanese companies are willing to discard older technologies as fast as newer ones can be developed, while financing the development of the new technologies by gaining strong and sometimes dominant positions in the world market for older ones. Japan's Overseas Economic Cooperation Fund provides very low interest loans to Latin Americans to finance large technological purchases, particularly of whole manufacturing plants (60 percent of Japan's Ex-Im Bank loans are aimed at selling whole plants). Japan's tax laws provide additional incentives for technological transfer. And Japan provides its companies with generous insurance against foreign losses. American foreign policy, obsessed with military and diplomatic advantage, is blind to this dynamic competitive process.

* * *

The same failure to understand international competition is affecting the very development of American high technology. The Pentagon now funds nearly one third of all the research and development undertaken by American corporations—almost twice the proportion funded by the Japanese government. For basic research, concerned with broad-based and theoretical experimentation that may have few immediate commercial applications, U.S. government funding exceeds two thirds of the total.

The Pentagon is now funding research and contracting for very large scale integrated circuits (the next major stage in the evolution of semiconductors), computer-aided manufacturing technologies appropriate to a "factory of the future," advanced fiber optics, lasers, supercomputers, superconductors, and new materials technologies. The Pentagon also has become the leading purchaser of many of these same technologies. As of 1988, the Pentagon employed more than 40 percent of the nation's scientists and engineers with advanced degrees. And since more than half of the Ph.D. engineers who now graduate from American colleges and universities are foreign nationals and thus frequently ineligible for employment by defense contractors, defense work actually commands an even larger share of American engineering doctorates.

Japan's Ministry of International Trade and Industry is pushing the same technologies. But unlike MITI, the Defense Department has no interest in the successful marketing of these new technologies. The Pentagon wants new and ever more advanced weapons systems. The two goals have begun to diverge sharply.

The marketing of new commercial products is stimulated by domestic competition, which forces firms to improve their performance and aggressively seek foreign outlets. Although MITI allows firms to cooperate on specific basic research projects, it ensures that they are fiercely competitive in marketing. For example, thirty-two Japanese companies now produce semiconductors, and the competition is intense. But the Pentagon is relatively unconcerned about competition within American industry. Over 65 percent of the dollar volume of U.S. defense contracts is awarded without competitive bidding. And even where competitive bidding occurs, the bids are often rendered meaningless by large cost overruns. The Pentagon seems most comfortable with large, stable contractors who are relatively immune to the uncertainties of competition.

Marketing new products successfully also requires long lead times, during which firms can apply new technologies and make sure they have adequate capital, labor, and productive capacity to meet anticipated demand. Many MITI projects span a decade or more. But Pentagon programs are subject to relatively sudden changes in politics and in perceptions of national security needs. The precipitous rise in U.S. defense spending during the 1980s created bottlenecks in the production of key subcomponents and capital goods, and shortages of engineers and scientists in advanced electronics and machinery.

Marketing of high technology requires a global strategy. MITI encourages exports through low-interest financing, subsidized insurance for risks overseas, and subsidies to international trading firms for establishing new markets. By contrast, Washington has imposed strict export controls on commercial high technology, requiring that purchasers ensure against transfer of their products to communist countries.

Finally, and most important of all, commercialization requires that new technologies be transferable to commercial uses at relatively low cost. MITI sees to it that new technologies are diffused rapidly into the economy and incorporated into countless commercial products. But the advanced designs required by tomorrow's elaborate military hardware —designs incorporated into precision-guided munitions, air-to-air missiles, cruise missiles, night-vision equipment, and missile-tracking devices —are not as easily applicable to commercial uses as were the more primitive technologies produced during the defense and aerospace programs of the late 1950s and early 1960s. Indeed, it is precisely *because* America's commercial high technologies are not likely to be adaptable to defense needs in the years ahead that the Defense Department has launched its own research and development programs to produce advanced gadgets designed expressly to meet its own needs. Rather than encourage American commercial development, defense spending on emerging high technologies has had the opposite effect over the long term, diverting U.S. scientists and engineers away from commercial applications. And Pentagon jitters about leaks to the Soviets have cast a veil of secrecy over commercial high-tech research.

Commercial spin-offs depend on quick, efficient access to new technology, but the door is rapidly closing. For example, during the 1980s, the Pentagon increased, from 13 to 20 percent, that portion of its research budget deemed so secret it won't even disclose what it is funding. Ever more research has fallen under a new executive order that makes it relatively easy to classify government documents without considering the public's need to know.

Even unclassified research has been controlled. The Pentagon routinely insists it has the right to review university-based research before the results are published and includes prepublication-review clauses in its research contracts. (Between 1980 and 1988 government officials pulled scientific papers from academic conferences a dozen times.)

In all these ways the United States is sacrificing the nation's high-tech future to the short-term exigencies of national defense and the parochial demands of domestic producers. America continues to regard the rest of the world through the foggy lenses of cold war diplomacy rather than through the clear glasses of commercial competition. Our international economic policies in the 1980s have consisted almost entirely of trade embargoes, tariffs, quotas, dumping complaints, antitrust challenges, and an occasional sensational arrest for alleged theft of trade secrets. And rather than encouraging our emerging industries and nurturing our high technologies, we are distorting their growth through exorbitant defense expenditures on esoteric military hardware.

* * *

It is ironic that the Reagan and Bush Administrations, whose laissez-faire rhetoric comes to us almost intact from the nineteenth century, should stymie free and robust international trade and cripple American industry in the process. But the conservative mind still sees the world as a vast chessboard on which subtle games of power politics are to be played—another vestige of the nineteenth century. The international economy is of secondary importance. Foreign policy is the bailiwick of the State and Defense Departments; the Commerce Department plays third fiddle. We have no equivalent of Japan's MITI, which is concerned primarily with the future of the national economy and its place in a changing world economy.

This international myopia is having grave consequences. America is losing the high-technology race. The nation's economy is not evolving rapidly enough for American companies to capture a significant share of the world's emerging markets. Already the Japanese have most of the world market in memory chips. They are gaining significant market shares in fiber optics, communications equipment, sensing devices, and composite materials. They are substantially ahead in robotics, computer-aided manufacturing, and photovoltaics. They completely dominate consumer electronics—videocassette recorders, camcorders, fax machines, and high-definition television. America's declining competitiveness in these emerging technologies will be accompanied by a decline in our relative standard of living. The decline has already begun.

Some will say that all this is well and good. Americans have lived too high on the hog for too long, and it is fitting and right that other industrialized nations should reach and surpass us. Who cares about high technology anyway? The problem is twofold. First and most obviously, if our national economy is no longer growing and many Americans therefore come to feel poor relative to what they once had and relative to what citizens in some other countries now have, it will be harder than ever to convince them to share their wealth with their less fortunate fellow citizens. All too often, history teaches us, a society's capacity for compassion and civic virtue exists in direct proportion to the rise in its citizens' real incomes.

The second problem with a declining position in international competition brings us full circle, back to national defense. For our ability to maintain peace and deter aggression depends on our overall prosperity; the resources and commitments that national defense requires over the long term can be sustained only amid a growing and buoyant economy. Perhaps even more to the point, America's best guarantee of national security over the long term is a buoyant world economy in which the fruits of prosperity are widely shared. Trade embargoes, tariffs, quotas, dumping complaints, arms sales, and all the other ways in which American foreign policy distorts international trade add nothing to the real wealth of the world. Unlike the military and diplomatic contest that has preoccupied the Reagan and Bush Administrations, the contest in commercial high technology at least in some respects pays a dividend to the rest of the world in the form of a higher quality of life.

The United States can meet the Japanese challenge in high technology only through policies calculated to spur American high-tech producers to commercial success in world markets: generous funding of commercial research and development; low-interest loans to less-developed nations to finance their technological purchases; education loans and grants to ensure an adequate supply of engineers and teachers; awards of defense contracts to smaller, innovative high-tech companies; more defense contracts channeled toward generic technologies with commercial applications; and an open world trading system that eschews embargoes and import barriers. In short, we need an affirmative industrial policy for American high technology. By taking precisely the opposite tack in each of these areas, the Reagan and Bush Administrations have threatened our economic future and, in the process, jeopardized our national security.

13

THE PENTAGON
AND THE GOSPLAN

I HAVE A FRIEND WHO CAN TALK NONSTOP FOR SEVERAL HOURS ABOUT computers without using a single word found in Webster's dictionary. Even verbs and gerunds are transmogrified into technicalese. I dimly understand him, but only because his highly animated hand and body movements communicate something of the functions and relationships he's describing; and the exercise is exhausting.

We live in a world where technical complexities and possibilities are advancing faster than is our ability to communicate about them. High technologies are shifting the ground on which our economy and our national defenses are built. They are altering relations among nations and tilting the balance of power. Most of us technological illiterates still think in terms of gross national products, numbers of missiles and divisions, and the extent of command over people and natural resources. But the real balance of power is coming to have less to do with these static aggregates than with a less tangible measure: the speed with which a nation's people comprehend and employ the latest technologies. And none has a greater stake in the potential of high technologies to shift the balance of power than three nations of remarkable technological prowess: the United States, the Soviet Union, and Japan. Each, in its own way, has been striving to match or exceed the technological eminence of the others.

The Soviet Union's successes in this competition among the technological superpowers should not be underestimated. The Soviets were the first to orbit unmanned and manned satellites. The Soviets' successful launch of the first Sputnik in 1957 stimulated America to equal, and eventually to greater, exertions: the Apollo program, the passage of the National Defense Education Act, the creation of the National Aeronautics and Space Administration, and so on. The Soviets also managed to produce a hydrogen bomb without direct assistance from anyone else. And in the intervening years they have created a broad range of highly sophisticated military weapons.

The Soviets' technological sophistication extends to industry as well. They were the first to invent continuous casting equipment for producing steel. They have pioneered new technologies for welding, electroslag remelting, cement making, aluminum casting, the coating of titanium nitrides, and the application of ultrathin diamond films to various materials. They invented the many-lined weaving machine and several advanced consumer products and processes. (They also invented anti-nicotine chewing gum.) And they have shown themselves capable of planning and implementing enormously complex technological projects, often spanning decades—like the recently unveiled Energia rocket, which is able to propel heavy loads into space. The Soviets will use the Energia for unmanned missions to Mars, and they are well on the way to launching orbiting platforms covered with solar cells for converting sunlight into electricity to be beamed back to earth.

* * *

All these technological achievements notwithstanding, the Soviets are behind in many areas. They produce more machine tools than any other nation on earth, but they have failed to incorporate into their production system computerized machine tools, industrial robots, and the computers and communications gear necessary to link them all up. They pump more petroleum and natural gas than anyone else, and they produce more steel, but they haven't yet ventured into either advanced drilling and exploration equipment or new material technologies. They are woefully behind in very large scale integrated circuits, supercomputers, biotechnology, personal computers, even copying machines. And the near meltdown at Chernobyl revealed a perilous shortcoming in the safe use of nuclear power.

Most important, the Soviets are losing ground in advanced technologies relative to Japan and the United States. And in terms of the balance of world power, relativity is everything. Although the Soviets have continued to maintain an average growth rate in gross national income about equal to that of the United States, the Soviet Union's real product per work hour is now about one quarter that of Japan and one fifth that of the United States. It is falling further behind every year. Thus, the average Soviet citizen has to work longer and harder just to stay put. The system's capacity to extract huge savings and apply them to new investment is no longer yielding the spectacular growth of decades ago.

Part of the problem is a depletion of natural resources. Energy supplies have become less plentiful and less accessible; the remaining stocks of oil and natural gas are at much deeper levels or in more remote regions. The Soviets are also up against a declining birthrate in European Russia, where most of the nation's industrial capacities are located. But the larger problem is the Soviet Union's inability to incorporate new technologies into its production system. Capital accumulation can only take the economy so far. Unless the Soviets do a better job utilizing technology, they will fall further behind, and they know it.

* * *

The modern Soviet economy owes much of its structure and philosophical underpinnings to Joseph Stalin's relentless drive toward modernization. Stalin's chief economic aim was to expand heavy industry. To do that, he had to expropriate massive amounts of capital from the agricultural sector and create a highly centralized planning system capable of directing the capital to large projects, such as steel mills, railroads, and factories. The objective was to produce high volumes of standardized goods so that the nation would both enjoy an adequate standard of living and be capable of meeting its military needs without undue dependence on imports. Such forced modernization required centralized direction. Ministries in Moscow set production targets and prices, allocated materials, and determined how the resulting goods were to be distributed.

Stalin's economic organization was remarkably successful. Right up until the mid-1960s, industrial production boomed. Steel production, for example, grew by about 9 percent a year throughout the 1950s. When Nikita Khrushchev visited the United States in 1959, he could credibly boast that—at the rates by which the two economies were growing— the Soviet Union would overtake the United States within twenty years.

But an economy that is planned at the center, and premised upon mass production and heavy industry, is an inflexible economy. It can generate large amounts of identical things, but it cannot shift easily into the production of new goods. Nor can it adjust for quality. As an industrial economy becomes more complex, the number of adjustments needed to ensure that the right things of the right quality are produced at the correct time in the right place increases logarithmically. Prices that are allowed to rise and fall with changes in supply and demand automatically signal to everyone how to make these sorts of adjustments. But central planning sends no such helpful instructions. Instead, planners drown in paperwork, and everybody else just drowns. According to 1988 calculations, Gosplan, the central bureaucracy responsible for most of the planning and allocation, handles about seven million documents and makes eighty-three million calculations each year. The State Price Committee sets two hundred thousand prices annually.

Even Khrushchev understood the limitations of central planning. In 1957, in an attempt to decentralize some of these adjustment decisions, he abolished most of the industrial ministries at the center. Many of the displaced Moscow bureaucrats migrated to the regional councils, or *sovarkhozy,* that were to take over from the center. But those who remained kept tight rein, and they never fully allowed the reforms to take effect. After Khrushchev's ouster in 1965 Alexei Kosygin restored much of the central bureaucracy. Not until almost two decades later did a Soviet leader again attempt decentralization, by which time the inefficiencies of central planning had taken a severe toll on the Soviet economy.

One of Khrushchev's reforms had a more lasting influence. In an attempt to spur productivity, he gave certain enterprise managers a bit more discretion over the assortment, the styles, and the prices of the goods their plants produced. The continued resistance of Moscow bureaucrats notwithstanding, this reform took root; by 1970 it was extended to all firms.

Still, Soviet planners have always resisted change. History has recorded few bureaucracies more entrenched than the bureaucracy that plans the Soviet economy. The *nomenklatura* comprises about four hundred thousand people, most of them in Moscow. Their livelihood and status depend on maintaining strict control over allocation and pricing decisions. They are conservative by belief and by instinct. Their deep-seated reluctance to experiment with economic reforms is shared by many other Soviet citizens: by minor bureaucrats in the fifteen republics and the 159 regions of the republics, by military officers, by Party officials, and by average workers, all of whom think they have little to gain and a great deal to lose by change, and many of whom have experienced the disruptions and the inconveniences brought on by previous efforts to alter the system.

* * *

Enter Mikhail Gorbachev. No other Soviet leader has ever been able to assume such extensive control of both the Party and the government in so short a time. Within one year of his election as Party general secretary, Gorbachev had removed almost half of the directors of ministries and state commissions and had altered the same proportion of top leaders in the Central Committee departments. He had extruded Party chiefs in one quarter of the republics and almost one third of first secretaries in the 159 regions of the republics and had shifted the membership of the Central Committee in his direction. He moved with equal speed in filling all these vacancies with people supportive of his reforms.

Can Gorbachev reform the system? More important, what does "reform" mean to Gorbachev? He is too wily a politician and bureaucratic infighter to define "reform" so radically that it cannot be accomplished. First, he wants to reduce the size of Moscow's top planning bureaucracy, thus cutting back the number of power centers with a vested interest in maintaining economic controls. He has announced his intention to halve the fifty-thousand-employee staff of Gosplan and to cut the number of Moscow ministries from eighty to twenty. Planning ministries would no longer have day-to-day responsibilities for prices and output. They would focus more of their efforts on planning new technologies, promoting foreign trade, and training personnel.

Second, Gorbachev would give enterprise managers more control over prices and output targets and more responsibility for the day-to-day implementation of plans. They would retain a share of the profits and use it for salaries or enterprise improvements. Unproductive enterprises would be shut down and unneeded workers laid off. In addition, managers would be elected by workers. Third, he wants to consolidate enterprises within larger, vertically integrated associations, thus enabling suppliers and their industrial customers to adjust to one another's needs directly, without too many external plans and directives. And fourth, he seeks a relaxation of tensions with the West so that more resources can be freed from military requirements and shifted to new investment and so that the Soviet Union can obtain credits, consumer goods, and technology from the United States and its allies.

Debate rages in the Soviet Union about whether these reforms go

too far or not far enough. Top officials who have been Gorbachev loy-
alists in the past—Politburo member Nikolai I. Ryzhkov, who heads the
Council of Ministers, and Gosplan chief Nikolay V. Talyzin—have spoken out against the bureaucratic cuts. Others say the reforms do not go
far enough. Nikolai Shmelyov, a prominent Soviet economist, has proposed that subsidies and price setting be abolished, central planning be
eliminated, the ruble be devalued to its real price in world money markets, and that the nation accept some unemployment as a natural
by-product of a free-market economy. Shmelyov noted recently that
Gorbachev's proposals were inadequate: "We are again dooming ourselves to halfhearted measures. And halfheartedness, as we all know, is
often worse than inactivity."

The very fact of this debate—so much of it in public, within official
publications—is remarkable. The Soviet Union is now openly arguing
about the merits of capitalism. The debate illustrates the fifth plank in
Gorbachev's reform strategy: getting the broader Soviet public involved
in such deliberations, and thus gaining their support for whatever economic reform emerges.

* * *

Gorbachev the politician is likely to prevail over Gorbachev the
economist. He is too cunning to push the bureaucracy too far too fast.
Thus, the reforms that are actually put into effect during the next few
years will, in all likelihood, be more modest than those many Soviet
economists are now advocating. Initially, Gorbachev said that he was
committed to "a profound transformation of the economy." But since
then, his language has been more moderate. He has talked only of "perfecting the economic mechanism" and has gone out of his way to stress
that his proposals signal no major change with the past. He was even
quoted as telling a group of automobile workers of "the enormous advantages of a centrally planned economy." As if to reassure the bureaucrats, he added that "we will even have to strengthen the principle of
centralization, where necessary."

But here's the rub: Improvements in productivity, in the form of
greater quantities of goods, aren't enough to rescue the Soviet economy.
These days an ever increasing proportion of the value of consumer products and military equipment alike derives from the application of advanced technologies. This trend is apparent in all advanced industrial
nations. The world's leading economies are shifting out of jobs tradition-
ally associated with heavy industries (such as steel making, large-batch

chemical production, and assembly) toward jobs that require the manipulation and application of knowledge (making and marketing high-strength ceramics, new alloys, specialty chemicals, computers, and integrated circuits). These new products fulfill many of the same functions as the old, but with far greater efficiency and flexibility and thus at far lower cost. Most important, these new products, and the services related to them, continually change as technologies evolve.

At best, the reforms that Gorbachev is seeking will render the Soviet economy administratively more efficient. This is no small feat. Stories are recounted of new milk plants installed in areas where there are few cows, petrochemical plants where no oil pipelines reach. But Gorbachev's reforms will not fundamentally alter the incentives operating on workers and managers. In all likelihood, poor quality will continue to haunt the production system. Every Soviet manager and worker knows how easy it is to measure, and thus to be rewarded for, quantity—and how difficult it is to measure, and to be disciplined for, poor quality. Gorbachev hopes to reverse this by administrative fiat. He has announced a new bureaucracy, the State Acceptance Service, charged with quality control. But as long as the old incentives remain in place, there is no reason to suppose that quality will show much improvement.

A bigger problem is that a centrally planned economy, even one that allows local administrative discretion, creates no incentives to innovate. Every Soviet manager and worker is aware of the risk that an innovation might slow the flow of products and thus reduce the year's bonus, while a successful innovation is unlikely to have any effect other than to increase next year's production quota. The result, not surprisingly, is that Soviet enterprises are extraordinarily reluctant to try something new. Not even the proposed Law on State Enterprise will affect these incentives very much.

The Soviet Union is not without occasionally dramatic technological breakthroughs, but these typically occur in laboratories far removed from the workplace. Some of these new inventions eventually find their way into enterprise plans, financed by a central Fund for the Development of Science and Technology. But by the time bureaucrats in Moscow discover that a new invention might be useful and then decide precisely where it should go, years may have passed. None of Gorbachev's reforms will speed the pace of technology transfer from the laboratory to the factory.

*   *   *

There is a still more fundamental barrier to technological innovation in the Soviet Union. Technological innovation can thrive only in an environment that invites, or at least tolerates, dissent. Technological innovation is largely a process of imagining radical alternatives to what is currently accepted and sharing these new possibilities with others. Problems must be openly recognized, and ferment must be generated among creative minds to find solutions. These are, in effect, acts of subversion. They almost invariably stir things up. And no clear boundaries exist between different categories of imagination, between different realms of subversion. The scientific, the managerial, the economic, the philosophical, the cultural, the political: They have a way of running into each other. It is no accident, as the Marxists used to say, that many of the Soviet Union's most brilliant scientists and artists are also political dissidents.

Moreover, many of the new technologies are themselves subversive. Computers, word processors, and telecommunications equipment not only incite unorthodox ideas; they also allow them to be exchanged instantly. They inspire communities of dissent. Totalitarian regimes understand this; they monopolize the technologies of communication—the press, radio and television, telephones, and now the computer. Nothing threatens a police state's legitimacy more than private and robust debate; nothing ensures its survival more than the isolation and fragmentation of the citizenry.

These ironies lie at the core of Gorbachev's dilemma. For more than a half century the Soviet police state has maintained tight control over communications among Soviet citizens. Even today senior scholars and scientists are loath to use copying machines: In most enterprises and universities copying departments are staffed by the KGB. How, then, can the Soviet Union be expected to adapt technologies that will unleash so much communication? How could the Soviets embellish and improve the new technologies without simultaneously inviting political and social dissent? To gain technological sophistication, Soviet economics and politics would have to be transformed. This the Soviet bureaucracy will not allow. Technological sophistication is essential to the Soviet Union's economic and political survival. Technological backwardness is essential to the Soviet Union's system of government.

* * *

Not since Stalin forced the Soviet Union into becoming an industrial state has any nation sought economic development with as much determination—and achieved it with as much success—as Japan. Many people can remember a time, not so many years ago, when "Made in Japan" was synonymous with cheap, shoddy workmanship. (During the 1950s, American regulators filed charges against a toy manufacturer from the Japanese town of Usa whose products bore the label MADE IN USA.) During the past twenty-five years, however, Japan has concentrated almost exclusively on improving productivity and shifting production to more advanced goods. Rather than trying to preserve its industrial base, Japan has sought to propel it into the future, at the same time casting off older industries in which Japan's competitive position was declining.

Thus, the Soviet Union is not the only superpower now falling behind technologically. For Gorbachev, the technological challenge potentially implies a fundamental transformation in the Soviet economic and political system. What does the Japanese technological challenge imply for America?

There are interesting parallels. Both the Soviet and the American military bureaucracies are the major users of advanced technologies in their respective economies. Both initiate and sponsor vast programs of research and development. Neither military bureaucracy worries much about ensuring competition among suppliers.

The Pentagon is also America's largest purchaser of high technology. The means by which the Pentagon decides what technology it wants to buy and then goes about obtaining it bear remarkable similarities to the nightmarish planning and allocation system centered in Moscow. According to a 1987 study by the Center for Strategic and International Studies in Washington, each year the Pentagon undertakes fifteen million separate contracts, overseen in the first instance by 150,000 acquisition officers. On top of them are nearly twenty-five thousand auditors and inspectors. The Pentagon floats on a veritable sea of paper. Procurement regulations themselves total thirty thousand pages and are issued by seventy-nine different offices. The direct cost of monitoring all this flow of paper is approximately $10 billion annually.

The Pentagon, no less than the Soviet military bureaucracy, is subject to wondrous inefficiency, along with more venal intention. Few months elapse in America without another story about the apparent deceit or gross negligence of a defense contractor. In recent years General Electric admitted to defrauding the Air Force of $800,000 by forging workers' time cards on a contract for upgrading the warheads on Minuteman missiles. More recently, the company admitted that it had overbilled the Pentagon by $10 million. McDonnell Douglas produced fighter jets the tail fins of which develop unusual cracks. Hughes Aircraft's missiles were found to be faulty. Texas Instruments' semiconductors didn't work as they should. And then there were the $500 hammers and $7,000 coffee makers. Between 1986 and 1989, more than five hundred contractors were suspended or permanently barred from doing business with the Pentagon because of poor workmanship or questionable billings. Forty-five of the nation's one hundred largest military contractors have come under criminal investigation for kickbacks, illegal overcharges, and other nefarious activities.

Every major cost overrun, scandal, or mistake in military contracting has elicited two powerful political reactions. On the one hand, Congress and the public have been eager to identify wrongdoers. There are typically elaborate criminal investigations, grand jury indictments, and stories in the press suggesting egregious instances of venality and cupidity. Most of these end in charges being dropped for want of adequate evidence of criminal intent or in watered-down plea bargains that at least temporarily satisfy the public's desire to place blame.

On the other hand, with every new scandal or revelation, the Pentagon is pressured to add still more layers of checks, monitors, and inspectors—to clog the procurement process with more paperwork, red tape, bureaucracy. In the wake of disclosures that the Defense Department was paying $400 each for $8 claw hammers, for example, the military added seven thousand additional staffers to solve its spare-parts problems. This bureaucratic propensity, too, resembles the Soviet response.

Secrecy is an important aspect of high-technology development within both bureaucracies, the Pentagon's and Gosplan's. Some of America's most modern factories, outfitted by the Pentagon with computer-integrated manufacturing systems—such as LTV Corporation's Vought plant, which produces the B-1 bomber—are now shrouded in Pentagon secrecy. No commercial entrepreneurs are allowed in to see how to do it.

There are other parallels. Like the Soviet Union, the United States continues to excel at technological breakthroughs but finds it difficult to move them quickly from lab to factory. Unlike Japan and the Soviet Union, we are blessed with an army of technological entrepreneurs, concocting extraordinary inventions in their basements and attics. But a significant percentage of their inventions never make it into production on our shores. American manufacturers haven't been particularly interested in new technology. Having succeeded so well for over fifty years in large-batch and mass production, American manufacturers haven't wanted—or understood the need—to shift to more knowledge-intensive forms of production.

Of course, the technological parallels between the Soviets and us should not be overstated. American productivity continues to be the highest in the world—far higher than Soviet productivity, still a bit higher than Japanese productivity. But both the Soviet Union and the United States are slipping badly in the global technology race. The reason is simple. Success depends less on big discoveries than on a widely diffused, continuous, and incremental drive toward application and refinement.

*　　*　　*

Technology development in all three nations—the Soviet Union, the United States, and Japan—is, to a large extent, planned. It must be. Private enterprises, which depend on profits for their continued survival, are rarely in a position to experiment with radically different ways of doing things. The risks are too great; the costs of shifting over the production system are too high. At best, these enterprises will wait until some other company tries out the new technologies. But such caution will badly hobble the pace of technology development overall. Thus, every industrialized government is in the business of technology planning, development, and transfer. The critical question is not whether such planning occurs, but how it is carried out.

In the United States, as noted, the tasks of technology development and transfer have been consigned largely to the Pentagon, which, not unlike the Soviet system of central planning, is a bureaucracy, with a bureaucracy's rigidities and concealments. In Japan, by contrast, technology development and transfer entail a close partnership between profit-driven enterprises and a range of quasi-independent agencies halfway between public and private sectors. The notorious Ministry of International Trade and Industry (MITI) is more coordinator than planner: It establishes joint research ventures among private firms and convenes endless councils and conferences of engineers and managers to parcel out risks and responsibilities more efficiently. Of equal importance are financial institutions, like the Japanese Development Bank, that provide low-interest loans to enterprises seeking to experiment with new production technologies. And then there is the array of institutes and semi-official laboratories that comb the world for new inventions and, after licensing them, organize groups of Japanese firms to find ways of utilizing them.

Of the three planning systems, Japan's is by far the most successful at transferring new technologies into the production system. It is the least bureaucratic and secretive, the most flexible. Consider, for example, the latest rage in high technology, superconductive alloys capable of transmitting electricity with virtually no loss of energy. If all the hoopla can be believed, these wondrous materials promise to revolutionize both goods and weapons. They are still in the labs, but they will find their way into production within the next few years. Which nation will take the lead? In Japan superconductive applications are now being pursued in dozens of institutes and joint research ventures, involving every major industry group and hundreds of smaller businesses and subcontractors. In the United States, by contrast, superconductive applications are being pursued within only three major institutions—IBM, AT&T, and the Office of the Strategic Defense Initiative in the Department of Defense— and most of the funding is coming from the Pentagon. Nobody knows exactly what the Soviets are now doing about superconductivity, but it's a fair bet that the central ministries and the military bureaucracies are in charge. We will have to wait for years to discover which of these three nations will prevail, but the odds strongly favor Japan.

*   *   *

If Darwinism could explain the evolution of political economies— such that the most successful economic organizations predominate until more adaptive, and thus more successful, ones come along—we might be able to predict the direction in which Gorbachev's reforms will eventually lead. We could make the same prediction about America's response to Gorbachev's reforms, indeed about the evolution of the American political economy itself. The prediction is that Japan will amass so much power that the United States and the Soviet Union will have no choice but to copy its decentralized, open planning system. The politics and the economics of the three superpowers would converge in a kind of managed, democratic capitalism.

But political economies don't follow Darwin's rules. Pesky things like culture, values, and beliefs intrude. It is here, perhaps, that Japan enjoys its most important advantage, for its political culture, institutions, and public values all tend toward the rapid utilization of new knowledge. By contrast, the military-encrusted bureaucracies of the Soviet Union and the United States tend toward the preservation of the economic status quo. As Gorbachev proceeds with his strategy and the United States responds, only one prediction seems reasonably safe. Increasingly, and in highly subtle ways, changes in these nations' relative technological prowess will lead to changes in the balance of world power and thus in the strategies employed by both the Soviet Union and the United States toward one another. But both nations' strategies will be affected by their technological prowess relative to Japan's. And more and more, the balance of power, at least as it is determined by technology, will tilt toward Japan.

14

BEYOND FREE TRADE

THE AMERICAN IDEAL OF FREE TRADE, WHICH EMERGED FULL-BLOWN IN the postwar era, assumed a steady expansion of capital-intensive standardized production within all industrialized nations. This was a heroic assumption. Comparative advantage among nations was perceived to depend on differences in the relative abundance of capital and labor, which in turn depended on national differences both in willingness to defer consumption and accumulate capital, and in the historic inheritance of capital stock. It was assumed that this comparative advantage would change over time; even less-developed nations eventually would adopt capital-intensive industries. But the process would be evolutionary —adjustments would be slow, regular, and predictable. It stood to reason that the best policy for ensuring both expansion and steady change would be a gradual reduction in trade barriers. That way, each nation could exploit large economies of scale in the type of production in which it currently enjoyed a comparative advantage, while incremental changes in investment and capital accumulation slowly altered the terms of trade.

Neoclassical trade theory itself was built on a much older, and even more heroic, assumption. Adam Smith and David Ricardo had based their potent arguments for free trade principally on geographic differences in *natural* endowments, implying a quite static distribution of advantages and disadvantages. A nation had no real choice but to realistically accept the economic station its land and climate had assigned it. As machine-based industry developed and spread, later theorists refined the model to accommodate the importance of physical capital. This "factor-proportions" model turned on the observation that some peoples were better than others at making and using machines for reasons that had little to do with natural resources. Comparative advantage became less a matter of given endowments, more a matter of chosen investments. Yet because it grew out of an era when technologies changed gradually, and when colonialism and devastating world wars stifled or distorted international economic adjustment, neoclassical trade theory never fully acknowledged the profound difference between comparative advantage as a fact of natural endowments and comparative advantage as an ever-changing product of social organization and choice. Until very recently, observing that the United States was rich in capital while Korea was rich in unskilled labor seemed as comfortably solid a basis for trade as observing that Portugal was sunny and suited for grapes while Ireland was verdant and suited for sheep. This was the theoretical basis of the free-trade principle that underpins American trade policy today.

Just as the Ricardian model had viewed world trade from the perspective of the textile industry—in which Britain then enjoyed a dominant position—so, by analogy, did the United States' postwar trade policy take the perspective of America's dominant industries: steel, chemicals, automobiles, rubber, and electrical machinery. Stability and predictability, to ensure that the fixed costs could be recovered, were the only principles of public policy necessary to spur further investment in these industries. Potential efficiencies in world-scale production promised to preserve American dominance of these industries, since the marginal costs of making the last mass-produced unit were quite low.

The postwar free-trade ideal was appropriate to its time, an era of unprecedented mass consumption of standardized goods. A new, relatively homogeneous generation of consumers was gorging itself on new homes, cars, and all sorts of steel and plastic gadgets. Throughout the 1950s and 1960s the American economy grew not by innovating but by expanding the scale of its basic production processes and thus reducing unit costs. Western Europe followed that lead. There were few breakthroughs in new products or processes and very little real competition. But prosperity reigned, as demand seemed insatiable. Free trade was a means both of enabling the rest of the world to partake in this bounteous expansion and of permitting the United States to preserve its economic preeminence.

The ideal was codified in the General Agreement on Tariffs and Trade, signed in 1947, and articulated in more detail in the subsequent rounds of tariff negotiations. It was expressed in principles of nondiscrimination (all nations to be treated the same), reduced government intervention, and the formal negotiation of trade disputes. The GATT structure succeeded reasonably well because all parties (except the less-developed nations) had a stake in making the system work so they could share in American-led prosperity and, not incidentally, because the United States possessed sufficient economic and political power to enforce its vision. The volume of world trade rose dramatically, exceeding gains in world production. Between 1913 and 1948 world trade had risen 2.5 percent per year on average; world production, only 2 percent; between 1948 and 1973 trade increased by 7 percent per year, and world production by 5 percent.

*   *   *

The principal departures from the free-trade ideal were agricultural commodities and textiles—largely because these two categories of trade threatened American producers from the start. United States representatives to GATT insisted on an exception for primary commodities. The United States already had restricted imports of dairy products, wheat, and peanuts. Sugar quotas went into effect in 1948. Later came "voluntary" agreements with Taiwan on mushrooms, with Australia and New Zealand on beef, and with Mexico on strawberries and tomatoes. Farm subsidies similarly were exempt: In 1955, when the contracting parties to GATT adopted provisions limiting the use of export subsidies, they effectively excluded primary commodities from coverage.

Policies to preserve the textile industry followed a related logic of escalating preservationism. In 1957 Japan agreed to limit its textile exports to the United States. This was followed five years later by a multilateral agreement (the Long Term Arrangement) designed to protect North America and Europe against cotton textiles from Japan and other developing nations; it has been extended and enlarged since then.

These two exceptions to the postwar ideal of free trade contained the seeds of its demise. Agriculture and textiles were the only significant sectors where genuinely free trade would threaten American producers. The world market for farm goods was limited. Competitors in Canada and Australia had not been crippled by war. And American agricultural interests expected that once the worst of the devastation was repaired,

Europe and Japan would soon become largely self-sufficient in food and even become exporters. Thus, American farmers saw little to gain and much to lose from free trade and simply rejected the principle. (There is an irony here. The potential world market and the American competitive edge have both proven greater than expected, and for decades the United States has tried unsuccessfully to recant its own exception and bring agriculture under the banner of free trade.)

In textiles the causes were different, but the effect was the same: Some American interests foresaw sizable immediate losses from free trade, and U.S. negotiators dutifully obtained exemptions from the rules. The world market for textiles, unlike the market for food, *was* expected to grow, but early in the postwar era it was clear that low-wage countries were better suited for most textile manufacturing.

In both cases, where free trade would have called for substantial immediate adjustment on the part of significant economic groups in the United States, the principle was unceremoniously abandoned. There were no public policies to guide adjustments of this magnitude. Nor were there mechanisms for international trade agreements to shape such policies. It was far easier—and more expedient—simply to declare each of these sectors to be special cases warranting unique decisions and relationships *outside* the framework of an open trading system. The ideal of free trade—and the codes and institutions that were growing up around it—had no response to the problem of structural adjustment. These early failures of the ideal foreshadowed its widespread breakdown today.

*   *   *

Even when the adjustment problems of the United States and Western Europe loomed larger in the 1970s, the United States continued to view the issues narrowly in terms of the free-trade ideal. Government interventions were seen as always regrettable but occasionally unavoidable concessions to buy off opposition to continued liberalization. At the instigation of the United States, the European (OECD) Council of Ministers in June 1978 adopted a hortatory document entitled "Policies for Adjustment: Some General Orientations," which emphasized that whenever governments intervened to ease the pain of trade adjustments, across-the-board policies affecting all industries were superior to targeted ones, and that in any event such interventions should be temporary. There was no mention of the importance of ongoing programs for stimulating emerging businesses, retiring excess capacity in older businesses, and retraining workers for new jobs.

During another round of negotiations in the late 1970s, the United

States continued to seek international agreements to limit government interventions that "distort" international trade. Several of the codes that emerged—governing public procurement practices and nontariff barriers —were informed by the free-trade ideal. But the subsidies code reflected no consensus on what sorts of subsidies were out of bounds; the code did little more than establish processes to ensure that one nation's retaliation against another for such subsidies was not disproportionate to the offense.

*   *   *

Trade accords became progressively less coherent and conclusive because the premises on which the postwar free-trade ideal had been founded were no longer applicable to large segments of industrialized economies. Comparative advantage was no longer a relatively static phenomenon based on slowly evolving capital endowments. The hourly output of workers in certain less-developed nations like South Korea and Taiwan was catching up to the output of workers in the United States and other industrialized nations because they were starting to use many of the same machines, purchased from international engineering and capital-equipment firms with money borrowed from international banks.

The pace of structural change was dramatic. As recently as the mid-1960s Taiwan, Hong Kong, Korea, Brazil, and Spain specialized in simple products that required large amounts of unskilled labor but little capital investment or technology—clothing, footwear, toys, basic electronic assemblies. Japan's response was to shift out of these products into processing industries like steel and synthetic fibers, which called for substantial capital and raw materials but still used mostly unskilled and semiskilled labor and incorporated relatively mature technologies not subject to major innovations. Ten years later, the newly industrialized countries had followed Japan into basic capital-intensive processing industries. Japan, meanwhile, had become an exporter of steel technology instead of basic steels and moved its industrial base into products like automobiles, color televisions, small appliances, consumer electronics, and ships—businesses requiring considerable investment in plant and equipment, as well as sophisticated new technologies.

By 1980 Taiwan and the other rapid industrializers had themselves become major producers of complex products like automobiles, color televisions, tape recorders, CB transceivers, microwave ovens, small computers, and ships. South Korea now has the largest single shipyard in the world; South Korea's Pohang steel mill is one of the most modern in the world. Almost all the world's production of small appliances is now centered in Hong Kong, South Korea, and Singapore. At the same time, Malaysia, Thailand, the Philippines, Sri Lanka, India, and other poorer countries are inheriting the production of clothing, footwear, toys, and simple electronic assemblies. India is fast becoming a center for computer programming.

Far from halting this migration of high-volume standardized production, automation actually has accelerated it. Sophisticated machines are readily transported to low-wage countries. Robots and computerized machines are substituting for semiskilled workers. Automated inspection machines are reducing the costs of screening out poor-quality components—and thereby are encouraging firms in industrialized nations to farm out production of standardized parts to developing nations.

*   *   *

In the face of this rapid movement into high-volume standardized production, Japan, and to a lesser extent West Germany, has sought to shift their industrial bases to products and processes that require skilled workers—precision castings, new materials, special chemicals, and sensor devices, as well as the design and manufacture of fiber-optic cable, fine ceramics, lasers, large-scale integrated circuits, advanced semiconductors, and advanced aircraft engines. Skilled labor has become the only dimension of production where advanced industrialized nations can create and retain an advantage.

These nations' governments are working with their businesses and labor unions to accomplish the shift. They are ensuring that managers obtain long-term capital and that workers obtain retraining. They are selectively raising entry barriers and reducing costs in an effort to alter the pattern of national investment, and thereby to accelerate structural change in their economies. They have undeniably made mistakes. On occasion, they also bow to the demands of older industries to maintain the status quo. Often they find it difficult to achieve consensus about the best strategy for adjustment. They are having problems coping with the current recession while trying to maintain flexibility. But these nations understand the inevitability and urgency of structural change, and the central importance of easing and accelerating the transition.

As the free-trade ideal has become hopelessly inadequate to guide these shifts, international economic agencies and formal trade processes sponsored by the United States have been progressively bypassed and enfeebled. Only the easiest of disputes are now settled within the GATT system; most major issues of global economic change are dealt with outside it. Bilateral export agreements have become the rule rather than the exception. Japan now "voluntarily" limits its exports to Western Europe of automobiles, machine tools, television tubes, and videocassette recorders; and its shipments to the United States of steel, automobiles, machine tools, semiconductors, and many other items. Western European nations limit their sales of steel to the United States. Quotas, tariffs, and other barriers are being imposed on a wide range of products. The European Economic Community maintains a tariff of 17 percent on integrated circuits. Australia, South Africa, Spain, Mexico, and twenty-six other nations require fixed percentages of domestic content in automobiles assembled within their borders. France is restricting imports of videotape recorders by subjecting them to detailed inspections and delays.

* * *

The free-trade ideal also has been crumbling within the United States. In many respects its erosion here has been more dramatic than elsewhere and has set a precedent for other nations. Since the late 1960s, the pattern has become well established: American industries suddenly faced with foreign competition have threatened to file complaints with the government alleging foreign "dumping" in the United States of goods priced lower than production costs, or foreign subsidies that render the imports "unfairly" cheap. Eager to avoid protracted litigation and the trade and diplomatic frictions accompanying it, the exporting nation often has responded by negotiating "voluntary" agreements with the United States, setting a limit to the volume of exports shipped to these shores. As structural changes continue and the exporter adapts by becoming more efficient, the drama repeats itself, with the resulting restrictions becoming even tighter than before.

In 1969 U.S. steel producers pressured the government to obtain voluntary limits on the tonnage of steel that could be exported to the United States from Western Europe and Japan. When these failed to stem the tide, the industry filed antidumping petitions. In 1978 the Carter Administration agreed to impose a "trigger-price" mechanism, which effectively barred imported steel at any price below the computed cost of production by Japan's most efficient producer plus transport charges, overhead, and a stipulated profit margin. After the steel industry filed new antidumping petitions in 1980, the trigger price was increased by 12 percent. After the steel industry *again* filed countervailing duty cases in 1982, alleging that steel-exporting nations were unfairly subsidizing their industries, the Reagan Administration negotiated a formal quota on steel exports from Western Europe, limiting sales to 5.44 percent of the U.S. market. Other steel-exporting nations received similar quota shares of the U.S. market.

In 1977 the U.S. government negotiated a marketing agreement with Japan, limiting Japanese imports of assembled color televisions to just under 1.6 million units annually. Similar agreements subsequently were negotiated with Taiwan and South Korea. In 1978 the U.S. government substantially increased tariffs on CB radio transceivers. In the 1980s the Reagan Administration forced Japan to limit its automobile exports to the United States to 1.68 million vehicles—a move that encouraged other importing nations to demand similar assurances from the Japanese. Meanwhile, American officials pressured Japanese electronic equipment manufacturers to limit their exports to the United States and to provide assurances about minimum prices.

American industries threatened by foreign competition also have been propped up by a wide assortment of government subsidies, special tax provisions, and subsidized loans and loan guarantees. These forms of assistance have mushroomed since the late 1960s, as global competitive pressures have increased. Finally, as has been noted, the United States continues to grant substantial subsidies and impose severe trade barriers under the pretext of national security.

Some connections to national defense are farfetched, but the connection continues to serve as a useful pretext. Merchant shipping is assumed to be a "strategic" industry in the United States; as a result, foreign merchant ships are barred from U.S. coastal trade, while the U.S. government spends approximately $500 million per year subsidizing the shipbuilding industry. Crude oil from Alaska's North Slope may not be shipped to Japan for fear that such trade will compromise America's "energy independence." Recently, the U.S. government pressured AT&T to award a large fiber-optics contract to a U.S. company rather than to Fujitsu, the lowest bidder, out of fear that the United States might otherwise grow too dependent on Japan for this strategically important product. (Protection of the U.S. watch industry was once defended on the ground that only watchmakers had the skills necessary for designing bomb sights, and recent demands for barriers against Chinese textiles warn of the danger of inadequate domestic capacity for making military uniforms.)

* * *

The practical choice facing the United States and every other industrialized nation is whether (and to what extent) to preserve existing jobs and industries *or* to help move capital and labor to higher value-added and more competitive production. The point is this: Both choices imply an active role for government. But the first is politically and administratively easier to accomplish than the second, at least in the short run. Most people are afraid of change, particularly when they suspect that its burdens and benefits will fall randomly and disproportionately. By the same token, many policies to preserve the status quo—policies like trade barriers protecting against foreign competition and special tax benefits propping up deteriorating balance sheets—do not entail active and visible government interventions; no bureaucrats intrude on corporate discretion; Congress votes no budgets. The costs do not appear on any national accounts, and those who bear them are seldom aware of the source or extent of the burdens.

On the other hand, policies designed to ease and accelerate an economy's transition to higher value-added and more competitive production often necessitate that governments work closely with business and labor to ensure that the sharp changes required do not impose disproportionate costs on some or windfalls for others; that workers have adequate income security and opportunities for retraining; that communities on the rise have adequate public services and systems of transportation, communication, and energy; that declining communities have help in phasing down; that emerging industries have sufficient capital to cope with the high costs and risks of starting up, beyond the costs and risks that private investors are willing to endure; and that industries in difficulty have sufficient resources to reduce capacity in their least competitive parts and restructure their most competitive. All of these activities entail an active and explicit government role.

The more attractive option is obvious. The future standard of living of Americans depends on rapid adjustment both within the United States and among our trading partners. Preservationism, here or abroad, imperils our future prosperity and that of the rest of the world. Efforts merely to preserve jobs and industries invariably give rise to "zero-sum" international games in which improvements in living standards for one nation come at the expense of another. Such zero-sum games are unstable. They often deteriorate into trade wars, as each nation scrambles to maintain its own living standard by blocking others from exercising their own competitive strengths. Mounting import barriers and subsidies are obvious manifestations of this decline. More subtle are the situations in which poorer nations, whose expectations for higher living standards are dashed by the protectionist policies of industrialized nations, no longer can maintain their growth momentum and thereby stop importing complex products from industrialized nations; shrinking Third World markets in turn reduce the growth of the industrialized nations.

The international economy can be compared to a mill wheel driving the process of structural change in each national economy, pushing each into higher-valued production and generating, ultimately, an ever richer world. The current that propels the wheel is the flow of goods and services from country to country. Any attempt to dam up the current—say, to maintain jobs in the U.S. steel industry by blocking imports of Brazilian steel—reduces the current's force and slows down the wheel. Brazil has smaller earnings with which to repay its international loans, and its growth is stalled. It thus imports fewer U.S. products, and America's growth is slowed. Once the mill wheel begins to decelerate, it is difficult to restore the momentum short of unblocking all the dams and letting the current surge. But the sort of convulsive economic adjustments required to get the world economy moving again under these circumstances are far more difficult to arrange. In periods of slow growth and high unemployment, a progressively larger proportion of firms and workers become hostage to protectionist policies.

* * *

The United States' interest lies in promoting the rapid transformation of all nations' industrial bases toward higher value-added production, while discouraging zero-sum efforts to preserve the status quo. But this strategy requires that the United States abandon its condemnation of all government interventions as illegitimate departures from the free-trade ideal.

U.S. trade policies have had just the opposite effect—discouraging positive adjustments at home and abroad. Part of the problem is that America's failure to discriminate between desirable government interventions and undesirable ones—treating them all as somehow illegitimate and thereby forcing them outside the channels of international scrutiny and negotiation—has ceded much of the initiative to political coalitions bent on preserving the status quo. Informal, voluntary export agreements of the sort now covering substantial portions of the world market for steel, automobiles, textiles, and consumer electronics are almost certain to be undertaken as last-ditch efforts to save jobs. Negotiated piecemeal, without any overarching framework to guide them or any adjustment strategies against which to measure them, these agreements often fall prey to short-term political demands. One bilateral restraint provokes the next, as each nation feels itself progressively more endangered by the possibility that world output will be diverted toward it.

America's formal trade policies also have signaled to our trading partners that we reject the notion of active adjustment. For example, when the U.S. Commerce Department determined in the early 1980s that Britain was unfairly subsidizing British steel—but failed to consider that the subsidies were being used by British steel to reduce capacity and retrain redundant workers—the United States appeared to reject this adjustment strategy outright. Yet capacity reductions and retraining programs organized by affected industries with government help are among the most effective ways of easing the shift of capital and labor out of declining sectors. Indeed, the American steel industry itself stands to gain substantially from such reductions in world steel-making capacity.

Perhaps the saddest irony is that our formal machinery for responding to the allegedly unfair practices of our trading partners has tended perversely to block industrial change at home. America's primary instruments of trade policy have been antidumping levies and countervailing duties, both of which can only shield domestic producers from foreign rivals. As international competition has intensified in recent years, many U.S. firms have used these mechanisms to shield their domestic market and avoid the pressure to adapt. Congressional demands for "reciprocity" against foreign trade barriers and subsidies—and the Reagan Administration's "get tough" policies threatening retaliation against these allegedly unfair practices—suffer from the same perversity. Even if a foreign trade barrier or subsidy is patently a zero-sum attempt to preserve the status quo, it makes no sense for the United States to express its opposition in a way that retards industrial change in this country as well.

* * *

What sorts of principles might guide a new trade policy to encourage positive adjustment at home and among our trading partners? A new trade policy designed to accommodate structural change in the world economy would distinguish between two distinct categories of trade friction, each linked to a different type of business: low-skilled standardized businesses, or high-skilled emerging businesses. A strategic trade policy would be designed to facilitate adjustment within each category.

Low-skilled standardized businesses can be found in basic steel, cotton and simple synthetic textiles, metalworking, most shipbuilding, and basic chemicals. These businesses are characterized by long runs (or large batches) of fairly simple commodities, technologies that are evolving slowly, a relatively low level of skills demanded in the production process, and often intensive use of energy. Notwithstanding that capital costs may be high in some of these businesses, it is relatively easy for newly industrialized nations like South Korea, Taiwan, Hong Kong, Singapore, Brazil, and Mexico to pursue them and become strong competitors. Their labor costs are low, they often have access to cheap raw materials, and their markets for such standardized products often are growing rapidly.

The task for the United States and other advanced industrial nations is to ease the adjustment of their firms and workers out of these businesses as quickly as possible. The least competitive firms should be induced to close, thereby giving the more competitive firms time in which to consolidate operations and shift to higher value-added production. Underutilized plant and equipment should be scrapped or put to other uses. Workers should be retrained. New businesses should be encouraged to move into affected communities. All this often requires an infusion of extra resources, since distressed businesses and their communities are unlikely to possess the wherewithal to do it themselves.

Thus, government subsidies linked directly to these adjustments should be encouraged, both within the United States and in other advanced industrial nations. A similar case can be made for some protection from lower-cost imports for a limited time during the transition—but *only* if specifically linked to a plan for capacity reductions and retraining. Domestic consumers will pay higher prices for these goods in the interim, but the higher prices may be viewed as a justifiable tax to help finance the transition.

For example, Japan's recent efforts at redeploying people and capital out of low-skilled standardized businesses have been relatively successful. Since 1978, the government has helped businesses organize adjustment cartels to scrap excess capacity and find alternative employment for their workers. Other advanced nations are installing such adjustment mechanisms with varying degrees of success. If the United States is to have any workable alternative to protection, it must create similar instruments for easing the transition. At a minimum, the United States should refrain from countervailing against foreign subsidies or retaliating against foreign trade barriers, when these practices are directly tied to capacity reductions and retraining programs.

On the other hand, the United States can legitimately object to certain of our trading partners' practices—like subsidizing exports and setting prices below production costs—which merely retard the shift of capital and labor out of these businesses. Such preservationist policies complicate adjustment and concentrate its costs. They can make it harder to design and implement national transition strategies. Even more objectionable in terms of the goal of continuing economic advance, these policies often end up slowing economic growth within developing nations (which otherwise would shift into these low-skilled standardized businesses) and thus retard the expansion of export markets for more complex goods produced in advanced nations.

The United States should seek international agreements with other advanced industrial nations, establishing targets and timetables for capacity reductions, the scrapping or conversion of existing plant and equipment, and retraining of workers. America might go even further—initiating the creation of an international adjustment fund to help finance these transitions. Payments into the fund would be proportional to a nation's current employment in designated low-skilled standardized businesses; drawing rights would be proportional to a nation's agreed-upon capacity and employment reductions.

Agreements among advanced industrial nations to targets and timetables for phasing out low-skilled standardized businesses would need to be complemented by trade policies encouraging adjustments of developing nations into these same businesses. For example, while no legitimate function is served in advanced nations by granting these businesses export subsidies or in pricing these products below production costs, trade practices like these actually might help *developing* nations quickly gain the production scale necessary to become profitable. For developing nations shifting into standardized businesses, export subsidies and below-cost pricing policies are more accurately viewed as being analogous to investments in new plant and equipment. At the least, therefore, a trade policy geared to adjustment would not impose countervailing duties or antidumping levies on these developing-nation imports.

* * *

Emerging businesses in advanced industrial nations are characterized by rapid technological change. All depend largely on skilled labor. Examples include the design and fabrication of optical fiber cable, large-scale integrated circuits, advanced aircraft engines, complex polymer materials, and products derived from recombinant DNA. Many of these businesses are found in the higher-valued, more specialized segments of older industries—for example, automobile transaxles, aramid fibers, and corrosion-resistant steel. In many of these businesses the traditional line between goods and services is becoming blurred—for example, office communications and computer-aided manufacturing. In short, these are the businesses of the future on which our standard of living and that of every other industrialized nation is growing dependent.

Every industrialized nation is racing to gain scale and experience in these businesses; national strategy, not natural endowment, is the key to competitive advantage. Every nation—including the United States, through the back door of NASA and the Department of Defense—is subsidizing research, development, and commercialization. Some nations also are erecting import barriers on the theory that these businesses represent "infant industries" that must be temporarily sheltered. Finally, in anticipation of burgeoning markets, some firms are setting prices substantially below current production costs. Which of these practices should the United States oppose? Which should it emulate?

Subsidies to spur development should be welcomed. New, higher-valued products and new processes for generating them add to the world's wealth. Even if every nation aims for leadership in the same field, this will not become a zero-sum game, since an infinite range of variations and improvements can be achieved, and intense competition will spur even greater progress.

For emerging businesses even below-cost pricing should be welcomed as a positive-sum strategy. Such pricing is undertaken in anticipation of a substantial drop in prices with greater scale and experience. The producer thereby gambles that there will be sufficient demand for the product to generate a healthy return when and if the producer gains a dominant market position—a gamble made all the more risky by the possibility that a competitor will bring out a new product generation in the meantime. Because this form of competition keeps prices low, all consumers benefit. Moreover, given the dynamic nature of the market, below-cost pricing under these circumstances is not predatory—any competitor can leapfrog to a new and better product.

The United States has two handicaps in this race. The first is its significant spending on defense-related research and development, which leads only occasionally and by accident to commercially competitive products or processes. This problem, as I have already suggested, is best addressed by boosting support for nondefense research and development and by ensuring that to the extent possible, defense needs are met by technologies and products directly applicable to commercial, civilian markets. The second handicap takes the form of antitrust policies that discourage research joint ventures among domestic firms in international competition. This can be remedied by altering the antitrust laws explicitly to permit such joint ventures when the world market share of the relevant U.S. firms is under, say, 25 percent.

But there is no reason why the United States should erect trade barriers against foreign emerging businesses that enjoy targeted subsidies or set prices below production costs. Barriers only reduce domestic competition and thereby retard the shift of domestic producers into these businesses. So long as markets are growing and changing rapidly, the financial health of domestic firms in these businesses is not dependent on heavy investment in existing production capacity or on a stable pool of customers; it is dependent on rapid adaptation and quick exploitation of new opportunities—a set of organizational skills that can be honed best in a highly competitive global market.

Nor does the "infant industry" argument provide a reason to protect emerging businesses in today's global economy. Such protection rarely will help a domestic firm catch up to a foreign competitor enjoying a head start in scale and experience. Since technologies are changing rapidly, a better strategy for the domestic firm is to leapfrog to the *next* product generation and establish a leading position there. Domestic producers intent on making such a leap may need government subsidies but not protection from imports of the product they aim to surpass.

Import barriers also may jeopardize the international competitive positions of domestic industrial purchasers—who must now pay more for their components or settle for components of poorer quality. U.S. pressure on Japan to reduce exports of semiconductors surely placed American computer manufacturers at a competitive disadvantage relative to Japanese computer manufacturers, who have ready access to better and cheaper chips; similarly, were the President to disallow investment tax credits for the purchase of numerically controlled machine tools manufactured in Japan, as some American machine-tool manufacturers have urged, U.S. producers of automobiles and construction equipment no longer would have access to superior Japanese machine tools at a low cost.

For these same reasons the United States should strongly oppose the erection of foreign trade barriers that block U.S. exports of high-technology products. But because such tactics are apt to hurt these other nations at least as much as they do U.S. producers, the United States has an opportunity through international negotiations to convince these trading partners that the route to competitive success in emerging businesses lies more with subsidies than import barriers.

A final aspect of U.S. strategy for emerging businesses concerns investments in the education, training, and group learning that now define advanced nations' comparative advantage and determine their capacity to adopt emerging high-value businesses. This subject has been discussed. The quality of public education will continue to be critically important. But since many of the most relevant skills can best be learned on the job, it is becoming increasingly important to develop and attract emerging businesses that will invest aggressively in the training and development of their employees.

* * *

The goal is to change the nature of the debate and the focus of attention. Rather than preoccupy ourselves (and our trading partners) with endless and empty disputes over whether a particular practice constitutes an unwarranted subsidy, or a firm is engaged in "dumping," or a certain domestic industry has suffered an injury, or certain nontariff barriers are disruptive to free trade—these new trade strategies would focus the debate on the central question of whether the practices in question serve to accelerate adjustment *or* to maintain the status quo. And to answer that question, we would need to know how particular businesses fit within the evolving world economy.

The international economy is changing too rapidly to expect that we can discover any immutable principles to guide it automatically on its way. Structural changes are painful, and the vagaries of politics inevitably will play a larger role in setting trade policy in the United States and in every other nation in the years ahead. Thus, we need a set of strategic concepts that are consistently applied and that clearly alert our trading partners to what we conceive to be our interest. For the same reason a formal, courtlike apparatus for fact finding and disposition of trade disputes will prove to be less useful than an ongoing process of political debate and negotiation, in which all sides are permanently engaged.

The choice is clear. The forces of preservation will continue to gain ground without firm U.S. leadership in the opposite direction. The United States should approach our trading partners in full awareness that adjustment is inherently difficult, that active government intervention is inevitable and sometimes desirable, and that—through explicit strategies and an ongoing process of negotiation and compromise—we can change zero-sum international conflict into a positive-sum enterprise for world growth.

15

THE UNSPECIAL RELATIONSHIP

ON MARCH 5, 1946, WINSTON CHURCHILL, SPEAKING BEFORE A GROUP of farmers and local businessmen in Fulton, Missouri, referred to the "special relationship" between the United States and Great Britain—a relationship that had led the allies to victory and would continue to lead the world in the postwar era. Assuming without question Britain's continued status as a leading world power, Churchill regarded the alliance as between equals; any shortfall in Britain's economic influence would be compensated by its political skills and historic wisdom. Every subsequent British prime minister has expressed similar sentiments. Anthony Eden likened the relationship to that between Austria and Britain after 1815. Harold Macmillan invoked a more classical analogy, somewhat less flattering: "We . . . are Greeks in this American empire. You will find the Americans much as the Greeks found the Romans—great big, vulgar, bustling people, more vigorous than we are and also more idle, with more unspoiled virtues but also more corrupt."

The idea of a "special relationship" between Britain and the United States was from the start more a hope than a historical description. The hope was largely Britain's—that America would accept and underwrite Britain's status as a coequal world power in an era in which Britain's actual power was waning. The idea never had the same appeal in the United States. Before the wartime alliance most Americans had regarded Britain as a quaint, or even occasionally menacing, imperial power. For more than a century, the deepest instinct of the United States in foreign affairs had been to isolate itself from Europe. America remembered, too, that Britain had been an enemy in two wars. The Irish who flooded into America in the mid- and late-nineteenth century did little to soften this hostile view.

* * *

From America's side the "special relationship" since World War II has been founded in mutual defense against the Soviet Union. The wartime alliance merely had shifted its concern from one common enemy to another. The Soviet Union's first atomic explosion in the autumn of 1949 hastened the process by which the postwar relationship was transformed into a military alliance supported by massive force. The special relationship thereafter took the form of efforts to contain Soviet aggression—through joint leadership of the North Atlantic Treaty Organization, coordinated action in the United Nations Security Council, the sharing of political and military intelligence, Britain's willingness to devote a high proportion of her national product to military purposes, and its acquiescence to American jet fighters based on British soil and nuclear submarines in British ports. Although the United States rarely treated Britain as an equal partner in making strategic decisions, American officials nevertheless consulted closely with their British counterparts during these early postwar years, and Britain was responsible for suggesting many of the initiatives that marked NATO's response to the Soviets.

Britain's enthusiastic cooperation in containing the Soviets was reciprocated by America's willingness to trust Britain with nuclear weapons and to subsidize their cost. In 1958 Britain became the only American ally (to the lasting distress of President De Gaulle) to receive technical information on the production of nuclear warheads and fissile material. Subsequently, the United States allowed Britain to buy the Polaris submarine and then, in 1980, the Trident. No other American ally was given access to these advanced nuclear systems.

This military and strategic relationship took root precisely as Britain's economic and political power in the world began to wane. The decline would, over time, both enhance Britain's dependence on the United States and reduce America's interest in Britain. Both consequences would be unfortunate. As the "special relationship" became increasingly one-sided, Britain grew ever more fearful of either becoming a pawn of or, alternatively, being abandoned by the United States. As America began losing interest in its foremost ally, American policy makers grew less sensitive to the needs and desires of all its allies.

* * *

World War II had set the two allies on different economic trajectories. While the war pulled America out of the Depression, instigating a production boom that lasted twenty years and extending America's economic influence around the world, it had had a very different effect on Britain. Britain sacrificed a quarter of its national wealth to the war and, ultimately, its economic hegemony over a significant part of the globe. The trend would not be apparent for a decade or more. In 1950 Britain's gross national product had just ceased to equal that of France and West Germany combined. As late as 1959, though far behind the United States, Britain still possessed the second-largest GNP in the world. But by 1970 Britain had been overtaken by West Germany and was easily matched by France. By 1985 Britain's GNP per capita was less than that of Italy.

Given how far Britain has fallen, it is easy to forget the extraordinary degree of economic power the nation exercised on the eve of the war. In 1939 the British Empire and the United States together accounted for about 60 percent of the world's industrial production and controlled roughly three quarters of the globe's military wealth. At the war's end the two were the only industrial economies still largely intact. It was natural that Britain and America would now take joint responsibility for redesigning the world economy—developing a system of fixed exchange rates to minimize currency fluctuations, an International Monetary Fund to ensure liquidity, a World Bank to aggregate and direct development finance, a General Agreement on Tariffs and Trade to ensure an open trading system. And it was by dint of their joint commitment to this system that it worked so well for a quarter of a century. The years 1945 to 1970 witnessed the most dramatic and widely shared economic growth in the history of mankind. World GNP grew from $30 billion to over $300 billion. Even allowing for inflation, real incomes tripled, world trade quadrupled.

Since the 1970s, Britain's decline as a world power has, in the eyes of American policy makers, begun to overshadow Britain's reliability as a military ally. Simultaneously over the last fifteen years, and especially during the 1980s, Britain has begun to view America as less the leader of the free world than a frustrated actor seeking to impose its will upon it. It is in this respect that the gradual undoing of the "special relationship" has had the most unfortunate of consequences, both for the United States and for the world.

* * *

Few nations in history have combined such raw military and economic muscle with so parochial a view of the rest of the globe as does modern America. The vast majority of the citizens of the United States speak no foreign language, read little or nothing about happenings beyond their borders, and are decidedly ignorant of the history, culture, or policies of the rest of mankind. In one recent survey 40 percent of American high school seniors had difficulty finding Canada on a world map. This attitude of benign neglect of the rest of the species is a luxury that only a large, naturally wealthy, and geographically isolated nation could have maintained for any length of time. Before World War II its consequences for the rest of the world were relatively harmless. Since then, American ethnocentrism has had more unfortunate effects. The biggest impediment to America's effective leadership of the free world has been its limited ability to understand and collaborate with the rest of the free world.

It is precisely here that the "special relationship" with Britain played such an important role in the quarter century after the war. In Britain the United States found another nation whose citizens spoke the same language, who shared similar legal and political institutions, not to mention many of the same ancestors, but who, by virtue of geography and history, possessed a different and perhaps broader vision of the world. Here was a people whom Americans could trust: friends and confidants in an unfriendly and confusing world, who provided another perspective, and thus helped America overcome its chronic tendency toward parochialism. Although the evidence is scattered and anecdotal, there is little doubt that during this era American officials often sought the counsel of their British counterparts and obtained the sort of frank and confidential advice that one can get only from an old and trusted friend whose judgment is deeply valued. To be sure, the two allies at times reinforced each other's delusions. But Britain's advice often comprised a different viewpoint, causing Americans to think again and to refine or abort a course of action that might not have been adequately thought through.

Yet as Britain's economic and political power has waned, each subsequent American administration has come to view Britain more as one among several constituents whose assent is sometimes necessary or useful to legitimize a policy, or who must be mollified and cajoled into accepting a particular American initiative, and less as a special counsel. (American culture has long tended to discount advice coming from the impecunious: As the Yankee homily goes, "If you're so smart, why ain't you rich?") Notwithstanding the personal friendship of Margaret Thatcher and Ronald Reagan, the generation of experts and bureaucrats that now populates the higher reaches of the White House, the National Security Council, the State Department, the Treasury, and the Defense Department has no direct experience and little memory of the "special relationship" in its golden days. To them, increasingly, Britain is just another pestering voice.

This gradual transformation from a special to a not-so-special relationship has in turn loosened the subtle constraints on American foreign policy, rendering it less sensitive to the needs and views of all of America's allies, with the result that the policies that have issued from Washington in more recent years have too often been unilateral, peremptory, and wide of the mark. And as American policy has appeared in Britain to diverge ever more from the judicious and responsible path, and American officials seem ever less inclined to consult seriously and in advance with their British counterparts, Britain has understandably begun to withdraw from the relationship, to distance itself from America.

The new and more popular form of anti-Americanism in Britain, as in the rest of Western Europe, is, I believe, attributable to what appears to be America's growing indifference to its European allies and to the effects of her policies on world politics and economics. Sadly, examples abound: The postwar system of international economic institutions set up by America and Britain is now coming apart, and U.S. economic policies are largely to blame. America refuses to tame its yawning budget deficit, which has undermined the stability of world currencies; it continues to contrive bilateral "voluntary restraint agreements" and "orderly marketing agreements" with trading partners, with the result that world markets for steel, automobiles, consumer electronics, and other goods are rapidly becoming cartelized; and it is unrelenting in imposing harsh conditions on the repaying of the Latin American debt to U.S. banks, thus drying up these potential markets while destabilizing their new democracies.

American defense policy reveals similar insensitivities. The Reagan Administration fluctuated between complete lack of interest in negotiating reductions in either strategic or intermediate-range nuclear weapons (the inclinations of allies notwithstanding) and then, as at the Reykjavik

summit meeting in 1987, sudden—and shocking—willingness to eliminate offensive ballistic missiles altogether, without any advance warning
to allies. Toward the Third World, the United States of the 1980s seemed
to have adopted a strategy of supporting anticommunist rebels wherever
they operated. And America chose to lead the free world against terror-
ism by solemnly instructing its allies not to bargain with terrorists while
secretly sending arms to Tehran for the release of American hostages in
Lebanon.

* * *

Ironically, the age-old American ideal of a pristine nation, separate
from the rest of the world, which can either assert its will unilaterally
upon the world or withdraw from it, has less relevance to the situation
in which America finds itself today than at any time in the past. American unilateralism has boomeranged, setting off a series of reactions that
have come back to where they began. When the United States has stimulated its economy while other nations have opted for restraint, it has
summoned a flood of imports and risked inflation and unemployment.
When the nation has unilaterally raised interest rates, it has ravaged
debtor nations and invited a global recession. When America has closed
its borders to foreign goods, it has crippled its debtors' efforts to pay
back their loans. When it has lent support to any dictator or revolutionary distasteful to the Soviets, America has lost whatever moral advantage
it possessed in the Third World.

Faced with these awkward realities, there has been a temptation in
America to lash out—to be ever more assertive toward the rest of the
world. American politicians increasingly describe international relations
as a series of tests of America's credibility, determination, and resolve.
They warn of becoming a "patsy." The assumption is that either we win
or they win.

Britain's shift toward Europe, away from the "special relationship"
with America, is understandable in this new context. So, too, are the
doubts being expressed in Europe these days about the reliability of
America's nuclear umbrella, and about America's willingness to maintain free trade and cooperate on macroeconomic management. By 1992
Europe will achieve a new economic identity; a new political independence cannot be far away.

Thus, as Britain moves away from America in response to America's
having moved away from Britain and its allies, Britain will be leaving
America more alone than this nation has been at any time over the last
half century. It is a solitude that is at once poignant and dangerous.

16

WHOSE CARS?

ON FEBRUARY 17, 1983, GENERAL MOTORS AND TOYOTA ANNOUNCED plans for the joint manufacture of a subcompact car in the United States. General Motors would contribute its assembly plant in Fremont, California, and $20 million in cash. Toyota would kick in $150 million in cash. The car, a front-wheel-drive version of the Toyota Corolla, which Toyota already produced and sold in Japan, would be called, in its American version, the Chevrolet Sprinter. About 250,000 cars would be produced annually.

The only thing unusual about this arrangement was its two participants. These were not mom-and-pop operations. General Motors is the largest manufacturer of cars in the world. It sells 40 percent of the cars people buy in the United States. Toyota is Japan's largest carmaker and the third largest in the world. In the U.S. market Toyota ranks number four, just after Chrysler. In sales of subcompacts within the United States Toyota ranks number three, ahead of Chrysler. Both GM and Toyota have long set the pace for the other automobile companies in their home markets in prices, styling, and innovation. Not surprisingly, the two companies are the most profitable auto manufacturers on the globe.

For the past ninety-four years the U.S. government has enforced, with varying degrees of ardor, laws that prohibit companies from monopolizing or restraining trade. Antitrust concepts have a certain charming obscurity about them, and no two lawyers who specialize in this fascinating corner of the law share precisely the same notions about what is or is not permissible. But of this much we can be sure: When the largest and near-largest firms in a market comprising just a few large firms collude with one another, agreeing on a price at which to sell their goods and exchanging information about products and marketing strategies, something questionable is happening in the eyes of the law. At the very least, an arrangement has been made that might easily cause prices to rise.

And so the Federal Trade Commission spent a year investigating the planned joint venture between General Motors and Toyota. A majority of the commissioners then concluded that the plan (ever so slightly modified) was fine. Their logic, spelled out in a public statement, represented one of the first in government decisions expressly modifying traditional law in light of international competition. It marked the beginning of a more explicit national industrial policy. And sadly, it was wrong.

*   *   *

The commissioners were persuaded of the wisdom of the venture primarily on the grounds that it offered General Motors a "valuable opportunity" to learn firsthand about Japanese manufacturing and management. GM could thereby become a more efficient company. "If GM can learn how to build significantly lower-cost cars, as Japanese producers can now do, it will attempt to implement those lower-cost methods at its other plants," noted the commissioners. In recent years the interpretation and enforcement of antitrust laws have demonstrated increasing respect for whatever efficiencies might possibly be imputed to an agreement among firms, but this particular sort of efficiency—learning by colluding—has never before been thought of sufficient merit to pass even the mildest muster. Applied generally, this new principle of antitrust analysis would seem to permit any two companies to combine so long as one was better at doing something than the other.

But the commissioners had something rather more special in mind. The benefits of learning how to produce cars efficiently presumably would extend beyond General Motors. GM would show other U.S. automakers that "the Japanese system can work in America." This would lead inexorably to "a more efficient, more competitive U.S. automobile industry." At last, we get to the logical core of the argument, the new rule being enunciated. The real justification for allowing America's largest car company to team up with Japan's largest car company was to improve the international competitiveness of the U.S. automobile industry. According to the commission's majority, this long-term national benefit outweighed whatever risk that the arrangement might cause car prices to rise in the near term.

The commissioners' goal was unobjectionable. To be in favor of enhancing U.S. competitiveness is not exactly controversial. But to their real credit, these Republican appointees managed to transcend the White House's ideological revulsion toward industrial policy and accurately perceive that a decision either way would affect the structure of American industry for years to come. The question to be addressed in this case —as in countless government decisions about tax rules, tariffs and quotas, federal procurement contracts, loan guarantees, and research grants —was, What is our national competitive strategy to be?

They asked the right question. It was their answer that was wrong. To understand why, we have only to examine how the world automobile industry has been evolving.

*　*　*

The world automobile market was then a $250-billion-a-year business, not counting sales of parts, secondhand cars, repair, and service. World car production peaked in 1978 at 31.8 million vehicles and was inching back from the 1982 trough of 27.5 million. Japan then accounted for roughly 25 percent of this output; the United States, for 23 percent. (Since then, the percentages have changed only slightly, with Japan moving up and the United States moving down.) The industry is a major employer in all industrialized nations. If subcontractors, component manufacturers, dealers, advertisers, mechanics, and other related occupations are included, automaking still employs about 15 percent of all Japanese workers and 17 percent of Americans. Many of these jobs, moreover, pay quite well. Relative to other industrial workers worldwide, auto workers are highly productive.

The most dramatic development in the world automobile industry over the past decade, as in so many other industries, has been the success of the Japanese. But it would be wrong to conclude from this that Japan's national economic strategy turns on automobile production. The auto industry in Japan is no longer a particularly favored sector; it enjoys none of the special tax preferences, low-interest credit allocations, antitrust exemptions, or consumer subsidies that are had by fledgling companies in such fields as biotechnology or computers. Strength in the world automobile market is not an end in itself for the Japanese. Their long-term goal is not simply to sell more cars. It is to gain world dominance in the knowledge-intensive industries of the future. Automobile production—or more accurately, the design and fabrication of complex auto parts and the processes necessary to put them together—is a means toward that end. This point bears further elaboration.

Regardless of whose nameplates grace their exteriors, today's automobiles increasingly are multinational creations. Economies of scale and experience, together with political exigencies, are coming to require that parts be produced wherever on the globe they can be manufactured most cheaply and assembled in the region of the globe where the finished cars are to be sold. It is a safe bet that twenty years from now General Motors cars will bear no special relationship to the United States and Toyota no special connection with Japan. One no longer will be able to speak with pride (or derision) about an "American" automobile any more than about a "Japanese" or "West German" automobile. Regardless of where corporate headquarters is located, shareholders, lenders, managers, workers, and consumers alike will be drawn from all over the globe.

But there will be at least one important difference among nations. Workers' real wages—their standard of living—will depend on the *portion* of the production process for which they have responsibility. Since assembly operations will be highly automated worldwide, with robots handling most tasks, the critical distinctions among national work forces will depend on which components they specialize in producing. Workers engaged in making such relatively simple parts as seatcovers, windshield wipers, and dashboards, for example, will not command the same rewards in the global economy as those engaged in more complex tasks. Indeed, the proportional contribution of world auto sales to a nation's wealth will turn on the relative value added to automobile production by that nation's work force. National competitiveness in the automobile industry, as in many other global industries, will come to depend on national prowess in the higher-valued aspects of production.

The Japanese understand this prospect. They are bent on capturing the highest-valued portions of world auto production. They are specializing in such parts as engines, transaxles (front-wheel-drive transmissions and axles), electronic fuel injections and monitoring systems, precision ball bearings, and in such processes as robots and computer-controlled systems for putting all the parts together. These products and processes, in turn, rely on advanced microelectronics and on strong but lightweight synthetic materials and alloys. They thereby represent specific commercial applications of Japan's emerging knowledge-based industries.

The overall strategy is clear. It is the same strategy that underlies Japan's recent, rapid shifts into aircraft engines, videocassette recorders, telecommunications devices, and personal computers. These products are launchpads for gaining scale and experience in the world's newest technologies. Attaining immediate profits from these products is less important than becoming the largest and most experienced world practitioners of the advanced methods that lay behind them. A Japanese labor force so attuned will easily come to dominate the highest-valued portions of any global industry. There is nothing sinister about this; consumers all over the globe continue to benefit from Japan's advances, although Japan eventually will enjoy the world's highest standard of living. Viewed in this light, the Japanese automobile strategy is part of an overall national strategy by which the Japanese will become the design engineers for the world.

* * *

Japan's automobile strategy is by now well under way. GM buys its diesel engines from Isuzu; Chrysler, many of its transaxles and engines from Mitsubishi. Ford gets its complex parts from Mazda. In Ohio and Britain Honda is assembling cars, the designs and more sophisticated components of which come from Japan. Nissan is assembling trucks in Tennessee and cars in Britain and Spain; their designs and highest-valued parts also come from Japan.

This trend is particularly apparent in the production of the smallest cars, which must be designed and manufactured especially carefully in order to minimize costs and maximize comfort. As the Japanese have learned in producing everything from televisions to semiconductors, innovations in products and manufacturing processes often occur at the most compact end of a product line, where the engineering challenges are the greatest. For the same reason, development expenses often are highest at the compact end. If your strategy is to gain scale and experience in applying new technologies, then you will gladly bear these costs; the investment will pay off in a work force better able to innovate in the future. But if your strategy is to maximize profits over the next three or four years, you will buy the compact technology from someone else. Accordingly, the Japanese are developing it; the Americans are buying it.

Subcompact automobile technology—including the design, advanced parts, and machines for assembling the parts according to the designs—is being ceded to the Japanese. GM is importing subcompacts from Suzuki and Isuzu and assembling "R" cars produced by Isuzu; GM's futurist Saturn model is still on the drawing board. Chrysler has quietly abandoned its planned replacement for the Omni/Horizon family of cars and is looking to Mitsubishi to fill out its subcompacts. Ford has invested $500 million in Mexico, where it will assemble a Mazda subcompact.

* * *

The joint venture between General Motors and Toyota fits this pattern exactly. The cars that roll out of the Fremont, California, assembly plant are designed in Japan; their engines, transaxles, and other advanced components, manufactured in Japan; many of the robots and computerized machine tools used to assemble them, designed and produced in Japan. Left to American labor are the lower-skilled assembly tasks, production of the simpler parts, and of course, advertising, sales, and repair services to be offered in the United States.

GM, Ford, and Chrysler have grown more profitable largely by cutting their costs and selling bigger cars based on older models. During the past decade, the three companies have closed assembly plants, shut down vast networks of parts plants, and laid off a sizable portion of their work force. They have canceled or delayed at least a dozen new products. They are now "lean and mean," which is the way corporate managers in America like to describe the newly dismembered companies over which they preside. They are investing in new models only gradually, extending the lives of older models by making slight alterations.

General Motors leads this timid pack. Its costs are the lowest, its profits highest. But it worries about the next downturn in the business cycle. Its "planning horizon" is three years. If GM finds a new way to cut its costs, Ford and Chrysler must follow suit or else run the risk of losing even more of the market. GM has decided that it is cheaper to buy subcompact technology from Japan than to invest in it at home. And the cheapest way to buy subcompact technology from Japan is to get the Japanese to foot part of the bill for jointly assembling Japanese cars in America. That is what the joint venture with Toyota is all about. It is a white flag of surrender. Other U.S. automakers will see it and follow.

Joint ventures like this one fit nicely into Japan's automobile strategy, making it worth the extra cost. They create an immediate demand for Japanese designs, sophisticated components, and high-technology manufacturing systems. Yet because they appear to save American jobs, they also forestall mounting political pressures in the United States to protect against Japanese imports. Indeed, the United Auto Workers was quite supportive of the GM–Toyota plan. Never mind that the jobs preserved or created in America are lower skilled and routine, eventually to be replaced by robots and computers. In the immediate future at least, there are jobs. To American workers, the obvious alternative seems far less salutary.

* * *

Is there any other alternative? Surely not the proposal, touted by the United Auto Workers Union, that cars sold in the United States must contain a high percentage of components produced in America. Even if 90 percent of the value of cars sold here were produced here, Japan still would be supplying the most sophisticated 10 percent and simultaneously supplying the rest of the globe (including GM, Ford, and Chrysler operations abroad) with an even larger percentage—thereby maintaining superior scale and experience at the highest-valued end of world auto production. More to the point, the perennial "domestic content" proposal gives companies no real incentive to invest in advanced automobile technologies within the United States. When pressed, they can simply duplicate whatever technologies already have been perfected in Japan. Meanwhile, everyone who buys a car in the United States gets stuck with a huge price tag reflecting the higher cost of making cars in America. We lose both ways.

There is no simple solution. Japan's competitive strategy embraces its entire industrial base; America's strategy is the by-product of individual corporate strategies whose goals may have little to do with enhancing the standard of living of Americans. To reverse the present trend and gain predominance in the highest-valued portions of world auto production would require that auto companies operate under a very different set of incentives than they do today. At the least, such a reversal would entail changes in tax laws, international trade laws, and antitrust rules. For example, Congress or the special trade representative might have linked Japan's "voluntary" export restraint to explicit agreements by U.S. automakers to invest in advanced automobile technologies and to train their workers in these emerging fields. We missed this opportunity; the automakers got the benefits of the export restraint with no strings attached.

The GM–Toyota joint venture represented another small opportunity to move the auto industry in the right direction. To be sure, had the Federal Trade Commission rejected the proposed venture, that would not have stemmed the tide; at best, it might have slowed it down a bit. Antitrust law is a crude means of fashioning industrial policy. But the commissioners might have used the occasion to announce a different direction for antitrust enforcement in the future, perhaps encouraging joint research ventures among American companies and clearly signaling the strategic perils for the American economy that lay in the path GM and Toyota had chosen. If they in fact believed the dubious contention that the venture would help the entire U.S. automobile industry, moreover, the commissioners might have called GM's bluff and required the arrangement be a public "demonstration project" in which Ford and Chrysler were invited to participate. But the commissioners did none of these things. By approving the venture instead, and doing so on such broad grounds, they opened the floodgates.

17

THE CORPORATION
AND THE NATION

IF THE CORPORATIONS AMERICANS OWN AND WORK FOR SUCCEED, THE American economy will too—or so we were brought up to believe. This assumption was given its most brazen expression thirty-five years ago by Charles Erwin Wilson, who was then the president of General Motors; he was nicknamed "Engine Charlie," in order to distinguish him from another Charles E. Wilson, "Electric Charlie," who was the president of General Electric through the 1940s. During the Senate hearing on his confirmation as Eisenhower's nominee for secretary of defense, Wilson was asked whether he could make a decision in the interests of General Motors' shareholders. Wilson said that he could but that such a conflict would probably never arise. "I cannot conceive of one because for years I thought what was good for our country was good for General Motors, and vice versa. The difference did not exist."

Engine Charlie's statement was widely criticized at the time as an example of corporate America's arrogance, but in fact it simply expressed principles already codified in American law and policy: The corporation existed for its shareholders, and as they prospered, so would the nation.

This root principle of our political economy is no longer valid. The corporations Americans own and work for are becoming disconnected from the national economy. The overall success of these corporations has less and less to do with America's continued growth and prosperity. Corporation and nation are growing apart, and American law and politics must adapt to this new reality.

*   *   *

When Engine Charlie uttered his dictum, it was easy to believe that what was good for corporations and their shareholders was also good for the national economy. At least, shareholders' interests were not so narrowly defined as to seem inconsistent with the nation's broader economic objectives. Shareholders were typically too widely dispersed to exert any real control over the corporation. Most shareholders faithfully held on to their shares, treating them as long-term investments and trusting that share values would continue to rise over time.

Top corporate executives thus enjoyed wide discretion to do whatever they pleased, including what they deemed to be socially responsible, as long as their expenditures could be justified as benefiting shareholders over the long term. This rationalization was capacious enough to encompass almost any activities that might improve the corporation's image. In fact, some of the expenditures they made—on basic research, the development of new products and technologies, employee training, various educational and philanthropic activities—had little positive effect on the corporation's bottom line, because the new knowledge easily spread to other firms. But these activities did help spur broader economic development within the regions the corporations inhabited. And many of the executives relished the role of the "corporate statesman," who mobilized private resources for further public gains.

These activities should not be romanticized. Managerial discretion was not always put to such noble purposes. But it could be, and the prevailing ideology held it to be an appropriate exercise of corporate power.

In the past few years, however, the stock market has become far more efficient at keeping the executives' attention fixed on the bottom line. First, the dispersed individual shareholders of yore have largely been replaced by a relatively few professional investment managers, who are responsible for investing enough billions of dollars of pension funds, mutual funds, and insurance funds to make up at least a third of all the equity in corporate America. These investment managers are responsible for some 70 percent of the trading on the New York Stock Exchange.

They compete against one another and are quick to shift funds from one corporation to another, depending on whose share prices are rising or falling at the moment. Second, the deregulation of brokerage fees and new technologies linking computers to trading floors have reduced the costs and increased the speed of such transactions; the computer linkages also give investment managers up-to-the-minute data on share prices. Third, financial entrepreneurs have refined techniques for acquiring controlling blocks of shares, sometimes even using the corporation's own assets as collateral. Because of these three developments, it has become relatively easy for an aggressive company or a few audacious individuals to seize control of even the largest of American corporations when they sense a failure by the corporation's executives to exploit some opportunity for increasing the value of their shares.

To deter raiders, every major American corporation is busily "restructuring" itself, to use the Wall Street euphemism. This has required eliminating or drastically cutting back on discretionary spending. "There are very few corporate statesmen anymore," laments James Joseph, the president of the Council on Foundations, which monitors corporate giving. "CEOs no longer want to spend their time on social issues." As one executive put it recently, "It becomes positively un-American to look at anything except their own bottom line."

* * *

Executives no longer argue that what is good for shareholders is necessarily good for the nation. In fact, many are now insisting that the stock market's unrelenting demand for higher share value is actually harmful to the nation and that raiders should be restrained. Their warnings are being heard. In one recent *Business Week*–Harris poll 64 percent of the people surveyed favored new government restrictions on hostile takeovers. States are taking the lead in protecting their corporations. Earlier this year Delaware—where almost half the firms on the New York Stock Exchange are incorporated—became the twenty-ninth state to limit takeovers, thus in one swoop effectively shielding half of corporate America. Congress is considering legislation to discourage hostile mergers nationwide.

What may have escaped notice by America's business leaders is the logical consequence of their new argument. One of the great advantages of the Engine Charlie principle to American business was its implicit rejection of any formal means of holding corporations accountable for the nation's continued prosperity. In benefiting shareholders, the corporation would necessarily spur the economy forward. But once it is granted, even by business leaders, that this is not always the case—indeed, that *too much* attention to shareholders' demands may in fact detract from the nation's long-term vitality—then the presumptive link between corporate executives' responsibilities to their shareholders and to the nation is severed. What is good for the shareholders is not necessarily good for the nation.

The question that in Engine Charlie's day had been submerged under the vague rubric of "long-term" shareholder interests thus arises: By what means should corporations be held accountable to the public for contributing to the nation's prosperity?

*   *   *

As ever more of corporate America is bought by foreign nationals, another divergence appears between the interests of the corporation and its shareholders and the interests of the nation.

In Engine Charlie's time virtually all major corporations doing business in America were owned by Americans. Thirty years later, this situation has changed. Other national economies are catching up with that of the United States; a few are on the verge of surpassing it. American-owned corporations are no longer the only global enterprises of significant power and scale, nor even the largest ones. And in a historic reverse, foreign ownership of American capital now stands at over $200 billion, more than double what it was in 1980, and it is rising rapidly.

The low dollar has made bargains of American corporations, as if corporate America were having a fire sale, with every company marked 35 to 50 percent off its regular price. The companies that have been bought include some sporting familiar names, like Doubleday, CBS Records, Purina Mills, Mack Truck, Allis-Chalmers, and Firestone. Foreign capital is also pouring into the American stock market. Major banks and investment houses—BankAmerica, Shearson Lehman, Paine Webber, and Goldman, Sachs—are now partly owned by Japanese banks intent on breaking into the American financial market.

The wave of foreign acquisition of corporate America is having an effect in the United States similar to that felt in other nations when they faced American investment years ago—when charges of American "imperialism" were in the air and fears that American multinational corporations would exploit host nations were acute. A trade bill passed in 1988 by the House of Representatives requires foreign investors to report to the government any "significant" interest they had acquired in an

American corporation. The version passed in the Senate authorizes the administration to review any proposed acquisition of an American corporation by foreigners. American business leaders, although delighted to have foreign investors bid up the prices of their own shares, have expressed mounting concern about the number of foreign-owned corporations popping up in their midst.

Here, too, the implication is that the interests of the shareholders of the corporations in our midst are no longer the same as the nation's. In this instance, it is not enough that a corporation produces goods and services within the United States and employs American workers. To guarantee that corporate success will translate into national success, the corporation must also be firmly under the control of *American* citizens —so the argument goes. American shareholders and executives, it is assumed, can be trusted to act in the nation's interest under circumstances in which foreign shareholders and executives cannot be trusted. But a step is missing from this argument, just as a step was missing from the previous argument, that corporations protected from takeovers will act in the long-term interest of the economy. Here the unanswered question is, Why and under what circumstances should American citizens be expected to forgo profits in pursuit of national goals?

* * *

In Engine Charlie's time almost everything that American-owned corporations sold here or abroad—particularly anything involving the slightest complexity in design or manufacturing—was produced in the United States. This is no longer the case. American-owned corporations are now doing all sorts of technologically sophisticated work outside the United States. A significant proportion of America's current trade imbalance is due to this tendency.

Look closely at almost any major American corporation that sells complex gadgets and you are likely to see a foreign producer in disguise: In 1986 IBM imported $1.5 billion worth of data-processing equipment and General Electric half a billion dollars' worth of cassette recorders, microwave ovens, room air-conditioners, and telephones. Apple Computer's Asian plants make all Apple II computers, which in 1986 accounted for more than half of the company's sales. Eastman Kodak now sells, under its own name, Canon photocopiers, Matsushita video cameras, and TDK videotape, and it has farmed out the production of its thirty-five-millimeter cameras to Haking Industries, in Hong Kong, and Chinon Industries, in Japan. And so on.

All such goods that American corporations buy or make abroad and then sell in the United States are counted as American imports. The current frenzy in Washington over allegedly unfair foreign trade practices has obscured this reality. Consider Taiwan, which now exports some $19 billion more to the United States each year than it imports from the United States. The imbalance has provoked the indignation of American politicians, some of whom are demanding that Taiwan take steps to improve the balance or incur stiff penalties. But on closer examination the real culprit emerges. Several of Taiwan's top exporters are American-owned corporations—RCA, Texas Instruments, and General Instruments. All told, more than 30 percent of Taiwan's trade imbalance with the United States, and more than half of its imbalance in high-technology goods, is attributable to American-owned corporations buying or making things in Taiwan and exporting them back to the United States. Taiwan's only sin is to have a highly skilled population that is willing to work for relatively low wages (Taiwanese engineers earn a quarter of the salary of American engineers, and Taiwanese technicians a fifth of their American counterparts' wages).

Even Japan's notorious trade surplus with the United States is in substantial part the handiwork of American-owned corporations. Fully $17 billion, or about 40 percent, of Japan's $39.5 billion trade surplus with the United States in 1985 (a year in which the trade imbalance surged) was the result of American corporations' buying or making things in Japan to be sold in the United States under their own brand names. One of the ironies of our age is that an American who buys a Buick or an RCA television is likely to get *less* American workmanship than if he had bought a Honda or a Matsushita TV.

Americans who live and work in the United States continue to consume more than they produce and to import more than they export—hardly the path to prosperity. But American-owned *corporations* are doing quite well, regardless. They are not only raking in nice profits by buying or making things abroad for sale here but also doing well by buying or making things abroad for sale everywhere else. In 1985 American-owned corporations sold the Japanese over $53 billion worth of goods that they made in Japan—a sum greater than the American trade deficit with Japan that year (Japanese companies, meanwhile, sold us only $15 billion worth of goods that they made in the United States). IBM Japan is huge and prosperous in its own right, with eighteen thousand employees, annual sales of $6 billion around the world, and research and production facilities that are among the most advanced anywhere.

In fact, American-owned corporations have remained competitive worldwide. A recent study by Robert Lipsey and Irving Kravis, of the National Bureau of Economic Research, suggests that while the fraction of world markets held by U.S. corporations exporting from the United States has steadily dropped during the past twenty-five years, such losses have been offset by the gains of American-owned corporations exporting from *other* nations.

*   *   *

One conclusion that might be drawn from all this is that America's competitive decline does not stem from any inherent deficiency in the top management of American corporations. The stream of books exhorting managers toward excellence notwithstanding, American managers have done well by their shareholders (although not so well by America). Unsurprisingly, this insight has been welcomed by American business leaders eager to shift the blame for our competitive woes onto someone else. Mobil Oil Corporation made the argument succinctly in a 1987 advertising pronouncement:

> American multinational companies can, and do, compete successfully all over the world. While the U.S. trade balance became a shambles, these companies continued to operate successfully in world markets. They did so by producing in those countries with the best business climates. . . .
> So to argue that American businessmen have lost their management and technological skills, or grown fat and lazy, is neither true nor relevant. We should be looking to ourselves to learn why this country has provided a less favorable business environment than some of our trading partners. And then we should act to improve the climate.

Stripped to its brutal essentials, Mobil's message is this: American corporations and their shareholders can now prosper by going wherever on the globe the costs of doing business are lowest—where wages, regulations, and taxes are minimal. Indeed, managers have a responsibility to their shareholders to seek out just such business climates. If America as a whole wants to be a successful exporter, it must compete with other nations to be the location where American corporations find it profitable to set up shop.

This lesson is well understood by state governments. Consider, for example, the Hyster Company, an American-owned corporation that makes forklift trucks used to shuttle things around factories and warehouses. In 1982 Hyster informed public officials in five states and four nations where it built trucks that some Hyster plants would close. Operations would be retained wherever they were most generously subsidized. The bidding was ferocious. Within six months Hyster had collected $72.5 million in direct aid. Britain is reported to have offered $20 million to ransom fifteen hundred jobs in Irvine, Scotland. Several American towns—including Kewanee, Illinois; Sulligent, Alabama; and Berea, Kentucky—surrendered a total of $18 million in direct grants and subsidized loans to attract or preserve around two thousand jobs.

The same underlying problem emerges. Subsidies and tax breaks are offered with no strings attached—no means of holding corporations accountable to the public. Executives of the Hyster Corporation are under no more legal obligation to direct corporate efforts toward spurring the American economy than are the executives of companies shielded from takeovers by recent state laws, such as those passed by Delaware, or than are the executives of American-owned corporations in general. Hyster can take the subsidies and tax breaks and do with them whatever it wants. Indeed, just last August Hyster announced another wave of closings. The Engine Charlie principle, as this example illustrates, is no longer valid, but nothing has replaced it to reestablish the link between corporation and nation.

* * *

The privileged place of the corporation in America has been justified for more than a century by the assumption that corporations automatically fuel the nation's economic growth—that what is good for shareholders is necessarily good for America. In the past few years, however, as corporate America has become simultaneously more attentive to the immediate demands of shareholders for high returns and more international in its ownership and operations, its links to the national economy have seriously weakened.

How *should* the corporation be bound to the nation in the future? Should it be bound at all? The struggle to define a new relationship between corporation and nation will be one of the central economic and political tasks of our era, and it will defy easy solutions. Only the contours of the emerging debate can be seen.

On the one side will be those who argue that any divergence between corporate strategies and national goals is perfectly OK. The world economy as a whole will be stronger if corporations are free to attract investors from anywhere and undertake production anywhere, with the sole objective of rewarding their shareholders with the highest possible returns. In this view, any special relationship between particular corporations and a particular nation will result in an inefficient use of resources overall. As the world economy grows ever more integrated, the nation-state is becoming outmoded and irrelevant anyway. A nation's only legitimate concern with corporations doing business within its borders should be to guard its citizens from harmful side effects of corporate activity, such as pollution, unsafe products, monopolization, and fraud.

But this view fails to take into account the positive side effects of corporate activity for a nation—in particular, the training of a nation's work force in new skills applicable outside the company, and technological discoveries with broader potential. Such corporate investments in the skills and knowledge of a nation do not necessarily benefit shareholders, as has been noted, because the benefits often leak out of the company as the new knowledge spreads and as employees take their skills elsewhere. But they are critical for moving an economy forward. Positive side effects like these are as relevant to the welfare of a nation's citizens as are the potential harmful side effects. In a world in which nation-states continuously compete for economic power and the influence that flows from it, decisions about where investments are undertaken, by whom, and of what sort can have profound political consequences as well.

On the other side of the debate will be those who argue that corporations should be tightly bound to the nation. In this view large corporations in particular should be firmly under public control. It will be urged, for example, that representatives of the public be placed on corporate boards; that some corporate shares be held by publicly appointed trustees or by public authorities; that American corporate investments in other nations, and foreign investments here, be reviewed to ensure compatibility with national economic goals; and that transfers of American capital or technology across the border be carefully monitored. But this view suffers from the opposite infirmity—it sacrifices market efficiency to public accountability. Without the hope of maximizing profits, the spur of competition, and the fear of loss, enterprises have a tendency to stagnate. Too much of this, and entire economies can decline. There is a growing consensus, now apparently extending all the way to the Kremlin, that public ownership and centralized controls are not the path to progress either.

*   *   *

The best solution would be to focus specifically on what things we want corporations to do that are apt to be unprofitable to shareholders and then to induce corporations to do them. What is it we want corporations to do? Not to preserve jobs in the United States that can be done far more cheaply by foreign workers eager to do them. The costs of trying to keep such jobs here—as reflected in higher prices for consumers and onerous burdens on Third World workers deprived of work—would far exceed the benefits. We should ask corporations instead to help propel the American economy forward by training American workers in new skills and investing in new knowledge. America's economic future depends not on the old jobs we used to do but on the new contributions we can make to an increasingly integrated world economy.

Our overriding goal should be to ensure that America is a place where enterprises of whatever nationality perform sophisticated tasks and thus give large numbers of Americans valuable experience. There are several ways of inducing corporations to undertake complex production in America. The first and most obvious is to ensure that our citizens are capable of learning quickly on the job so that Americans will be the kind of workers global corporations want to train. This will require that we as a nation invest more than we do now in education—in preschool programs, in basic literacy and numeracy, in scientific and technical competence, and in foreign-language training, to name only the most critical areas. Numerous recent studies reveal the ignorance of American schoolchildren relative to those in Japan and other industrialized nations, and the extent of illiteracy and innumeracy in the society. In recent years there has been much handwringing over reading and math scores in certain locales, and even some progress in raising them. The important point is that America's future productivity is directly related to our collective capacity to learn on the job, which depends in turn on how well we are prepared to learn. No corporation, however well intentioned, can afford to make up for a lack of basic education.

In addition to the general lure of a competent work force, however, we will need more-substantive inducements. They could take several forms. We might, for example, subsidize corporations that do certain kinds of advanced design and manufacturing in the United States, with the amount of the subsidy depending on the numbers of employees so engaged. Or the inducement might take the form of a tax credit, similarly structured.

Inducements like these would also be costly, resulting in higher taxes or prices for most Americans. But unlike the open-ended initiatives now commonplace, these inducements would feature a quid pro quo: Corporations receiving them would be delivering benefits to the American economy, through on-the-job training and new knowledge. And the greater the benefits to the economy, the greater the inducements to the corporation.

These inducements would not hobble international trade or shelter American corporations from competition. They would be made available to any corporation—headquartered anywhere, owned by anyone. Corporations would thus be held accountable for what we as a public sought from them yet would have a continued incentive to allocate resources to their most profitable uses. Such inducements would have the additional virtue of pushing us to clarify our long-term development strategy—forcing our government representatives to define the categories of experience and skills we think will be most important to the nation's future.

* * *

The difficulties in the way of administering such inducements, or even gaining sufficient political support to launch them, should not be underestimated. It has been hard enough to strengthen public education and ensure a minimal level of competence in the American work force; this program of on-the-job training and research is far more ambitious. Moreover, many Americans lack confidence in government's capacity to accomplish public purposes wisely and efficiently and already feel overwhelmed and overtaxed by public needs.

But the alternatives are even less attractive. Our national strategy for economic development clearly must be more than, and different from, the sum of the strategies used by the corporations our citizens own or work for. To repeat, this is not because these corporations are irresponsible or unpatriotic, but because their widening global opportunities for making profits—and shareholders' mounting demands that they exploit such opportunities—are coming to have no direct or unique bearing on the nation's continued growth. The direction in which we are heading —blocking takeovers, hobbling foreign owners, and granting tax breaks and subsidies indiscriminately—seems far riskier and costlier than the direction I have proposed.

The growing divergence between corporation and nation is part of a larger quandary. As our economy becomes so entwined with the world's that the nations' borders lose their commercial significance, Americans need to understand and recognize the subtle ways in which our citizens are connected to one another—not through the corporations we own but through the skills and knowledge we absorb. Without this understanding we cannot expect to elicit the sacrifices required to gain greater skills and knowledge. Corporations are no longer the building blocks of the U.S. economy; our citizens are.

IV

THE
ROAD
TO
QUAYLE

18

THE REDEFINED PRESIDENCY

WHY DID GEORGE WIN? JUST BECAUSE HIS CAMPAIGN WAS ESPECIALLY vicious? No. Michael Dukakis threw his share of mud. Because of peace and prosperity? No. The public knows the peace is fragile, and prosperity uneven and vulnerable. Because America has turned conservative? No. Most Americans still want government help with education, day care, health care, housing, and the environment.

Then why did it happen? Simply, George Bush was elected because he demonstrated during the campaign that he could better fulfill the role of President as that role is now understood by the American people. George Bush campaigned for Ronald Reagan's job, and that's what he got. Michael Dukakis campaigned for a job that no longer exists.

The President used to be the government's chief executive, responsible for solving problems and implementing laws. He had a symbolic function, to be sure, but we all understood that his primary duty was to run the executive branch of government. We held the President accountable for the decisions he made. We demanded that he respond to the press, tell the truth, and take responsibility for major decisions.

But under Ronald Reagan, the Presidency was transformed, and the press and the public gradually accommodated to the change. The President has become our nation's toastmaster, the host and narrator of our country's unfolding TV docudrama. As redefined by Reagan, the President's function is to welcome home brave soldiers, comfort the families of fallen heroes, celebrate the birthdays of national monuments, exult our friends, and condemn our enemies. He is the reflection of our preferred national self-image—bountiful, buoyant, effervescent. His chief function is to make us feel safe, proud, and happy.

Ronald Reagan rarely met with the press, since this isn't required of the redefined President. A 1989 report by the Commission on the Presidential News Conference notes that Reagan's two immediate predecessors averaged one press conference every month, but Reagan averaged only six per year. Instead, he sought carefully staged visuals, photo opportunities, ceremonial pageantry. According to the report, "[e]very morning Reagan's team would meet to determine what images of the President they wanted to get on the nightly news." Thus, with each passing night we grew more accustomed to seeing our President on television, with the stirring or soothing message of the day.

Nor, in the redefined Presidency, is the truthfulness of White House statements a matter of major concern. Truth or falsehood isn't the point of such pronouncements. At the start of the Reagan Presidency the press and the public were upset about gross inaccuracies. But most people now accept that the President needs a wide degree of factual latitude. Made-up facts are accepted as illustrations, useful for the President's broader messages of uplift and inspiration.

Nor, finally, do presidential decisions matter very much. The redefined Presidency is separate from the day-to-day business of government. Ronald Reagan allowed others to make the decisions of state. To this, we have also accommodated. The public now accepts that the President should attend to sculpting the larger vision, rather than the details of governing. Since he makes no decisions, the redefined President can make no mistakes—outside his realm of symbol and image.

George Bush campaigned precisely for the job that Ronald Reagan left. Bush's campaign was a microcosm of the redefined Presidency—insulated from the press, carefully staged and scripted for the evening news, wondrously immune to the confusion of real issues. Bush had few press conferences, for fear that he might say something silly or embarrassing. He did not anguish over the accuracy of his statements. His handlers met each morning to decide on the day's theatrical backdrop—a flag factory, a crowd of police chiefs, Boston Harbor. "We are running a campaign that is designed for network TV," said Roger Stone, a senior

Bush adviser, in the weeks before the election. "That means only one message a day. . . . It means not allowing anything unplanned."

It should come as no surprise that George Bush was better qualified than was Michael Dukakis to take on Ronald Reagan's job. Bush had the advantage of seeing Ronald Reagan do it, close up, for eight years. And most of the people who guided Bush through the campaign—who gave him the scripts, told him where to stand, what to do and say—were the same people who guided Reagan as he redefined the Presidency.

Michael Dukakis campaigned for the old job. Nobody told him such services were no longer required. So he spent too much time proposing policies for educating our kids, ensuring our health, or restoring our technological lead. He talked too much with the press, and he resisted the advice of his packagers. When he tried to drop substance for symbols —like the time he rode around in that tank—he just looked silly. When he tried to spin visions, his words fell flat. He is altogether too serious, too somber, too dull for the redefined Presidency.

The tragedy of Michael Dukakis is that he wanted to be the nation's chief executive, while the open job was as Ronald Reagan's replacement. When it came time for Americans to ask which one of the two candidates would be better at doing what we have come to expect of our President, the choice was clear. We couldn't possibly envision Michael Dukakis as our national toastmaster. But George had proven himself a natural.

19

THE SPIRIT OF THE LAW

"YOU KNOW THE RULE: NO SUGARY SNACKS BEFORE DINNER."

"But Daddy," my son said plaintively, chocolate all over his face, "it wasn't a snack. It was just a few cookies. It wasn't sugary. The package said it was natural. And besides, I didn't eat them before dinner. It's five o'clock and dinner isn't till half past six." Since then, the family snack rule has become more specific.

When the spirit of the law is disregarded, the letter of the law expands until it claims attention.

In recent years the same drama has been played out on a larger stage. Investigations into wrongdoing at the highest levels of American business and government are turned over to prosecutors and defense attorneys, who argue over narrow definitions, while Congress seeks to prevent recurrences by enacting ever more detailed constraints.

Item: A coterie of Wall Street bankers and their friends stands accused of insider trading. The Securities and Exchange Commission, charged with enforcing the law, has defined insider trading broadly as a type of fraud. But in response to elaborate arguments by the bankers, there is pressure on the SEC to be far more explicit.

So it now recommends to Congress a new law barring the use of insider information if "it has been obtained by, or as a result of, or its use would constitute, theft, bribery, misrepresentation, or espionage through electronic or other means, or a breach of duty to maintain such information in confidence or to refrain from purchasing, selling or causing the purchase or sale of, the security which duty arises from any fiduciary, contractual, employment, personal or other relationship with . . . " and so on, for five turgid pages.

Securities lawyers think this clarifies and closes loopholes in the old standard and thus will be easier for the SEC to enforce. Maybe. But there was never any doubt about the purpose of the former law: to make sure that no one profits from information unavailable to the public, lest investors eschew a market that seems rigged. And the bulwarks thrown up in the new version will pose little challenge to defense attorneys skilled in the art of legal circumnavigation.

Item: A gaggle of former presidential assistants stands accused of using public office for personal gain. The Ethics in Government Act of 1978—itself a post-Watergate effort to render explicit what had always been understood as inappropriate conduct—bars former officials from lobbying their old offices within a year of leaving them, especially on matters that were pending when they left.

But one of the accused—a former White House deputy chief of staff—says the law doesn't apply to what he did. He had a right to lobby the Office of Management and Budget on behalf of a private client as soon as he departed his office, he claims, since OMB is not technically part of the White House, where he worked.

Another recently indicted White House aide argues that he did no wrong even in lobbying the White House, since the White House isn't a place where matters are ever "pending" anyway; it's where they're decided. In response, Congress is now trying to tighten the lobbying law, no doubt rendering it as convoluted and picayune as the SEC's proposed ban on insider trading.

Item: A band of high-level military officers is suspected of having violated several laws in funneling money to the contras. In late 1985 Congress expressly barred "any agency or entity of the United States involved in intelligence activities" from doing so. (This law, by the way, was an effort to close loopholes in earlier laws intended to stop military aid to the contras.)

But the officers, who were then staff members of the National Security Council, argue in court that the NSC is an advisory body to the President, not an intelligence agency, and thus was not included in the ban. Next time, Congress will be sure to close this loophole.

* * *

Regardless of who wins in the courts, we all lose. When the law degenerates into cat-and-mouse games of discovering and closing ambiguities, it loses its moral force, without which no set of detailed proscriptions can ever be detailed enough.

The cumulative effect is to loosen the bonds of mutual trust and responsibility on which a free society depends. And this exacts a real cost from all of us, as our society becomes as rule bound as a potted plant no longer able to grow.

The solution is not to be found in more niggling rules, which even a small boy intent on chocolate cookies can elude. It lies in a society that focuses on why laws are enacted rather than how they are phrased and thus demands adherence to the law's purposes as well as to its literal constraints.

Fines or imprisonments, or even impeachments, are appropriately reserved for those who transgress the letter of the law. Those who violate its spirit deserve a less official but no less sure form of punishment: They should stand disgraced in the court of public opinion.

20

A SENTIMENTAL EDUCATION

THERE WAS A PARADOX AT THE HEART OF THE REAGAN ADMINISTRATION.
In his book* Martin Anderson, Ronald Reagan's first domestic policy adviser, portrayed a White House that was the very model of efficient and thoughtful policy making. "All major policy ideas had to pass through a gauntlet of committee meetings, ranging from formal meetings of the full Cabinet or the Cabinet councils, to smaller, more informal gatherings," he wrote. Each of the six Cabinet councils had jurisdiction over an area of policy that cut across departments—like trade, natural resources, and defense. In addition to the relevant Cabinet members, each had its own staff and executive secretary. Below these were a number of working groups, developing specific policy options in each area and tracking the implementation of decisions already made. The councils and working groups, in turn, were supported by "the best research facilities in the world," comprising a "level of available expertise, facts, and studies . . . [exceeding] that of even the most sophisticated research institutions," including an endless stream of classified information pouring in from the four corners of the globe.

* *Revolution* (New York: Harcourt Brace Jovanovich, 1988).

To say nothing of the talent. Anderson spared no superlative in describing most of his White House colleagues. David Stockman, then director of the Office of Management and Budget, had attracted "probably the most talented team to ever head the budget office . . . unrivaled in OMB's history." The White House speech writers were "the most talented group assembled since the days of Kennedy and Nixon." He even quoted Robert Strauss, who in a (characteristic) fit of nonpartisan enthusiasm called the White House staff "simply spectacular . . . the best I've ever seen."

For Anderson, moreover, this extraordinary system was a logical extension of Reagan's 1980 presidential campaign, in which "the largest and most distinguished group of intellectuals ever assembled for an American political campaign" had been organized into forty-eight policy task forces, each producing detailed reports on what the Reagan Administration should do once in office. George Shultz alone presided over six economic policy task forces, whose membership totaled seventy-four "highly talented" individuals. The subsequent transition to the White House was "the most carefully planned and effective in American political history." The personnel operation, through which two thousand gifted young men and women were chosen to fill the highest levels of the Administration, "was easily the best in the history of the United States."

Let us assume even a small element of truth to Anderson's hyperbole. Compared with other recent administrations, the one that came to office in January 1981 did appear to be unusually competent and well organized. It knew what it wanted to do, and it had thought about how to do it.

But, the paradox: How could such a beautifully designed policy process have generated the remarkable stream of blunders that marred the Reagan Administration? Why the unprecedented budget deficits, culminating in over $400 billion owed to the rest of the world? Why the foreign policy debacles—the disaster of the Marines in Lebanon, the Bitburg folly, the foolishness of the "disinformation" campaign, the Iran–contra fiasco, the humiliation by Noriega? Why the seemingly endless series of scandals, improprieties, forced resignations? Even the Administration's claimed successes, like the Soviet withdrawal from Afghanistan and the treaty on intermediate-range ballistic missiles, seemed to depend less on any carefully conceived strategy than on events and personalities over which the White House had no control, and on luck.

* * *

Donald Regan, the President's secretary of the Treasury during the first term and chief of staff for two years during the second, offered one explanation for this arresting divergence between input and output. In his titillating memoir,* he blamed Reagan's fantastic passivity. The book made headlines for its revelations that a clairvoyant in California determined Reagan's schedule, but Regan's criticism of the President was more fundamental than anything merely celestial. Regan wished to demonstrate that Reagan simply wasn't interested in the substance of policy.

The campaign task forces, the working groups, the talented advisers notwithstanding, when Regan took the Treasury job, he had no clue what he was supposed to do. After several months he confessed in his diary: "To this day I have never had so much as one minute alone with Ronald Reagan! Never has he, or anyone else, sat down in private to explain to me what is expected of me, what goals he would like to see me accomplish, what results he wants. . . . How can one do a job if the job is not defined?" Lacking any guidance from above, Regan felt it necessary "to figure these things out like any other American, by studying [Reagan's] speeches and reading the newspaper." Thus was the economic policy of the United States divined by the secretary of the Treasury.

What did the President want to do, for example, about taxes? Regan could only guess, based on the President's facial expression, on presidential fidgets, when the issue of taxes was raised. "I had the impression, based on observation of his body language rather than any words he had spoken in private, that he wanted to hold the line against new taxes." Should Regan and James Baker swap jobs? When they proposed it to the President, he simply smiled approvingly. "I did not know what to make of his passivity," Regan recalled. "He seemed to be absorbing a fait accompli rather than making a decision."

Regan was consistently stunned at the President's lack of involvement. Reagan never issued an order. He rarely asked a question. He provided no guidance at all. A Potemkin Presidency, according to Regan, all form and no substance. Reagan only acted the part of President; he wasn't really President at all. Regan tried to explain:

> As President, Ronald Reagan acted on the work habits of a
> lifetime: he regarded his daily schedule as being something like
> a shooting script in which characters came and went, scenes
> were rehearsed and acted out, and the plot was advanced one

---

* *For the Record: From Wall Street to Washington* (New York: Harcourt Brace Jovanovich, 1988).

day at a time, and not always in sequence. The Chief of Staff
was a sort of producer, making certain that the star had what
he needed to do best; the staff was like the crew, invisible
behind the lights, watching the performance their behind-the-
scenes efforts had made possible. . . . Checking off each event
with a pencil after it ended and preparing himself for the next
gave [Reagan's] life a regularity and tangible measure of
accomplishment that . . . was deeply pleasing to him.

The result was "an environment where there seemed to be no center,
no structure, no agreed policy." The policy-making talent generated
huge amounts of paper, but no final decisions ever seemed to emerge
from all this apparatus. In Regan's account there was simply nobody at
the top who made final decisions.

During his tenure at the Treasury, Regan found himself increasingly
critical of the way the President's staff seemed to encourage such passivity in the chief executive. They wanted to protect Reagan from controversy and also to protect the public from the bold visions and the strong
opinions that Regan felt certain burned deep inside the President. Regan
agreed to become chief of staff because he wanted to allow Reagan to be
more assertive, more decisive, more presidential: to "let Reagan be Reagan." And he tried. Regan reduced the number of Cabinet councils,
centralized control over the chain of command, and sought to streamline
the decision-making process so that the President could be more directly
involved.

One of his first acts as chief of staff was to prepare a planning
memorandum for the President on a range of controversial subjects that
were likely to arise during the following year, including farm supports,
protectionism, Social Security, and Western European defenses. The
memorandum set forth overall priorities and included detailed policy
recommendations, specific presidential actions, and timetables. "What
do you think?" he asked the President, expecting a substantive dialogue
about the complex and somewhat daring initiatives he was proposing.
" 'It's good,' the President replied, nodding in approval. 'It's really good,
Don.' " Nothing more.

In the end, as we all know, Regan was fired. And he is bitter about
that. He blamed Nancy Reagan, other White House staffers, the news
media, national security advisers McFarlane and Poindexter, and above
all, Ronald Reagan. Regan's failed effort to get Reagan involved in the
substantive choices facing the President of the United States resulted in
Regan himself being made a target. Criticized by the media for his lax

supervision of the National Security Council staff (over which, he protests, the chief of staff has no direct control) and detested by insiders who resented his assertive role, Regan was scapegoated for the inevitable failings of an indifferent president.

* * *

At least, that's his story. But his story doesn't ring true, exactly. We have heard similar complaints before, with the same self-serving, self-pitying quality about them. David Stockman, in his own memoir, sought to place blame for the Administration's mammoth budget deficits on Reagan's failure to get involved. "He conveyed the impression that since we all knew what needed to be done, we should simply get on with the job," Stockman chided. But there was more to it, according to Stockman, than simply getting on with the job. Cutting public spending or raising taxes required hard choices that the President was unprepared to make. Politics triumphed, because Ronald Reagan wouldn't take the lead.

It is worth remembering that Regan and Stockman were on opposite sides of the economic debate during Reagan's first term. Regan was a confirmed supply-sider who assumed that tax cuts would generate more tax revenues, as people began to work harder and earn more money. Stockman insisted that tax increases would be necessary. Reagan did not shy away from this debate, however. Most of the White House staff was on Stockman's side, but Reagan ultimately sided with Regan. In other words, here is one instance in which Reagan was an assertive—indeed, a bullheaded—president.

There is a natural temptation to attribute lassitude to superiors who disagree with one's own wisdom. (How could he have been paying attention if he failed to comprehend the obvious superiority of my argument?) And there is a natural temptation to impute indolence to a superior who agrees too quickly with one's recommendations, without fully acknowledging their brilliance. (How could he have been alert if he failed to discuss the finer points of my argument?) Regan and Stockman ultimately came to the same conclusion about Reagan, but from opposite poles. All that they possessed in common were raging egos, which demanded of Reagan both complete acquiescence and sparkling attentiveness. When they failed to receive one or the other, they grew bitter.

In fact, the record will show that Ronald Reagan was quite a decisive president and deeply concerned about a whole range of issues. The paradoxical disparity between inputs and outputs—between the elaborate systems of policy formulation in the White House and the often ill-

conceived blunderbuss that emerged—was not due to Reagan's passivity. It was due, rather, to the peculiar character of Reagan's engagement.
If anything, Reagan was too personally involved in decisions—too pas-
sionate, too caring, too sentimental. Time and again, he decided issues
on the basis of emotion rather than reason.

Reagan's blunders owed to his failure to respect the process of
policy making. And his staff swiftly grasped that lack of respect. Forget
the Cabinet councils, working groups, panels of experts, the briefing
books. When Reagan's advisers wanted him to decide something in a
certain way, they circumvented these established channels and manipulated his feelings.

When Regan wanted the President's go-ahead to reform the federal
income tax system, for example, Regan devised a way to play on Reagan's emotions. As Regan told it:

> As a way of introducing the subject, I asked him a question
> about his old employer, the General Electric company: "What
> does General Electric have in common with Boeing, General
> Dynamics, and 57 other big corporations?"
>
> Reagan's interest was immediately aroused. He had fond
> memories of his days as a television host and traveling goodwill
> ambassador for GE, and a large number of anecdotes and
> stories about this experience.
>
> "I don't know," he said, leaning forward in his chair and
> smiling. "What *do* they have in common?"
>
> "Let me tell you, Mr. President," I replied. "What these
> outfits have in common is that not one of them pays a penny in
> taxes to the United States government."
>
> "*What?*" the President said.
>
> His shock was genuine. A dumbfounded silence settled
> over his economic advisers. What unconventional idea was I
> trying to plant in the President's mind now?
>
> "Believe it or not, Mr. President," I continued, "your
> secretary paid more federal taxes last year than all of those
> giant companies put together."
>
> The President flushed, a sure sign of surprise and
> discomfort. "I just can't believe that," he said.
>
> "I don't blame you for doubting it," I replied. "But it's the
> truth. . . . It's perfectly legal, but it's wrong, Mr. President,
> when a hardworking secretary pays more to support her
> government than 60 of the richest corporations in the land. The
> time has come to do something fundamental about the tax
> system. It's too complicated, it's grotesquely unfair, and it's a
> drag on the economy because it discourages competition."

By now the President's cheeks were carmine and there was
a spark of resolution in his eye.

He said, "I agree, Don, I just didn't realize that things had
gotten that far out of line."

I interpreted his words as an instruction to go full steam
ahead with a proposal to overhaul the entire federal tax
structure.

Martin Anderson offered another example, in some ways more
chilling, of the White House staff's shrewd tendency to bypass the nor-
mal channels of policy making through appeals to Reagan's emotions.
When the Israelis began to bomb Beirut in June 1982, Michael Deaver,
then deputy chief of staff, was upset. According to Anderson, Deaver
lurched into the Oval Office, and the following exchange ensued:

"Mr. President, I have to leave."

The President was startled.

"What do you mean?"

"I can't be a part of this anymore," replied Deaver, "the
bombings, the killing of children. It's wrong. And you're the
one person on the face of the earth right now who can stop it.
All you have to do is tell Begin you want it stopped."

Reagan stared at Deaver with a look, as Deaver later
described it, of "My God, what have we done?" and then asked
his secretary to get Menachem Begin, the prime minister of
Israel, on the phone. . . .

When the call to Israel came through, Reagan told Begin
bluntly that the shelling and bombing of Beirut had to stop.
Reagan's last words were, "It has gone too far. You must stop
it."

In 20 minutes Begin called back and said it was done. The
shelling and bombing was stopped. Reagan was somewhat
incredulous and said, "I didn't know I had that kind of power."

But the master of the emotional manipulation of the President was
William Casey, the crumpled wizard of the CIA. According to Anderson,
Casey never missed an opportunity to play upon Reagan's fears and
Reagan's sympathies. And here lies a clue as to why Reagan agreed to
sell arms to Iran, the protestations of his secretaries of defense and state
notwithstanding. William Buckley was the CIA's station chief in Lebanon when he was kidnapped on March 16, 1984. Anderson tells us that
Casey wanted Buckley freed at all costs. In order to wring concessions
out of the United States, Buckley's kidnappers had sent the CIA a videotape of Buckley's brutal torture, complete with agonizing sounds. "Appealing deeply to Reagan's emotional anguish," Casey then arranged for

Reagan to see the sickening videotape. And thereafter Reagan would share Casey's intense commitment to free the hostages, almost regardless of the consequences.

*   *   *

The White House that emerges from these memoirs was a palace of intrigue, but it had its own unfortunate coherence. The intrigue consisted, to be precise, in the attempts of advisers to outmaneuver one another to capture the heart, not the mind, of the President. Every conversation was an opportunity to play to his emotions; every chance encounter, an opening for an evocative anecdote to convince him to decide this way or that. The people surrounding Reagan continuously sought to make use of his feelings for their purposes. They fed him vivid stories and letters to illustrate particular positions, they filled his schedule with emotionally charged events and meetings, they prevented him from being along with one of their competitors who might use the same tricks for opposite purposes, they planted pointed newspaper articles that he was sure to read.

Regan hated Nancy Reagan for the simple reason that she understood this game so well. After all, she had been playing it for decades. Her fascination with astrology was a minor irritant, really. What irked Regan most was that Nancy could outmaneuver him. She could orchestrate her husband's sentiments far better than Regan could. That, and not the zodiac, was how she could determine what Reagan would decide, far more effectively than could the President's chief of staff. And all the cabinet councils, the working groups, the experts, the briefing books were irrelevant to this larger, inner drama. Regan understood this, and so did Nancy. In the end, the two of them found themselves in a tug-of-war over the President's heart. Regan's biggest frustration was he was not the wife.

Historians of the Reagan Administration will certainly record a bold and decisive president—not the weak, indolent creature caricatured by Regan and Stockman. But history will also reveal a president without any appreciable capacity to make thoughtful decisions. The White House's sophisticated apparatus of policy development, of which Martin Anderson is so proud, was superseded by Ronald Reagan's boyish heart. Decisions *were* made, but as a result of the manner in which they were made, they bore little relation to the facts, the analysis, and the expertise on hand. America had eight years of government by sentimental education.

21

THE DAY
I BECAME A FEMINIST

"I LOST, BY FOUR VOTES," SHE SAID, SIMPLY. "I'LL BE HOME SOON." I must have looked shaken as I put down the phone. Our precocious six-year-old, who had been eyeing me, summed up the situation: "They fired Mommy, didn't they?"

Sexism had always been something of an abstraction to me. I knew it existed, but I assumed that it was the product of backward and parochial cultures. It might show up in entrenched corporate bureaucracies dominated by old-boy networks, or in ethnic groups governed by male-dominated traditions, or in working-class communities in which Rambo still reigned. But surely no such noxious bias would be found in the overwhelmingly liberal, intellectual, worldly, and high-minded university community that we safely inhabited.

Yet a string of white males had been voted tenure just before her. Most had not written as much as she, nor inspired the same praise from specialists around the nation as had her work. None of their writings had been subjected to the detailed scrutiny—footnote by footnote—to which her colleagues had subjected her latest manuscript. Not one of the male candidates had aroused the degree of anger and bitterness that characterized her tenure decision.

Why? At first I was bewildered. I knew most of the men who had voted against her. A few I knew to be narrow-minded, one or two I might have suspected of misogyny. But most were thoughtful, intelligent men. They had traveled widely, read widely, had held positions of responsibility and trust. I was sure that they felt they had been fair and impartial in judging her work. They would be appalled at any suggestion of sexual bias.

Gradually, I came to understand. They were applying their standard of scholarship as impartially as they knew how. Yet their standard assumed that the person to whom they applied it had gone through the same training and had had the same formative intellectual experiences as they. It assumed further that the person had gained along the way the same understandings of academic discipline, and the same approaches to core problems, as they had gained. In short, their standard was premised on the belief that the people they judged had come to view the modes and purposes of scholarship—of the life of the mind—in the same way they had come to view it.

Through the years she has helped me to see the gender biases of these assumptions. Her experiences and understandings, and those of other women scholars, have been shaped by the irrefutable reality of gender. The values and perspectives she brings to bear on the world —and in particular, the world of ideas—are different from theirs, because she has experienced the world differently. In fact, it is the very uniqueness of her female perspective that animates her scholarship, that gives it its originality and intellectual bite. They had applied their standard as impartially as they knew how, but it was a male standard.

Not that they were incapable of appreciating her scholarship simply because they were men: after all, the experts in her field whose opinions had been solicited during the tenure review, and who had overwhelmingly praised her work, had been male. And the majority of the men on her faculty had voted to grant her tenure; she had failed only to get the necessary two thirds. Presumably, the men who supported her had been able to imagine the life of the mind from a different perspective than their own. They had been able and willing to expand their standard—not to compromise it or to reduce it, but to broaden it to include a woman's way of knowing. I suspect that those who did not, did not care to try.

And why would they not have cared to try? Here again, I was momentarily stumped. Apart from the few diehards, they were kindly men, tolerant men. But perhaps they did not feel that she had invited them to try. Early on, her closest friends on the faculty were a group of young professors who took delight in challenging the sacred cows of prevailing scholarship. Her early articles openly proclaimed a feminist perspective. She had not played at being a good daughter to the older and more traditional men on the faculty, giggling at their jokes and massaging their egos. Nor had she pretended to be one of them, speaking loudly and talking tough. They had no category for her, and to that extent, she had threatened them, made them uncomfortable. So that when it came time for them to try to see the world from her perspective, they chose not to.

* * *

Since the vote, she has remained strong and as certain of the worth of her scholarship as before. Many women colleagues, and many men, rallied to her cause. There were student demonstrations. She pondered a lawsuit. She was offered a faculty position elsewhere and is happy with her new job.

But the experience has shaken me. First came the rage and confusion. Only later came insight into the insidiousness of sexism even in our most enlightened institutions. It has made me wary, in addition, of my own limited perspective—of the countless ways in which I fail to understand my female colleagues and students and their ways of knowing the world.

I have begun to notice small things. A recruiter for a large company calls to ask about a student who is being considered for a job. "Does she plan to have a family?" he inquires, innocently enough. "Is she really—er—serious about a career?" It is not the first time such a question has been put to me about a female student, but it is the first time I hear it clearly, for what it is.

A male colleague is critical of a young woman assistant professor: "She's not assertive enough in the classroom," he confides. "She's too anxious to please—doesn't know her own mind." Then, later, another colleague, about the same young woman: "She's so whiney. I find her very abrasive." It is possible, of course, that she is both diffident and abrasive. But I can't help wondering if these characterizations more accurately reflect how my two colleagues feel about women in general—their mothers, wives, girlfriends—than about this particular young woman.

At a board meeting of a small foundation on which I serve, the lone woman director tries to express doubts about a pending decision. At first, several loquacious men in the group won't give her a chance to speak. When finally she begins to voice her concern, she is repeatedly interrupted. She perseveres and eventually states her objection. But her concern goes unaddressed in the remainder of the meeting, as if she had never raised it. It seems to me that this isn't the first time she was ignored, but it is the first time I noticed.

In my class I present a complex management problem. An organization is rife with dissension. I ask, What steps should the manager take to improve the situation? The answers of my male students are filled with words like "strategy," "conflict," "interests," "claims," "trade-offs," and "rights." My female students use words like "resolution," "relationship," "cooperation," and "loyalty." Have their vocabularies and approaches to problems always been somewhat different, or am I listening now as never before?

The vice president of a corporation that I advise tells me he can't implement one of my recommendations, although he agrees with it. "I have no authority," he explains. "It's not my turf." Later the same day, his assistant vice president tells me that the recommendation can be implemented easily. "It's not formally within our responsibility," she says, offhandedly. "But we'll just make some suggestions here and there, at the right time, to the right folks, and it'll get done." Is the male vice president especially mindful of formal lines of authority and his female assistant especially casual, or do they exemplify differences in how men and women in general approach questions of leadership?

If being a "feminist" means noticing these sorts of things, then I became a feminist the day my wife was denied tenure. But what is my responsibility, as a male feminist, beyond merely noticing? At the least: to remind corporate recruiters that they shouldn't be asking about whether prospective female employees want to have a family; to warn male colleagues about subtle possibilities of sexual bias in their evaluations of female colleagues; to help ensure that women are listened to within otherwise all-male meetings; to support my women students in the classroom, and to give explicit legitimacy to differences in the perceptions and leadership styles of men and women. In other words, just as I seek to educate myself, I must also help educate other men.

This is no small task. The day after the vote on my wife's tenure, I phoned one of her opponents—an old curmudgeon, as arrogant as he is smart. Without the slightest sense of the irony lying in the epithet I chose to hurl at him, I called him a son of a bitch.

22

THE FOURTH
WAVE OF REGULATION

ONCE EACH GENERATION, AMERICAN BUSINESS HAS AN OPPORTUNITY TO exert leadership—to set the public agenda rather than defend itself against the public. And once each generation, the American business community squanders the opportunity. It is doing so again, under the benign aegis of Ronald Reagan and George Bush.

The first generation of American business leaders had an opportunity to exert leadership in the mid- and late-1880s, when mass-production techniques began to transform the relationship of managers and workers and the modern diversified corporation was born. But the business community's inability then to understand and respond to the public responsibilities attendant upon large corporate size contributed to the Populist and Progressivist agitation of the last decades of the nineteenth century and the early decades of this century—to antitrust legislation and the establishment of the Federal Trade Commission, to laws governing hours and working conditions, and to legislation protecting consumers from dangerous drugs and unwholesome meat.

American business had a second opportunity during the 1920s, after joining in successful partnership with the government on the War Industries Board and thus earning a measure of public trust. Its failure then to respond to the postwar demands of labor, investors, and consumers foreshadowed New Deal programs to protect these groups—legislation establishing a framework for labor-management relations, regulations governing the securities and banking industries, and laws further protecting consumers from unsafe foods, drugs, and cosmetics.

Business had a third opportunity in the 1950s and early 1960s, when government fiscal and monetary policies appeared to ensure steady economic growth, and Americans enjoyed the prosperity that business and government—working together—seemed able to provide. But the failure of American business once again to seize the initiative in anticipation of a new set of emerging public concerns about the environment, health, consumer safety, equal opportunity, and political corruption set the stage for a third wave of regulation, beginning in 1965. This wave was manifested in thirty-five separate regulatory programs covering everything from unsafe toys and flammable fabrics to unsafe mines and toxic chemicals. The third wave ended in 1978 with the defeat of several proposed pieces of legislation—to establish a consumer protection agency, enlarge protections accorded organized labor, eliminate certain special tax advantages enjoyed by business, and bar conglomerate mergers of firms above a certain size.

*   *   *

There are remarkable parallels among the three periods. Each successive wave was marked by a further extension of government control over business—either enlarging the jurisdiction of agencies already established or establishing new ones. Of the twenty-eight independent regulatory agencies founded between 1887 and 1980, all but seven were established during one of these three periods.

Each wave was immediately preceded by dramatic accounts in the popular press of public harms or dangers attendant upon business activity—Upton Sinclair's revelations of unsanitary conditions in the meatpacking industry at the turn of the century; Ida Tarbell's ringing indictment of the Standard Oil Trust; Louis Brandeis's exposé of the banking industry; more recently, Rachel Carson's stirring account of environmental decay; Jessica Mitford's revelations about the funeral industry; and Ralph Nader's string of exposés concerning dangerous cars, drugs, and food additives. Complementing these journalistic efforts (dubbed "muckraking" before World War I and "investigative reporting" in the 1970s) were public scandals and disasters, which lent credibility to the exposés and further undermined public confidence in business: the Triangle Shirt Waist factory fire, Jay Gould's Wall Street manipulations, the elixir sulfanilamide disaster, thalidomide deformities, fatalities in General Motors' Corvair and Ford's Pinto, scandals over union pension funds and foreign bribes, Allied Chemical's dumping of a toxic chemical into the Chesapeake Bay, mine cave-ins, leaks from nuclear reactors.

In each period dramatic events and revelations spurred middle-income citizens into political action. In the Progressive era organizations first sprang up at the local level, promoting the environment, consumerism, and better government. During the New Deal, middle-income groups formed antibusiness coalitions with urban ethnics, intellectuals, and organized labor. In the most recent wave middle-income groups joined with the organized poor on certain issues affecting business and with students and labor on others.

Each wave endured for about a decade before the interest of the middle-income groups waned and the antibusiness coalitions, of which they were a central part, began to disintegrate. In the first two periods the immediate cause of the decline was an international crisis, culminating in the buildup of military armaments, and the outbreak of global hostilities. The most recent wave ended with an international economic crisis spurred by an oil embargo, and the need for a national economic mobilization (or "revitalization" as it was termed). In all three periods middle-income groups, whose economic survival was suddenly at stake, quickly forsook their antibusiness activities and joined in an unstable coalition with business.

I have simplified, of course. Lines of cause and effect were more complicated than this. Business leaders sometimes sought regulations in order to protect themselves against competition. But I think it fair to say that embedded within much of regulatory history has been a pendulum-like cycle—an almost predictable waxing and waning of antibusiness political activity the momentum of which has been maintained from generation to generation in large part by the business community's own defensiveness or indifference to public concerns.

* * *

Instead of actively anticipating the *next* wave of public activism and exerting leadership in setting the future public agenda, America's business leaders have been content to enjoy their temporary respite from criticism. They have merely awaited the inevitable series of scandals, disasters, and exposés that signal a return to the politics of confrontation. At most, they have resorted to public-relations devices—expensive media campaigns designed to create a corporate image of social responsibility.

The business community has been unable to see below the surface of public activism. The waves of regulation have not reflected sudden shifts in public opinion about business as much as they have represented shifts in the public's willingness to engage in political activity.

Public opinion toward business has been remarkably stable over time. In survey after survey, a majority of the public has continued to support government regulation. This is true even in our current period of regulatory quiescence. In one recent survey 81 percent of the respondents felt that business had a responsibility to control pollution, but only 40 percent felt that business was fulfilling that responsibility; 80 percent thought that business had a responsibility to advertise honestly, but only 37 percent felt that business was fulfilling that responsibility. The responses were more favorable with regard to providing safe products of good quality—66 percent felt that business was fulfilling its obligations here. But that still left a large minority—34 percent—who disagreed. In another recent poll 80 percent of the respondents felt that government must ensure that business clean up its air and water pollution, provide safe products and services, and provide safe working conditions.* These results are not substantially different from those of similar polls undertaken over the last thirty years.

This underlying public distrust of business manifests itself in a variety of ways. Even when there is not political support for increased regulation, as now, the public vents its latent distrust in lawsuits and in market decisions to forsake American-made products.

Notwithstanding that case-by-case litigation over liability is cumbersome, costly, and extremely time-consuming, it has increased dramatically as the third wave of regulation has receded. Asbestos cases forced Johns-Manville into bankruptcy. Injuries resulting from the use of Firestone "500" steel-belted radials have given rise to millions of dollars in personal damage awards; injuries from the Dalkon Shield IUD have resulted in millions more; accidents related to an allegedly faulty gear shift in several Ford Motor Company models spawned hundreds of lawsuits and resulted in several large awards; the accident at Three Mile Island resulted in nineteen class actions for damages to personal property with an estimated total liability of $1.5 billion and earned lawyers over

* Harris and Roper polls, July and September 1987.

$7 million in legal fees; disorders arising in connection with the drug DES, used to prevent miscarriages, have resulted in a large number of class actions involving more than one thousand lawyers. The list goes on: toxic shock from tampons, cancer from benzene and vinyl chloride, birth defects from endrin, suspected cancer from trichloroethylene (TCE) and polychlorinated biphenyl (PCB). In addition to these specific liabilities, and partly because of them, American business paid over $8 billion in liability insurance premiums in 1988, up almost 300 percent from 1975 and still growing.

Even as more citizens seek legal redress, the courts are extending the limits of business liability. The California Supreme Court has ruled that plaintiffs in DES suits need not prove which manufacturer provided the specific brand of DES that caused the problem; instead, all manufacturers can be held liable, since they all produce the same drug. This is a potentially far-reaching doctrine, which could make entire industries liable whenever specific responsibility for damages is difficult to discern.

The courts are also looking more favorably on punitive damage awards, in which victims are not only compensated for the damages they endure but are also awarded an amount designed to punish the company for having inflicted the injury. For example, the Minnesota Supreme Court has affirmed a $1.8 million award against a textile manufacturer for producing cotton pajamas that caught fire and badly burned a young child; $1 million of that amount was punitive. A Florida jury has awarded a dealer in business machines $5 million, of which $3.3 million represented punitive damages for injuries resulting from defects in the manufacturers' plain-paper copiers.

Business executives are not fortune-tellers, and in many instances it is extremely difficult—if not impossible—to foresee potential dangers or injuries resulting from the use of certain products. But in reviewing these cases, one is struck by the abundance of early warning signals. The first cases of asbestos-related injuries, for example, were reported over sixty years ago. There was a major conference on asbestos dangers in New York almost twenty years ago. The first cases of DES malignancies were reported more than fifteen years ago. In almost every case of unsafe autos or tires, the companies involved received accident reports long before there were many injuries. Hooker Chemical Company could have spent $1.5 million in the early 1950s to build a landfill for its toxic wastes; its use of Love Canal, and subsequent sale to the City of Niagara Falls, ended up costing the company three or four times that amount in liability alone.

All too often, American business leaders have taken the short-term view, placing immediate profits above potential problems that may be years away. The easing of regulations during the 1980s has further encouraged this sort of myopia, making it that much more difficult for company employees who are concerned about these matters to be heard.

* * *

There is another way the public is expressing its discontent with American business. Consumers who find that a product is of poor quality, that it demands inordinate repairs, that it falls apart too quickly or appears to be dangerous have an easy option: to buy a *competitor's* product. Since the early 1970s, consumers have been exercising that option in large numbers, deserting American-made manufacturers for Japanese and West German producers. Surely, consumers are attracted by lower price tags on many foreign items; but quality continues to be a key reason for the desertion.

American business has deluded itself into spending millions of dollars to stall new regulations and fight product recalls. For example, some time ago the U.S. government levied a fine—the largest ever assessed under the Motor Vehicle Safety Act—against a major U.S. tire manufacturer for its failure to recall voluntarily tires that it knew did not meet federal safety standards. Not by coincidence, even before the government knew that the problem existed, a foreign tire manufacturer captured a $500 million share of the U.S. tire market.

The lesson should be clear. American business can no longer afford to wait for the next wave of regulation and then use the same stratagems of legal delay and obfuscation used too often in the past to block new rules. America has grown more litigious; our citizens are far more willing to seek damages in court than ever before. The world has become smaller; consumers here and abroad are more willing to buy another nation's products if they perform better. And the public side effects of business have grown more substantial, with large populations now suddenly endangered by leaks of toxic chemicals or malfunctions in nuclear reactors.

Should there be a fourth wave of regulation, it is likely to be no less onerous than previous waves. Perhaps more so. The irony is that unless American business actively seeks to anticipate and respond to emerging public concerns in advance of that wave, business already will have been seriously eroded by the time it breaks. For regulation is only the most visible expression of the public's discontent; animosity toward business is manifest in many other ways. American business leaders can discover the size and direction of the next wave by merely examining the causes of their mounting legal liability and declining profits.

23

THE ECONOMIC
THEORY OF POLITICS

IN RECENT YEARS ECONOMISTS HAVE CAST THEIR IMPERIALIST SIGHTS ON realms far removed from the seductive curves of supply and demand. One area in particular has captured their fancy, perhaps because the domain is large—stretching, as it were, across the globe. It is the domain of politics.

The modern economist's fascination with politics is not a new one, of course, nor is it especially surprising. The way people work together to produce goods and services is intimately tied to the way they set and pursue public goals. Indeed, the notion that the economic and political spheres of our life can be separated is of recent vintage. The very word "economics" was not firmly established until 1890, when Alfred Marshall wrote his *Principles of Economics*. Before then the term was "political economy"—with the adjective serving as a reminder of the "economy's" origins and effects. The entire field branched off in the late eighteenth century from moral philosophy, the study of citizens' rights, duties, and obligations. In earlier eras it seemed impossible to consider economic relationships in isolation from their specific political and social contexts.

The new attention given to politics by economists proceeds, however, from different premises. Rather than envision economic phenomena as outgrowths of political and social life, the new approach views political phenomena as outgrowths of economic life.

Not surprisingly, politics seen from this end of the telescope is even more dismal than the "dismal science" itself. In the marketplace personal demands are mediated through competition for scarce resources. But in politics the demands of special-interest groups are forwarded, often covertly, through exclusive channels to legislative committees, agencies, and bureaus. Politics becomes a pipeline to the public trough.*

As the American welfare state has burgeoned, the economic theory of politics has gained adherents. It seems to offer an explanation both for the failure of the Great Society to eradicate poverty and for the poor economic performance of the United States in recent years. According to this view, popular expectations and group demands on government have reached extraordinary levels, resulting in a vast expansion of government responsibilities; not all of these commitments can be fulfilled. The only way out of this morass is to reduce government responsiveness to these demands—to amend the Constitution to limit public spending and taxes, revert to the gold standard to discipline monetary policy, and devise new governmental arrangements like public corporations and independent authorities, which are less vulnerable to democratic politics. Democracy, in other words, must be saved from its own excesses by dramatically reducing access to state benefits or by reducing the discretion of public officials to respond to political demands—which amounts to the same thing.

* * *

One of the most recent, and most engaging, proponents of the economic theory of politics is Professor Mancur Olson, author of *The Rise and Decline of Nations*.† As the title implies, Olson sought to account for why some economies grow quickly, others slowly, and still others

---

* The economist Joseph Schumpeter, in some respects intellectual father of this school of thought, sought to dispense with the "classical doctrine" of democracy and its presumption that people are capable of acting with the common good in mind. Instead, Schumpeter saw democracy as "an institutional arrangement for arriving at political decisions in which individuals acquire the power to decide by means of a competitive struggle for people's votes." See his *Capitalism, Socialism, and Democracy* (New York and London: Harper and Brothers, 1942).
† New Haven: Yale University Press, 1982.

not at all. His answer: politics. Since broad and dispersed interests find it hard to organize for political action, the likelihood is that small narrow-interest groups will engineer a redistribution of benefits toward themselves and away from everyone else. Moreover, since people discover the benefits of such group action and organize themselves only gradually, a stable society will steadily accumulate more and more special-interest groups. After a long period of stability, such groups will have disproportionate political influence.

The means by which special-interest groups redistribute national wealth to themselves reduce a society's overall efficiency. If the special-interest group succeeds in raising some price or wage, or in taxing some type of income at lower rates than other income, the extra resources that are diverted into the favored area add less to society's output than they otherwise would. Or the special-interest group may seek to establish a cartel in order to reduce output and thereby enjoy a higher price, and in so doing it imposes additional inefficiencies on society as a whole. Such activities slow a society's growth by reducing the rate at which resources are reallocated from one activity or industry to another in response to new technologies and conditions. Indeed, special-interest groups may simply block technological change.

Olson employed these ideas to explain the postwar "economic miracles" in the nations that were defeated or occupied in World War II, particularly Japan and West Germany. In Germany Hitler did away with independent unions as well as other dissenting groups; immediately after the war, the Allies eviscerated German cartels and organizations with right-wing origins. Japan's militaristic regime had suppressed left-wing organizations; after Japan's defeat, American occupiers cracked down on Japan's monopolies and purged an entire generation of the business elite. Thus, in these nations violence and repression wiped the slate clean of special-interest groups by the end of the 1940s and thereby opened the way to rapid growth. On the other hand, the United States and Great Britain—countries with comparatively long and undisturbed histories of democratic freedom—have experienced slower growth in the postwar era. Both nations are rife with special-interest groups.

Professor Olson's answer? Rather than reduce political access generally, he would have us reduce the influence of special-interest groups on the political process. Violence and repression are one means of eliminating special-interest groups, at least for a time; but Olson was not so cynical as to conclude that economic growth requires a bloodbath. He sought instead a cultural and ideological transformation. He expressed the hope that the schools and the mass media would create a widespread public antipathy to special-interest groups. The remedy would follow quite naturally from this change in attitudes.

> A society with the consensus that has just been described might choose the most obvious and far-reaching remedy: it might simply repeal all special-interest legislation or regulation and at the same time apply rigorous antitrust laws to every type of cartel or collusion that used its power to obtain prices and wages above competitive levels.

Then, presumably, society would alter irrevocably its political arrangements so that special interests would be prevented ever again from holding sway.

* * *

It is perhaps too easy to take issue with the evidence Olson invoked to bolster his thesis. For example, the eradication of special-interest groups is neither adequate nor indeed necessary to explain much of the postwar economic dynamism of Germany or Japan. The loss of physical capital (combined in Japan's case with relatively little to begin with) left these nations with very low productivity levels on which to build. Both countries thus could show enormous proportional strides as they caught up with other, less ravaged nations. Such advances were fueled by the shift of labor from agriculture to industry—a shift well under way in many other industrialized nations—and by the simple expedient of adopting technologies developed elsewhere. (The recent rapid growth of Southern and Western states within the United States can be similarly explained. Starting from a much lower level of productivity than Northeastern states, the Sun Belt has played catch-up to older industrial regions; this process of economic homogenization has been accelerated by generous defense spending and public-works projects during the postwar era.)

There is a more basic issue, however. Olson, like others of his persuasion, proffered the ideal of a democratic state devoid of special-interest politics. It is a state whose economy can be "naturally" adaptable and innovative. Olson did not discuss this vision in detail, but one can infer its key features: No organization stands between the individual and the government except perhaps large encompassing organizations that effectively neutralize partisan appeals. The only small groups are households and firms, which relate to one another almost exclusively through the market. Social relations are virtually coextensive with market relations. Workers no longer are organized in industry-wide unions; wage bargaining occurs instead at the level of the firm. A household's income depends on the market value of its members' labor. The government's chief responsibility, apart from providing for national defense and certain public goods like highways, is to police the market in order to guard against the possibility that any group of individuals, households, or firms might seek to distort it through collusion.

Some, no doubt, may find this sort of society attractive. But what about its economic neutrality? After all, there exists an infinite array of alternative market outcomes, each equally efficient, depending on the *initial* distribution of resources in the society. And that initial distribution is maintained and enforced not primarily by specific regulations blocking market entry into certain profit-making activities, nor by discrete price-fixing arrangements and restrictive practices within the private sector; it is maintained by determinations about the nature and form of rights in property, the allocation of public services, and the rules of liability and contract governing society as a whole.

These deeper judgments, framed by courts and legislatures, are conveniently neutral on their face. No special interests are explicitly deemed their beneficiaries. But their consequences are profoundly distributive. Different groups of people, facing different circumstances, are affected by them in different ways. One's access to clean air, police protection, and safe working conditions, for example, is apt to vary substantially, depending on one's geographic community, income, race, and other characteristics. While "membership" in a geographic community, racial group, or income class is not the sort of "membership" Olson had in mind, these less voluntary associations nevertheless shape the deeper pattern of rights and social privileges in modern societies.

As people experiencing similar disadvantages come to understand their common interests and exert their collective political power, these more fundamental rules, and the distributions to which they correspond, are sometimes amended through political action. Thus, to dismantle the system of interest-group politics is to freeze the particular distribution prevailing at the time that the dismantling occurs.

The mechanics of democracy, moreover, are at stake. By positing a society in which nothing mediates between state and individual but encompassing organizations, Olson would effectively cripple democratic institutions. Interest groups are conduits for democratic participation. They are seedbeds for democratic opposition. Because they create centers of power, influence, and mutual support that are independent of the state, interest groups help to check state power. Totalitarian regimes are quick to dismantle special-interest groups. Hitler banned independent unions, trade associations, professional associations, and civic groups; the Soviets cannot tolerate an independent trade union movement in Eastern Europe.

* * *

Is economic growth inconsistent with robust interest-group politics? It may indeed be, if politics is understood primarily as an instrument for appropriating shares of national income. The economic theory of politics, which attends only to the outcomes of self-interested actors' political behavior, ignores the effects of political action on the actors themselves. Yet it is precisely through broadly political activities—within local trade unions, civic groups, grass-roots political movements, town meetings, professional associations, parent-teacher associations, chambers of commerce, shop-floor organizations, charitable organizations, and election campaigns—that individuals discover the subtler dimensions of their own needs and learn about the needs of others. They begin to understand the relationship between self and society; the encounter itself shapes their social values. If political organization is understood as a source of social values as well as a conduit for political demands, there is no inherent conflict between interest-group politics and economic growth.

Economists generally decline to specify how preferences are formed. It is enough, for most analytical purposes, to assume that people simply have wants and display them through the choices they make. But what of those wants that people cannot or prefer not to express in market terms—patriotism, social justice, the well-being of family and friends, or certain aspects of the natural environment? Those who trumpet the economic theory of politics assume that such preferences, although perhaps difficult to identify and to measure, exist prior to and outside of any social interaction. Social institutions neither create nor alter them. The group interest is simply the sum of its individual members' preferences. Individuals engage in political activity precisely in order to maximize their preexisting self-interests.

* * *

A contrary view is that political preferences embody values that are conditioned by social experience. Within political organizations people reconsider and revise perspectives and opinions. Common interests are discovered. Disagreements and inconsistencies force individuals to balance and rank their wants. What previously had been assumed to be solely personal concerns are found to be shared ones, and this discovery often empowers participants to act on them. Thus, individual values are transformed into social values that extend beyond the confines of the group. Collective purposes are forged. Political movements are born. But even more important, through the group experience a social morality is defined and refined. Groups create citizens.

The economic theory of politics, which casts groups as mere aggregations of atomized individuals, posits no effective public restraint on selfish conspiracies of group members against the rest of us. The greater the number of special-interest groups, the more collusion against the common good. But the social theory of politics, which sees in these groups the vehicles by which citizens come to understand common interests, suggests that one of the most effective restraints on selfish demands against the state may be the understanding and sophistication that derive from political experiences within such groups. The wider and more active is the public's participation in politics, therefore, the sounder and deeper is the potential political commitment to the common good, including economic growth. The economist's ideal of a rationally self-interested individual enters politics only to further preexisting, strictly personal goals. But the goals of citizens are formed in part by their social experience. The economist's rational actor, if not restrained, inevitably exploits other individuals and stifles the economy; such a person cannot be trusted with real democracy. A virtuous citizen, on the other hand, can at least potentially embrace general prosperity as a common cause and lend energies to achieving it.

*　　*　　*

How can nations overcome the bias against economic change? One way is to reduce or eliminate political organization and political access, particularly for those who bear the brunt of the dislocations associated with economic change. Olson pointed to Taiwan as a "prototypical" example of fast growth and low inflation, due, he said, to "Taiwan's nearly complete absence of special-interest organizations." He also singled out South Korea and Singapore for special mention.

It is no accident that these nations lack special-interest organizations. The South Korean government periodically declares all political opposition to be illegal. Those outside the ruling coalition are effectively disenfranchised. Demonstrators expressing dissatisfaction have found themselves jailed or killed. The government of Singapore continues to bar most political opposition. Taiwan has no free press, and only a facade of multiparty representation; it periodically jails dissidents.

The alternative way to overcome a population's fear of economic change is to ensure that the burdens and the benefits of economic change are allocated in ways that most people deem to be fair. And to achieve this sort of consensus, a nation would have to democratize its system of economic planning. Economic democracy might take the form of devices like shop-floor participation in decisions governing plant and working conditions, labor-management committees to plot company investment strategies, community and regional planning boards to determine local development objectives, and national bargaining over wages and prices. The aim is not to politicize every economic issue, but to recognize that every important economic choice is by nature political, and therefore to open up political channels in which the substance of economic change can be debated explicitly.

No capitalist democracy has extended the concept of economic democracy very far, but several of the more successful trading partners of the United States have, over the past several decades, experimented with a wide variety of approaches. For example, the vast majority of workers in the United States have no financial stake in their companies nor any formal means of participating in company decisions. But in West Germany employees are represented on workers' councils and on supervisory boards. Even in Japan, whose formal politics is relatively insular, employees participate in companies through elaborate systems of consultation at all levels of the firm. (Indeed, in many respects, Japan's system of bottom-up economic planning is far more democratic than its top-down politics.)

This is not to suggest that companies in continental Europe and Japan are models of labor-management harmony; they are not. The difference is that workers in these nations understand that their fates are tied to the profitability and competitiveness of their firms. Therefore, they bargain for change—retraining programs, relocation assistance, new investment in plants and equipment. Their counterparts in the United States and Great Britain, meanwhile, seek to maintain the status quo, because change threatens their economic security. Similarly, while in Great Britain and the United States macroeconomic policies designed to restrain inflation impose unemployment on the segment of the population least able to cope with it, wage and price increases in many other industrial nations follow guidelines established in national negotiations.

Smaller-scale groups—local unions and industry associations—participate indirectly through their representatives.

One indication of the comparative effectiveness of these various
participatory mechanisms is found in the distribution of national income
and wealth. By 1985 (the latest year for which such data are available)
the poorest 20 percent of the population in the fast-growing nations
fared better than in the slow-growing ones. In Japan the poorest fifth
received 7.9 percent of after-tax national income. In West Germany the
comparable figure was 6.5 percent. In Great Britain the poorest fifth
received 6.3 percent of national income, and in the United States the
share was only 4.3 percent. Indeed, of twelve industrialized nations, the
United States ranks tenth in posttax income equality. Of fourteen industrial nations, the United States ranks fourteenth in the extent of social
insurance coverage.

Other data also tend to stand Olson on his head. For example, by
comparison with other more vigorous economies, a very small proportion of the working population in the United States is unionized. In 1988
only 17 percent of private-sector wage and salary earners belonged to a
union. The figure was 33 percent in Japan and 42 percent in West Germany. In certain respects, moreover, Americans appear to be *less* politically active than their counterparts in other industrial nations.
Comparatively few Americans actually take to the polls during national
elections. In 1988 George Bush won the Presidency with the votes of less
than 28 percent of the potential electorate.

These data are only suggestive. Yet together they frame a picture of
two nations, the United States and Britain, both of which have experienced comparatively poor economic performance over the last twenty
years, and both of which possess relatively few democratic mechanisms
for ensuring that the burdens and benefits of economic change are allocated in a politically acceptable way. Both nations draw a relatively rigid
delineation between economic decision making—whether within the
government or within large corporations—and democratic institutions.
Mancur Olson correctly observed that both nations possess a wide array
of legal impediments to economic change: licensing restrictions, professional associations, regulatory barriers, trade barriers. But if the argument developed here is correct, these various restrictions have grown up,
not in *consequence* of long-standing democratic institutions in these nations, as Olson would argue, but because of the inadequacy of these
democratic institutions to deal effectively with the social dimension of
economic change.

24

WHEN THE
WOMEN RETURNED HOME

She was searching for something she believed in—and look *what she found. Her husband, her children, her home, herself. She's the contemporary woman who has made a new commitment to the traditional values that some people thought were "old fashioned." Researchers are calling it the biggest social movement since the '60s.*

—*Advertisement for* Good Housekeeping
January 1989

IT SEEMS LIKE YESTERDAY, BUT DEMOGRAPHERS TELL US THAT THE RE-action set in a full decade ago, around 1990. It was then that American women began going back home.

You remember: George Bush was in the White House. General Motors, Ford, and Chrysler were still making a few of their cars on American soil. It was after Wall Street's Black Monday but before Apocalyptic Tuesday. And more than half of all women with infants or school-age children worked outside the home.

And then, the big switch. By 1995 the vast majority of women with children were back in the home. Indeed, the latest survey shows that 85 percent of married women do not hold paying jobs.

Why the turnaround? Sociology professor Ernest Schwein of Harvard's Center for Gender Studies thinks that the "back to the home" movement came as a reaction to the earlier era. "Social changes occur in cycles," he says. "Look at how rapidly women had swarmed into the workplace! In 1950 only 11 percent of women with children under six years old held jobs outside the home. By 1986 it was 52 percent! Inevitably, there had to be a rebound, a backlash of some sort, a return to traditional values."

As evidence, Dr. Schwein points to the advertisements, articles, and TV talk shows that began to appear around 1989, extolling the virtues of home life for women and predicting the dire consequences for children of maternal employment. These pronouncements had a common theme: Women were fooling themselves if they thought they could "have it all" —a career, a family, and a well-run home. And they didn't need to. They could choose. One perfectly respectable choice was to withdraw from the world of paid work and become a "homemaker" like women of the 1950s.

In fact, says Dr. Schwein, the movement back to the home fit the tempo of the times. The 1990s resembled the 1950s in many ways. After more than a decade of hearing Ronald Reagan's homilies and George Bush's bromides, the average American had sunk into a nostalgic stupor. The older values of family, home, and neighborhood had become wondrously appealing. By the start of the decade it was once again acceptable for women to opt for homemaking. They were no longer embarrassed when people asked about their jobs or careers. "I stay home!" was said confidently, even with a smile.

What has been the aftermath of such a rapid about-face? Financial analysts point to the near collapse of many industries. Convenience businesses—take-out food stores, same-day laundries and dry cleaners—were the first to go. Now that women don't have to manage their careers and their homes simultaneously, saving time is no longer worth the price. Same with products like microwave ovens, frozen food, and giant freezers. Sales of all of these have plummeted in recent years. And the entire child-care industry is in disarray. Says an incredulous Sidney Hirsch, president and CEO of Toddlers-R-Us, a national day-care chain, "We never expected this." The firm has just filed for bankruptcy.

Home construction is down from previous levels, as are sales of new cars. Families can no longer afford large-ticket items. Indeed, average family income has dropped about 30 percent since women went back home. There has been a corresponding rise in mortgage foreclosures, personal bankruptcies, and the number of families living below or near the poverty line. Says Theodora Meadows of the Commerce Department's Bureau of Working Women (which is being disbanded next month), "Many women entered the work force twenty-five years ago to prop up family earnings. Now that they've gone home, there's no prop."

In general, American women are now far more dependent on their husband's income than they were a decade ago, and advertisers have stopped courting them. Remember those ads of the mid-1980s featuring women driving sports cars or carrying rawhide briefcases? No more. Nowadays, men make all the major family purchases. In ads women are back scrubbing bathroom bowls and eradicating ring around the collar.

Another interesting result: The Census Bureau reports that the divorce rate is half what it was in the 1980s. Yes, marriages are holding tight—and sales of tranquilizers are soaring.

The drop in the rate of divorce, according to Dr. Rex Tyranous of Columbia's Institute for Sexual Studies, has nothing to do with marital harmony. "Women are sticking to men because they have to. They gave up their careers, so they can't strike out on their own, can't escape from bad marriages. Economically, they're trapped."

Indeed, sociologists note that many of the old hierarchies have returned. The renewed financial dependency of women has placed them in a subordinate position. Dr. Tyranous again: "Ten years ago, men were just beginning to share responsibilities at home—taking care of the children, cleaning, cooking meals. Now it's back to Ozzie and Harriet. All across America, men come home from a busy day at the office, grab a beer, sit in their favorite chair, and are waited on. They don't even interact with the kids."

Even in affluent suburbs adult men are going out drinking together. Neighborhood bars have reemerged, as have "men only" clubs.

There is a noted upsurge in "momism" among children, particularly boys. Dr. Bruno Heifetz, a psychiatrist at Cornell's Childhood Sexual Disorder Clinic, puts it bluntly: "With mommy now back in the home full time, the attachments are simply too intense. We are seeing just what we saw in the 1950s—young men who can't form mature relationships with women because they lack the emotional integrity that comes with full separation from the mother. And we see all the symptoms back again as before—rage, depression, acute competitiveness. I thought we were on the way to licking this problem a decade ago."

But the loudest warnings are coming from economists who worry about the nation's external debt, now hovering close to the $3 trillion mark. "America's competitiveness has worsened dramatically," says Robert B. Reich, director of the American Academy of Economic Pontification. "It was bad ten years ago, of course. But since then, the private sector has lost a huge portion of its talent, its brains, its capacity to innovate. The precipitous decline in productivity gains really dates from the late 1980s, when women started staying home."

The experts are stumped for a solution. There's no easy way to lure women back into the paid work force. "Once a social backlash begins, you can't readily stop it," says sociologist Schwein. "It has a predictable momentum. You have to let it play itself out."

Nevertheless, several states have been experimenting with subsidies and tax incentives designed to encourage women to go back to work. Wisconsin, for example, now offers employed women a four-month paid maternity leave. Minnesota subsidizes day care and gives tax credits for transportation and service expenses in connection with the job. Lieutenant Governor Susan Fromidge—one of the last of America's women still holding high public office—says the benefits are necessary. "Every woman we can get back into the work force generates three more jobs, reduces medical and public health costs, improves the quality of our young people, and adds to productivity. Clearly the investment is worth it."

Not all agree. Mrs. Nadine Kornfalb, a young housewife in Skokie, Illinois, thinks that the "back to the home" movement is a good thing: "True, we now live in a one-bedroom apartment. When I worked, we could afford our own house with separate bedrooms for the kids. And we used to eat steak once in a while, go to the movies occasionally, and take vacations. Now we eat a lot of potatoes and watch more TV. But I don't mind at all. My life is so much easier than my mother's was. That generation of women tried to do too much—family, home, career, personal development. They made themselves miserable, and everyone around them. My generation—we just make everyone happy."

25

THE FOUR PARABLES
OF AMERICAN POLITICS

THE NEXT PRESIDENTIAL RACE WILL START REMARKABLY SOON. IN SHORT order, we will be treated to a new round of speeches, debates, and interviews concerning America's most pressing problems. Some of the proposals will be original, a few of the perspectives even novel. But underlying the rhetoric will be stories we have heard many times before. They are the same stories we tell and retell one another about our lives together in America; some are based in fact, some in fiction, but most lie in between. They are our national parables.

These parables are rooted in the central experiences of American history: the flight from an older culture, the rejection of central authority and aristocratic privileges, the lure of the unspoiled frontier, the struggles for social equality. One can distill four central themes:

1. The Rot at the Top This parable is about the malevolence of powerful elites, be they wealthy aristocrats, rapacious business leaders, or imperious government officials. It is the story of corruption in high places, of conspiracy against the public. At the end of the century, muckrakers like Upton Sinclair and Ida Tarbell uncovered sordid tales of corporate malfeasance; their modern heirs are called investigative reporters. The theme arises from the American detective story whose hero—such as Sam Spade, Serpico, or Jack Nicholson in *Chinatown*—traces the rot directly to the most powerful members in the community. The political moral is clear: Americans must not allow any privileged group to amass too much power.

2. The Triumphant Individual This is the story of the little person who works hard, submits to self-discipline, takes risks, has faith in himself, and is eventually rewarded with wealth, fame, and honor. Consider Benjamin Franklin's *Autobiography,* the first of a long line of American manuals on how to become rich through self-denial and diligence. The theme recurs in the tale of Abraham Lincoln, log-splitter from Illinois who goes to the White House; in the hundred or so novellas of Horatio Alger, whose heros all rise promptly and predictably from rags to riches, and in modern success stories, such as *Rocky* and *Iacocca.* Regardless of the precise form, the moral is the same: Anyone can "make it" in America through hard work and perseverance.

3. The Benign Community The third parable is about the American community. It is the story of neighbors and friends rolling up their sleeves and pitching in to help one another, or self-sacrifice, community pride, and patriotism. The story is rooted in America's religious traditions, and its earliest formulations are found in sermons like John Winthrop's "A Model of Christian Charity," delivered on-board ship in Salem Harbor just before the Pilgrims landed in 1630. He envisioned a "city set upon a hill" whose members would "delight in each other" and be "of the same body." Three hundred years later, these sentiments echoed in Robert Sherwood's plays, John Steinbeck's novels, Aaron Copland's music, and Frank Capra's films. The last scene in *It's a Wonderful Life* conveys the lesson: Jimmy Stewart learns that he can count on his neighbors' generosity and goodness, just as they had counted on him. They are bound together in a spirit of dependence and compassion. The principle: We must nurture and preserve genuine community.

4. The Mob at the Gates The fourth parable is about social disintegration that lurks just below the surface of democracy. It is the tale of mob rule, violence, crime, and indulgence—of society coming apart from an excess of democratic permissiveness. It gives voice to the fear that outsiders will exploit the freedom and openness of America. The story shows up in Federalist writings about the instabilities of democracy, in

Whig histories of the United States, and in the anti-immigration harangues of the late nineteenth and twentieth centuries. Its most dramatic appearance in recent years has come in fictionalized accounts of vigilante heroes who wreak havoc on muggers—like Clint Eastwood's Dirty Harry or Charles Bronson in *Death Wish*—and in Rambo's messy eradication of platoons of communist fighters. The lesson: We must impose social discipline, lest the rabble overrun us.

* * *

These four parables are completely familiar to most of us. They shape our political discourse. They confirm our ideologies. Every American retells and listens repeatedly to all four stories; every politician and social commentator borrows, embellishes, and seeks legitimacy from them.

But the parables can be linked together in different ways, each arrangement suggesting a distinct political message. At any given time in our nation's history one particular configuration has been dominant, eventually to be replaced by another. The art of political rhetoric has been to reconfigure these stories in a manner that affirms and amplifies the changes already occurring in the way Americans tell the tales.

In the early part of the century, for example, leaders of the Progressive era emphasized the link between the parables of Rot at the Top and the Triumphant Individual. Big business—the trusts—blocked worthy citizens from their rightful places in society; corruption at the top was thwarting personal initiative. Woodrow Wilson put the matter succinctly in a speech during the 1912 presidential campaign, promising to wage "a crusade against the powers that have governed us . . . that have limited our development . . . that have determined our lives . . . that have set us in a straitjacket to do as they please." In his view, the struggle against the trusts would be nothing less than "a second struggle for emancipation."

By the 1930s, the parables had shifted. Now the key conceptual link was between Rot at the Top and the Benign Community. The liberties of common people were under attack by leaders of big business and finance. In the 1936 presidential campaign, Franklin D. Roosevelt warned against the "economic royalists" who had impressed the whole of society into "royal service."

"The hours men and women worked, the wages they received, the conditions of their labor . . . these had passed beyond the control of the people, and were imposed by this new industrial dictatorship," he warned in one speech. "The royalists of the economic order have conceded that political freedom was the business of the government, but they have maintained that economic slavery was nobody's business." What was at stake, he concluded, was the "survival of democracy."

The shift from the Progressives' emphasis on the Triumphant Individual to the New Deal's Benign Community was more than an oratorical device. It represented a change in Americans' understanding of social life. The Great Depression had provided a national lesson in social solidarity; nearly every American family felt the effects of poverty. The Benign Community became intimately relevant as relatives and neighbors sought to help one another, as government became the insurer of last resort, and then as Americans turned together to winning the "good war" against fascism. The Benign Community embraced the entire nation.

In the decades following World War II, however, the Benign Community became a less convincing parable. Much of the country's middle class began to enjoy a scattered suburban affluence, far removed from the experiences of mutual dependence that had characterized American life a generation before. The prewar images of the common people and the forgotten man were less compelling now that most Americans felt prosperous and not at all forgotten; the story of Rot at the Top was less convincing now that life at the top was within plain sight.

* * *

The descendant of the Benign Community was a feeble impulse toward social altruism. Lyndon Johnson's War on Poverty was sold to the American public as being relatively costless. The idea was that proper Keynesian management of the economy required substantial public expenditures, which might as well be for the benefit of the poor. The economy was buoyant enough that America could afford to enlarge its welfare state; the "fiscal dividend" could be spent on the less fortunate. And in any event, "we" were only giving "them" and "equal opportunity," simply allowing the Triumphant Individuals among them to come forth and find their true potential. Under the banner of civil rights and social justice, Triumphant Individuals joined the nation's Benign Community.

Once again, the configuration of stories Americans told one another began to shift. As the economy slowed in the 1970s, a public tired of belt tightening became less tolerant of social altruism.

Enter Ronald Reagan, master storyteller. His parables drew upon the same four American tales, but substantially recast. This time the Rot at the Top referred to career bureaucrats in government and liberal intellectuals. The Triumphant Individuals were America's business entrepreneurs. The Benign Community comprised small, traditional neighborhoods in which people voluntarily helped one another, free from government interference. And the Mob at the Gates was filled with criminals, pornographers, welfare cheats, illegal immigrants, Third World debtors and revolutionaries, ornery trading partners, and communist aggressors—all of them encouraged by liberal acquiescence. The Reagan Revolution would discipline "them," to liberate the Triumphant Individuals in "us." Political choices in this story were cast as how "hard" or "soft" we should be on "them." Hard always emerged as the only decent American response.

In the 1988 election, both Michael Dukakis and George Bush tried to claim the American parables for themselves, but Bush wielded them far more effectively. Dukakis sought to portray Bush as a wealthy preppy —the Rot at the Top—and himself as a son of immigrants who had lived the American dream of the Triumphant Individual; Dukakis also warned America of the Japanese Mob at the Gates, and he called for a Benign Community that would ensure good jobs at good wages for every American. Bush, on the other hand, portrayed Dukakis as a member of the Harvard liberal intelligentsia—the Rot at the Top—and himself as a Triumphant Individual who had come to Texas as a young man to make his fortune. Bush accused Dukakis of letting criminals out of jail to rob and rape honest Americans (the Mob at the Gates), and he celebrated America's "thousand points of light"—the generous, Benign Community of America, which would help the less fortunate among us through acts of charity rather than through central government.

Inevitably, the configuration of stories Americans tell one another will change yet again. The "us" and "them" recountings of the present era eventually may be superseded by a new version that reflects a more complex, interdependent world. Perhaps, in the next version, the parable of the Benign Community will be expanded to include more of the earth's peoples, and that of the Triumphant Individual will embrace our collective aspirations for freedom and dignity. Indeed, it is just possible that Americans already are telling one another these sorts of stories, and are only waiting for a new set of political leaders to give them voice.

V

THE
RESURGENT
LIBERAL

26

THE
IDEOLOGY OF SURVIVAL

AT THIS WRITING, GEORGE BUSH'S "KINDER, GENTLER NATION" IS STILL rather callous. One in four of our nation's children is now born into poverty, up from one in five a decade ago. One in six has no health insurance. Following years of progress in preventing infant death, improvements in infant mortality have stopped; our rate is now worse than in nineteen other nations (a black baby born in Boston or Washington, D.C., is more likely to die before his or her first birthday than a baby born in Jamaica). Twenty million Americans remain hungry; a half million children, malnourished. The average American's real wages have declined since 1980. For the poor and near poor, the drop has been more severe. Meanwhile, the share of household income of the richest fifth of the American population continues to rise. The gap between the two groups is now wider than at any time over the last fifty years.

Those who inhabit the left of the political spectrum are tempted to view all this as evidence of the continuing triumph of wealth and privilege. They dream of a new politics that would unite the poor and near poor and restore the liberal agenda long ago lost to Ronald Reagan and his unkind, ungentle ilk. Such populist notions have romantic appeal. But they will fail unless they transcend class interest and come directly to terms with American ideology.

Political discourse in America rests on ideals so long established that they have become encoded onto American life. It is this emblematic battle, rather than a debate over class interests, that has been lost by those who place great value on social justice. The logic of self-interest has never been far away from this contest, to be sure, but neither has it been a primary motivating force. Indeed, direct appeals to class consciousness have never gained much political currency in America. America's emblematic battles have instead been over the nature and meaning of the public interest.

It is easy to dismiss supply-side economics as a pretext for securing the wealth of the rich at the expense of the poor. It is by now apparent that tax breaks for wealthy people and for giant corporations do not "trickle down" to anyone else, because the rich are prone to spend their extra income on yachts, real estate, or Oriental carpets rather than saving it, and because large corporations are apt to spend their extra income building foreign factories or buying up other companies rather than investing in new productive capacity in the United States. And one could be forgiven for viewing America's obsession with its national security as a manifestation of the same underlying class conflict—to protect the rich from the poor—this time played out on a global scale, in which the rest of the world is perceived as coveting America's riches.

But these mercenary assumptions underrate the continuing appeal, to a broad spectrum of Americans, of Reaganism and its kinder, gentler incarnation in Bushism. Both derive from a strand of conservative social philosophy that was last prominent in America one hundred years ago. Although it has lived on in our political culture, that strand has had little to do with the dominant tradition of American conservatism, founded on the inviolability of property and profound distrust of popular social change. Instead, it celebrates change and often fails to respect established boundaries. While the main line of American conservatism has looked to the likes of Edmund Burke and Alexander Hamilton for intellectual sustenance, this minor strand, from which Reaganism derives, looks to Herbert Spencer and William Graham Sumner. Its central organizing principle is social Darwinism.

* * *

Few Americans living today have read any of Herbert Spencer's writings, but they had an electrifying effect on America during the last three decades of the nineteenth century—a far greater effect than in Spencer's native England. Their influence was so great, in fact, that they worked themselves into the folkways of American political philosophy

—into the everyday assumptions that many Americans still carry around in their heads about how social life is and should be arranged.

To Spencer and his followers, the marketplace was a field for the development and encouragement of personal character. Work provided people with moral discipline, which was critical to survival. Life, after all, was a competitive struggle in which only those with the strongest moral fiber could survive. It was through this competitive struggle that societies became stronger over time. Only the fittest were able to prosper, because only they were able to muster the necessary resources to sustain themselves and their offspring.

Even before Darwin's evolutionary theories were presented to the world in 1859, Spencer had developed the idea that the pressure of subsistence on populations would have a beneficent effect on the human race. The miserable social conditions of the early industrial revolution had provided data for Malthus's grim essay on the principle of population, but Spencer saw in the thesis a cause for hope. For the very process of impoverishment would place a premium on skill, intelligence, self-control, and the power to adapt through technological innovation. The inevitable pressure of poverty would itself stimulate human advancement by selecting the best of each generation for survival. It was Spencer, not Darwin, who coined the phrase "survival of the fittest."

An inevitable correlate of this principle was that government should do little or nothing to eliminate poverty. Charity was permissible; if the "fittest" wished to bestow gifts on some of the less fit, that would not contravene evolutionary forces and might indeed enhance the moral character of the giver. But state intervention to improve the lot of the poor would have disastrous results. Not only were the effects of public programs for the poor often vastly different from their intended consequences (since poverty was an infinitely complex social phenomenon that could never be eradicated), but the programs themselves interfered with natural selection. Spencer's follower, William Graham Sumner, a professor of political and social science at Yale, writing three years after Ronald Reagan's birth, put the case succinctly: "[I]f we do not like the survival of the fittest we have only one possible alternative, and that is the survival of the unfittest. The former is the law of civilization. . . . [A] plan for nourishing the unfittest and yet advancing civilization, no man will ever find."

Spencer and his followers publicly deplored poor laws, state-supported education, regulation of housing conditions, and the protection of the consumer against dangers and deceptions. They also found anathema any state-enforced effort to achieve equality, even equality of opportunity, because evolution depended for its force on *inequality*. Those who could not adapt themselves to their environment for whatever reason should not be artificially helped, so they thought, because the survival of the species depended on the survival of people who could adapt. Without natural inequalities, the law of survival of the fittest would have no meaning.

* * *

If all this sounds impossibly cold-blooded to someone living in the last decades of the twentieth century, it may be more because these sentiments have been disguised within socially acceptable rhetoric than because they have been totally discredited in the popular mind. Consider the oft-repeated charge by conservatives that the nation's poor can find work if they really want to (why, just look at the help-wanted columns in your daily newspaper), or the circumlocutions surrounding proposals to develop urban "enterprise zones," return welfare responsibilities to the states, provide tax credits for private schools, and eliminate the progressive income tax. The party line is that our society has grown fat, flaccid, and careless. We are soft from too much coddling. Only by trimming the fat, going back to basics, and enhancing our vigilance can we hope to return America to its former position of prosperity and strength. This suggests that the government's withdrawal will release all sorts of energies among those best able to adapt and survive, while forcing less-able souls to work harder. Those least able to survive should not be nurtured by the state, lest the entire society become demoralized as a result and the wrong habits and qualities be thereby encouraged in our citizens. (An important image in this symbolic argument is the welfare mother who has more babies in order to get a bigger welfare check.)

The subtle allure of social Darwinism finds its way into other policy arenas. One can detect its presence in recent discussions about foreign aid. Apart from contributions to Israel and Egypt, America is now providing an infinitely tiny portion of its GNP in aid to poorer nations—the smallest percentage of any industrial nation. After all, so the argument goes, there is very little that we or anyone else can do to relieve human suffering in sub-Sahara Africa or the Indian subcontinent. It is tragic, of course, but it is a fact of life. If we fed them, that would only make them more dependent and prolong their agony.

* * *

America's tepid responses to Soviet proposals to dismantle weapons and reduce troops can also be viewed most clearly through the myopic lens of social Darwinism. Notwithstanding that Herbert Spencer was a pacifist and an internationalist, the ideas he fathered are easily transmuted into demands for more weapons, bigger bombs, and trade embargoes. If only the fittest will survive, we must ensure our national strength. If survival is a bitter contest, then surely the Soviets will bury us should our vigilance wane.

One can also see the underpinnings of social Darwinism in this decade's hands-off approach to corporate acquisitions and buyouts. Let RJR-Nabisco borrow to the hilt, regardless of consequence to the larger economy. Drop antitrust charges against behemoths like IBM, since their market power arises by virtue of inherent superiority. Let corporations gobble up smaller companies and drive rivals into the sea. Their successes are to be encouraged, and weaker companies must be weeded out; that is the law of natural selection. Our economy will be all the stronger for it.

Social Darwinism's underlying concern with the development of moral character—and with the survival of those with the strongest fortitude, ambition, and conviction—suggests a connection between these economic and military policies and the moral crusades of the New Right. If prayer in the public schools builds moral conviction in our young, if proscriptions on abortions make people more responsible for their actions, if the possession of firearms encourages people to defend themselves and their families, then the nation and its citizens will be so much the stronger. And such moral strength is necessary both to keep our economy virile and to defend ourselves against the godless Soviets.

These ideas are not unique to Ronald Reagan or to George Bush. They have been with us, in one form or another, for more than a century. They have been a minor strand in America's popular political philosophy, to be sure. But Reagan did not single-handedly bring them to renewed national prominence. The teachings of Herbert Spencer and William Graham Sumner no doubt helped shape the political consciousness of many youngsters born around the first decade of this century, particularly in America's heartland, and so it is not surprising that they colored Ronald Reagan's own instinctive ideology. But they have resonated in the America of the 1980s because issues of survival have once again taken a central place in the nation's consciousness.

* * *

The current preoccupation with survival has its roots in America's fallen hopes. In the decade of the 1970s Americans' expectations for ourselves and our nation were dashed in a rude series of shocks, symbolized by Vietnam, OPEC, and Watergate. Perhaps even more significant than these discrete setbacks was the fact that a large and pampered postwar generation reached adulthood within an economy that could not deliver. By 1978 the standard of living of most Americans was beginning to decline for the first time in forty years. Survival seemed to be at stake for the simple reason that so many trends all at once sloped downward. For Americans who were accustomed to seeing the future as a more bountiful and better version of the present, the decade of the 1970s presented an ominous prospect.

It is difficult to be precise about the beginnings of a zeitgeist, but there is little doubt that as a nation and as individuals we now ponder our survival with a degree of concern not felt since the early 1930s, perhaps not since the turn of the century. Questions of survival are everywhere: Can our cities survive? Can democracy survive? Will our economy survive? Politics and economics in America have grown deadly serious. The presidential campaign of 1988 was devoid of specific issues but replete with dark warnings and accusations. Polls revealed that Americans are worried about the future.

*   *   *

The ideology of survival is enormously powerful, and Ronald Reagan and George Bush have exploited it at every turn. Their happy talk about America's future is matched by dark forebodings, should we lose our way. Liberals must respond to the apprehension about survival if liberalism is to speak to its time. The question that must be addressed by those who still place great value on social justice and democratic processes is not what type of political program will appeal to the selfish interest of a majority of voters. Granted, we need a new agenda on the left; Great Society liberalism has run up against a bureaucratic wall. But reformers are wrong to focus entirely on programs and policies at a time when the real challenge for those on the left is to enunciate an ideology appropriate to an era haunted by fears of survival.

Since the middle decades of the twentieth century, American liberalism has been preoccupied with issues of income redistribution. How the pie is divided among rich and poor continues to be a vitally important question, of course, but it is far less compelling than survival. If we are forced to choose between a more equitable distribution of our wealth and the continued vitality of our society—and this is precisely the choice that has been posed by Reaganism and the New Right—there is little doubt which side most Americans will take, for survival is a precondition to everything else.

The politics of class only cuts us off from one another; a new ideology on the left must join us together as one people facing a common challenge. That new ideology must be premised on the importance of the values of conciliation and community to the continued survival of the nation and the planet. It can take as one of its starting points the threat of nuclear holocaust that imperils us all unless we reach global agreement on arms control. If the "fittest" is assumed to be the nation that can amass the greatest nuclear arsenal, then the process of natural selection will doom us all.

In the economic sphere as well, communitarian values can be shown to underpin future prosperity. Economic survival is coming to depend critically on how well people collaborate within large and complex organizations. By the same token, cynical indifference to public values is corrosive, as each person or group becomes less willing to bear any burden on the supposition that others are avoiding their fair share. We see the dark side of this paradox in the $90 billion in taxes that the Internal Revenue Service estimates were unpaid last year; in the dishevelment of our parks and public facilities; in the reluctance of many people to report crimes or corruption. A collective commitment to social justice and democratic processes helps assure everyone that benefits and burdens are allocated fairly, and this assurance in turn is the very foundation of future prosperity and social security. A collective cynicism about the fairness of the system perpetuates itself in the opposite direction, impoverishing our life together.

The coming ideological debate is not over how the pie is to be divided; nor is it the old contest between efficiency and equity, property and state-enforced charity. It has deeper roots, and the stakes are higher. As the economies of America and all other nations slow down, and some begin to decline absolutely, many people are tempted to maintain their standard of living by expropriating a portion of the declining share of everyone else. But these beggar-thy-neighbor strategies, already apparent in America, will undermine civic virtue and ultimately reduce the prosperity and security of everyone.

The coming debate is over the ideologies of survival. A central concern with fairness is the flip side of social Darwinism. Such a concern is patently more relevant to America's future survival than is an ideology that celebrates competitive struggle. Those who value social justice must spread the message that in the long run the dog-eat-dog world hailed by the new social Darwinists will lack even the memory of a bark.

27

THE FADED
IDEAL OF EQUAL SACRIFICE

WHAT DO CITIZENS OWE ONE ANOTHER? YOUR ANSWER MAY COMPRISE A longer or shorter list of civic obligations, depending on your ideological bent. But most people would agree to two minimal requirements: You should pay taxes to support the common good, and you should help defend the nation from its enemies.

There will be disputes about amounts, conditions, and definitions, but most Americans would agree that the two burdens—to support and defend the common good—should be shared by all adult members of our democratic community. These burdens should not only be shared, but be shared equally. Equality of sacrifice is important to society's general perception of fairness—the foundation on which our entire system is built.

This idea isn't new. The principle of equal sacrifice is a cornerstone of modern liberal political thought. John Stuart Mill proclaimed that "[w]hatever sacrifices [society] requires . . . should be made to bear as nearly as possible with the same pressure on all." In defending the nation, the wealthier should stand shoulder to shoulder with the poor. In paying taxes, the wealthier should bear a comparable financial pain by ceding a larger proportion of their incomes. Even Adam Smith, the progenitor of free-market conservatism, saw the wisdom of a progressive tax: "It is not very unreasonable that the rich should contribute to the public expense, not only in proportion to their revenue, but something more in proportion."

Yet in recent years America has retreated from this central creed of civic obligation in two important ways: (1) In June 1973 the draft was ended. We now have an all-volunteer armed service, whose members are somewhat more likely than the population as a whole to be minority (as 27 percent of the armed forces now are categorized) and to lack any college education (79 percent). (2) In November 1986 the progressive income tax was substantially ended. Beginning in 1988, the federal government claimed no more than 28 percent of the highest personal incomes in the land, giving us the lowest top tax rate of all industrialized Western nations.

* * *

America's surrender of the ideal of equal sacrifice has occurred without much public debate or even awareness that we were doing it. It has come rather as a by-product of specific policies that seemed otherwise perfectly sensible.

In both terminating the draft and retreating from income tax progressivity, the logic was much the same. Four basic arguments were made against the rhetoric of equal sacrifice:

It was hypocritical. First, it was noted that the prevailing reality fell far short of the ideal of equal sacrifice. By 1973, when the draft was ended, it was clear that wealthier citizens had managed to create or exploit loopholes in the Selective Service System. The eleven million men who had served in Vietnam were drawn disproportionately from lower-income families. Similarly, by 1986 tax progressivity was shown to be a similar sham. Despite a top personal rate of 50 percent, for example, families earning over $200,000 a year paid on average only 22 percent of their income in taxes.

It was wasteful and bred cynicism. The tactics wealthier Americans used to escape these obligations had wasted valuable resources and bred a cynical and contemptuous attitude toward the law. In the late 1960s many draft-age men who had no intention of becoming preachers, doctors, or teachers were flooding into graduate programs that offered them relief from conscription. One 1972 survey showed "avoiding the draft" to be among the three most important reasons cited for attending college. Others sought refuge in fatherhood, feigned illnesses, or various forms of legal and bureaucratic chicanery.

In a similar vein high-income taxpayers of the 1970s and 1980s sought investment—in railroad boxcars, office buildings, and cattle feeding, to name a few—the attractions of which had far more to do with avoiding tax payments than gaining direct economic returns. In seeking tactical advice and legal counsel for avoiding the draft or reducing their taxes, wealthier Americans spawned entire service industries dedicated to outwitting the government.

It was naive. It was assumed to be politically unrealistic to expect any greater degree of sacrifice on the part of wealthier citizens than the actual extent to which they willingly accepted the burden. No more than a relatively low percentage of their sons could be coerced into the military; no greater than a relatively low fraction of their incomes could be captured by the Internal Revenue Service.

It was inefficient. Finally, reform entailed a kind of exchange. In return for explicitly affirming and legitimating the relatively low burdens that wealthier citizens actually bore, the system for recruiting military personnel or for gathering personal tax payments could be rationalized and streamlined. Loopholes could be eliminated, waste and distortions removed; an unworkable and hypocritical process could be replaced by one capable of recruiting dependable soldiers or of efficiently garnering tax receipts.

Thus the President's Commission on an All-Volunteer Armed Force argued in its 1970 report that abandoning the draft would require that the government pay its recruits salaries competitive with the private sector. But these higher personnel costs would be offset by the benefits flowing from more professionalization and dedication among enlistees, less turnover, and a more "rational" process of selection.

Ten years later, the cause of tax reform appeared doomed until Senate Finance Committee Chairman Bob Packwood offered to lower the top rate to 28 percent, at which point the bill moved toward swift passage. Advocates of tax reform conceded that the only way to broaden the tax base, eliminating the welter of deductions and exemptions, was to reduce the top marginal rate until it approximately matched the effective rate that wealthier citizens actually paid.

* * *

The logic in both instances was the same, and reformers were drawn to similar conclusions: No purpose was served in continuing to maintain the fictions of universal conscription or of progressive taxation. By accepting political reality and making official what had become the norm, each system could be strengthened and rendered more efficient.

But in both cases the reformers failed to consider that the ideals of universal service and tax progressivity had moral value in *themselves,* as social aspirations. They symbolized the equal sacrifices that Americans believed in. They represented the goal of social solidarity. That the ideal was not achieved in practice did not mean that we should no longer seek to achieve it.

In both instances the gap between the ideal of equal sacrifice and the reality of evasion had widened only recently, in response to particular events, and might have closed again as quickly had the ideal not been abandoned.

The move toward an all-volunteer army occurred at the end of an unpopular war. Overall, only 20 percent of the troops we sent to Vietnam had been drafted, and the ability of the Selective Service System to compel young men to serve steadily declined during the course of the hostilities. In a 1972 poll only 13 percent of the public said they supported peacetime conscription. But the situation had been quite different before Vietnam.

More than 60 percent of the Americans serving in World War II had been drafted, and the Selective Service System had functioned relatively well. Peacetime conscription remained popular after World War II. Even in 1969 fully 60 percent of the population was in favor of it. Since Vietnam, popular support for the draft has bounced back somewhat. In a 1984 National Opinion Research Center survey 42 percent of adult Americans said they would favor a return to the draft. Forty-four percent favored a wider system of compulsory national service for both men and women even if "such a program made it necessary to increase your taxes by a small amount—for example, by 5 percent."

Our more recent retreat from tax progressivity also occurred in an era when the public was especially unsympathetic toward the purposes their sacrifices would serve. Beginning with Watergate, Americans' confidence in government had steadily declined. Jimmy Carter and Ronald Reagan both campaigned against Washington insiders, meddling bureaucrats, and chronic government inefficiency.

The late 1970s and early 1980s had been marked by tax revolts in the states. As public support for taxation waned, tolerance for tax avoidance increased. And as the loopholes widened, the actual rates paid by wealthier Americans sharply declined. Years earlier, when Americans had greater faith in government, the top tax rate was much higher and exemptions fewer, with the result that the tax code was far more progressive in actual effect: In 1944 a family of four with an income of $100,000 (in 1986 dollars) paid about $40,000 in taxes; in 1966 the same family paid $30,000; in 1980 just $24,000.

* * *

The surrender of the ideals of universal service and tax progressivity was not costless, as reformers had assumed. The shift to an all-volunteer armed force and to a low marginal tax amounted to a renunciation of social aspiration. The retreat signaled an abandonment of an important goal and our sense of mutual responsibility and interdependence. From here on, there would be less of a shared understanding of the principle of equal sacrifice, less striving to narrow the gap between aspiration and reality.

The failure of reformers to recognize what they were abandoning was linked to the way in which they had defined the problems to begin with. In both cases "reform" meant accomplishing specific common acts more efficiently, rather than reinforcing our capacity for common action.

The conferences and commissions convened in the early 1970s to study the possibility of an all-volunteer armed service understood the goal primarily as ensuring a reliable supply of military personnel. Richard Nixon's concerns about meeting our "manpower needs" were echoed by liberal reformers. Similarly, various liberal organizations like Citizens for Tax Justice and The New Republic, which called for tax reform in the late 1970s and early 1980s, for the most part saw the challenge as broadening the tax base and simplifying the code.

The tendency for reformers in America to focus on administration rather than principle has often reflected a healthy pragmatism. We fix what we can, when we can. But the same tendency also can blind us to the broader consequences of our efforts and the cumulative ways in which they reinforce or undermine social norms.

At a time in American history when prophets of the right are busily claiming the high moral ground, attributing the decline of character and civic virtue to the temptations of the welfare state, it is perhaps appropriate for liberals to resurrect the venerable ideal of equal sacrifice as a core principle of public philosophy.

28

THE LIBERAL AS PLANNER

GROVER CLEVELAND CALLED HIMSELF A LIBERAL AND SPENT MUCH OF his time as President defending American corporations and financiers against the fulminations and protestations of workers, socialists, and Populists. Herbert Hoover identified his cause as liberalism in the 1928 presidential campaign. Robert Taft called himself a liberal to the end of his life. To this day, many European intellectuals and American leftists continue to identify liberalism with its nineteenth-century quest for economic and civil independence from the ancien régime, for the freedom of individuals to contract with whomever they wish and for whatever purpose.

For most Americans, however, liberalism has come to stand for something quite different: big government. The shift in meaning began during the first decades of the twentieth century and culminated in the New Deal. It was fueled, in part, by the rise of the giant American corporation and by the view that such large concentrations of economic power were the natural and inevitable consequence of technological change. Big government was necessary to tame the giant corporation, to ensure that it functioned in the public's interest, to counterbalance its awesome power on the side of the individual American.

* * *

Adolf A. Berle exemplified this new thinking. Like Robert Moses (a Republican) and David Lilienthal, he belonged to a generation of planners. Their monuments—the SEC, the Triborough Bridge, the Tennessee Valley Authority—are still with us. So too is their vision.

Born at the end of the last century, Berle grew up in the Progressive era, when it was assumed that men of good sense and broad perspective could rise above the rapacity of big business and the corruption of politics to lead the nation toward greatness. His was the vision of a confident, powerful, assertive, expansive government that would function as the senior partner of corporate America. Berle the man was as assertive and expansive (and arrogant) as the government he envisaged. In his many writings and in his numerous public activities, he represented an American liberalism that was as idealistic as it was grandiose.

Pushed by an ambitious and imperious father, Berle entered Harvard College at the age of fourteen, graduated with honors from Harvard Law School, promptly and presumptuously became an adviser at the Paris peace talks after World War I, practiced law and lectured on corporate finance, and then in 1932 collaborated with a young economist named Gardiner Means to write a book that shook the nation, *The Modern Corporation and Private Property*. By that time America was mired in economic depression, Hoover and the Republican champions of Wall Street were on the run, and America wanted to understand what had happened and what to do about it.

Most of Berle and Means's book was dry, filled with lawyer's arguments and economist's data; but taken as a whole, it told a tantalizing tale about the increasing concentration of American economic power in the hands of a relatively few giant corporations and their managers, who were accountable neither to their shareholders nor to the public at large. The authors concluded by demanding that "the modern corporation serve not alone the owners or the [managers] but all the society." The federal government must rein in unbridled captains of industry and put the modern corporation to work for the nation. Neither laissez-faire nor socialism was the answer. The real answer was to be found in a partnership between business and government, in which government had the senior role. Although few people ever read the book (in its first twenty years only thirty-five thousand copies were sold), *The Modern Corporation and Private Property* became, in the indubitable words of *Time* magazine in the spring of 1933, the "economic bible of the Roosevelt administration."

*   *   *

Berle had been drawn into Franklin D. Roosevelt's "brain trust" even before the election. His ideas and his influence were evident during the campaign, especially in FDR's notable Commonwealth Club speech, given in San Francisco in the fall of 1932. Reviewing the history of the American economy, Roosevelt pointed out that "in many instances the victory of the central Government was a haven of refuge to the individual." Hoover's protective tariffs and government loans had benefited big business at the expense of the individual. Wealth in America was far more concentrated now in 1932 than it had been in 1912. Roosevelt then described the nation's challenge in words that echoed Berle:

> Our task now is not discovery or exploitation of natural
> resources, or necessarily producing more goods. It is the
> soberer, less dramatic business of administering resources and
> plants already in hand, of seeking to re-establish foreign
> markets for our surplus production, of meeting the problem of
> underconsumption, of adjusting production to consumption, of
> distributing wealth and products more equitably, of adapting
> existing economic organizations to the service of the people.
> The day of enlightened administration has come. . . . [We
> should not] abandon the principle of strong economic units,
> merely because their power is susceptible of easy abuse. . . .
> Today we are modifying and controlling our economic units.

It was to this job—of modifying and controlling economic units through enlightened administration—that Berle turned with relish. Berle's prescriptions for the federal regulation of securities became the Securities and Exchange Act. His influence was felt in the creation of the National Recovery Administration and in the Temporary National Economic Committee hearings later in the decade. He argued for a branch banking act, for the coordination of all federal credit agencies, such as home loan banks, for the consolidation of railroads, for a federal incorporation act, for a national program of sickness and unemployment compensation, for a public-works finance corporation. In much of this, he was prescient. He urged that "women performing [for] equal income . . . [is] a field we have not yet entered but it is plainly foreshadowed by the modifications going on."

For the next three decades Berle hopped from office to office, from project to project, like a gourmet cook in a soup kitchen, stirring pots, bringing issues to a boil, advising and scolding lesser mortals, everywhere imperious and often insufferable. No sooner had the New Deal been launched than he left it to become an adviser to Fiorello LaGuardia, then mayor of New York during one of the city's periodic financial crises. There he took on the role Felix Rohatyn was to play four decades later, devising financial schemes to save the city and then, without undue modesty, accepting full credit for having done so. Then back to Washington as a State Department assistant secretary, running Latin American affairs, dabbling in civil aviation, working on a host of other weighty matters. Then to Brazil as ambassador. Then back to New York, and so on, continuing through the Kennedy Administration, in which he was briefly in charge of a task force on Latin America.

* * *

Berle's pattern was to set himself up as a fount of ideas but to leave the work of implementation to others—and then to fulminate over how badly his ideas were handled. He bruised egos wherever he went, and his short tenure in any single job was as much a function of others' impatience with him as of his impatience with everyone else. It never occurred to him that policies that could not be administered well were probably bad policies to begin with. For those who worked with Berle, "enlightened administration" was synonymous with arrogance.

There was an arrogance, too, in Berle's ambitions for America. He espoused a foreign policy intellectually consistent with his view of government's purpose and role in the nation. Just as Americans needed a strong central government to liberate them from the predations of giant corporations, nation-states needed powerful international institutions to liberate them from the scourges of colonialism, nineteenth-century imperialism, and then—after World War II—from international communism. In the absence of powerful international institutions, however, the job of ensuring national self-determination naturally fell to America. Berle never came to terms with the possibility that America-as-global-policeman would exercise imperial power itself. He was certain that no state would willingly become communist; where communism existed, he assumed that it had to have been imposed from the outside.

Then Cuba turned communist, and revolution threatened in other Latin American nations. Berle urged American intervention. Years later, he was an advocate of America's role in Vietnam, and in 1969 he described an antiwar strike at Harvard as directed by "a small group of organizers working primarily as political warfare agents for Maoist communism." Berle's rhetoric became more strident. In the end he disavowed his earlier commitment to self-determination in favor of communist containment. Berle the Progressive liberal ended his days as Berle the anti-communist curmudgeon.

*　*　*

The Progressivist origins of Berle's ideas were never far below the surface. Berle's vision of a powerful national government, guiding American industry and protecting individual rights, was the direct descendant of that of Herbert Croly. Croly had been the first editor of *The New Republic* during its visionary days before World War I. Almost a quarter century before Berle and Means produced their tome, Croly had offered in *The Promise of American Life** a stinging critique of the reformers' infatuation with trust-busting.

Foreshadowing Berle, Croly argued that big businesses "contributed to American economic efficiency" and that civilized society should aim, therefore, to substitute cooperation for competition. Corporations should be able to fulfill their "natural" growth, so long as federal powers were used to bind their activities to the national interest. And wielding these new federal powers were to be wise public leaders free from selfish interest. What was needed, said Croly, was a "New Nationalism" to direct individual efforts away from selfish pursuits, toward collective solutions to the nation's problems. This was the logic of Alexander Hamilton applied to an industrial America.

Theodore Roosevelt took up Croly's ideas and placed them at the center of his 1912 Bull Moose platform, in opposition to Woodrow Wilson's call for stricter antitrust enforcement. These two visions of reform—a cooperative system of national planning, or a competitive system of atomized economic units umpired by trustbusters—faintly echoed the much older Hamilton–Jefferson debate. But this was also a completely new discussion about the role of private power in an industrialized economy, and its terms were to guide subsequent liberal debates. Two decades later, Berle offered his generation a forceful restatement of Croly's position, and he spent much of his intellectual life battling with those on the other side—Felix Frankfurter, Benjamin Cohen, Thurmond Arnold—who shared the Wilsonian view.

The New Deal never resolved the liberal debate. To the end, the planners and the atomizers fought one another for control of the ideological agenda. The National Recovery Administration marked the high

---

* First published in 1909; Harvard University Press edition, 1965.

watermark of the planners; Arnold's reign at the Justice Department, of the atomizers. Nor has the debate been resolved since.

* * *

How should the economy be reorganized, and who should do the organizing? Liberals have never come up with a coherent answer. The problem with the liberal planners' vision has always been arrogance. How are the planners to know what the economy needs or in what direction it should move? How can the public be assured of their knowledge and impartiality? The problem with the liberal atomizers' vision has always been sentimentality and naïveté. How can a complex industrial economy function with only small businesses and dispersed sources of capital? Is there, as a practical matter, really such a thing as a free market?

Liberals have tended to forget this debate when times are good and then indulge in it once again when the economy is threatened. The labels may change and the prescriptions may differ in specifics, but the underlying controversy survives. In this decade, for example, some thoughtful observers have argued that America needs an explicit industrial policy to encourage older industries to reduce outmoded technologies, to channel research and development funds into emerging industries, and to help workers retrain. Otherwise, the necessary shifts in the nation's industrial base will come more slowly and be more painful, and in the meantime the United States will have lost out to other nations that have made the transition more smoothly (notably Japan). These arguments have been greeted by the predictable Wilsonian response—recently emanating from such august liberal enclaves as the Brookings Institution—that all we need do is maintain free trade and free-floating currencies, and the economy will fix itself.

The two views battled for Walter Mondale's allegiance during the 1984 presidential campaign. Neither prevailed. Nor, for that matter, did Mondale. Liberals were again in disarray over how the economy should be organized, until the ensuing recovery seemed to render the problem irrelevant.

Through it all, conservatives have sounded like Wilsonian liberals but acted like planners. Herbert Hoover as secretary of commerce in the Coolidge Administration, and then as President, rhapsodized over the wonders of the free market, but he suspended antitrust enforcement and proceeded to organize American business into powerful trade associations to plan industrial growth with the "cooperation" of the federal government. Sixty years later, Ronald Reagan waxed equally enthusiastic over the magic of the market and the heroism of entrepreneurs but followed Hoover's well-worn path toward business planning.

* * *

It should be noted that Reagan's plan to shrink old-line basic industries—forcing radical cuts in employment and wage concession, busting the unions—was quite successful. Standardized goods, such as steel, autos, textiles, commodity chemicals, and others that rest on mass or large-batch production, are particularly vulnerable to price competition. Thus, the easiest way to reduce the size of these industries was to increase the prices of these goods in world markets, making it difficult for them to be exported and making it relatively easy for foreign producers to threaten them at home. And the fastest way to increase the price of these goods was to raise the value of the dollar by keeping interest rates high. Presto: These older industries were forced to contract. Between 1981 and 1985, as the value of the dollar soared, some two million jobs were lost in old-line manufacturing businesses. Membership in industrial unions shrank dramatically. Steel, autos, and others were forced to reduce domestic capacity, set up operations abroad, and diversify into specialized niches. By 1985, when the dollar started to decline, old industrial America was a pale shadow of its former self.

Reagan's plan to promote high technology was equally ambitious. Between 1981 and 1988 about $600 billion was channeled into new weapons, most depending on advanced technologies. This demand for state-of-the-art products pulled these emerging industries down the learning curve to the point where commercial spin-offs were attainable. By the mid-1980s well over 50 percent of all the research and development funding for America's high-tech industries was coming directly from the Pentagon. In 1987 the Pentagon launched a major effort to develop practical applications for superconductors, special alloys that lose all resistance to the flow of electric current when cooled; it agreed to fund Sematech, a research joint venture comprising America's leading semiconductor manufacturers, designed to improve their competitiveness; and the National Security Agency poured money into parallel processing, the most advanced computer architecture, which may produce the fastest computers in the world. The Strategic Defense Initiative aimed to extend the frontiers of lasers, fiber optics, new materials, and computer technologies into the twenty-first century.

Viewed as a whole, Reagan's economic policy and military buildup constituted an extraordinarily ambitious plan for shifting America's industrial base. This was planning with a vengeance. But because Reagan was an avowed defender of the free market from the depredations of big government, there were few voices to his right denouncing Washington's vulgar intrusion into the temple of the marketplace. As only Richard Nixon could open relations with Beijing, so only Ronald Reagan (and Hoover) could make economic planning respectable.

But there are important differences between conservative planning and liberal planning. The former is done far more quietly, and it tends to be run by large corporations and Wall Street. Neither Hoover's trade associations nor Reagan's Federal Reserve Board and Pentagon are exemplars of open, democratic accountability. Conservative planning also has an uncanny way of making the rich richer and the poor poorer.

Were he alive today, Adolf Berle would be incensed at the hypocrisy of the present planning system and dismayed at the cynicism with which the public has come to view the federal government. He would, no doubt, get on the phone to his favorite Democratic candidate and presumptuously instruct him to tell the American people exactly what was happening.

29

HOW NOT TO
MAKE INDUSTRIAL POLICY

"INDUSTRIAL POLICY" IS ONE OF THOSE RARE IDEAS TO HAVE MOVED swiftly from obscurity to meaninglessness without any intervening period of coherence. Blame it on the business cycle. Before the recovery commenced in late 1982, neoliberals, progressives, leaders of organized labor, Democrats, and others to the left of supply-side economics thought they had found in that term a simple answer to Reaganomics— an answer that promised growth, equality, and some degree of democratic planning. But the recovery intervened too soon. Most people stopped worrying about the economy (although they have every reason to continue to worry). And by the time the 1992 depression gets under way, it may be too late to worry.

What would have happened to "industrial policy" had the recovery not happened? At some point many supporters would have discovered that their own definition of "industrial policy" conflicted with that of many other supporters. How *much* growth? What *sort* of equality? And especially, *whose* planning? Alas, there are no simple answers, even to the vacuities of supply-side economics.

Rhode Island offered a test case. By 1983 the recovery had all but passed it by. Unemployment was still high, relative to the rest of New

England. Average manufacturing wages were the lowest in New England, forty-eighth among the fifty states.

So a small group of civic leaders got together to plan a new industrial policy for the state. The "Greenhouse Compact," as it was called, featured $750 million in public aid for business, designed to help older companies restructure and newer industries grow (hence the name). In addition, organized labor would support legislation to modify strikers' benefits, business leaders would overhaul the state's antiquated unemployment insurance system, the banks would invest more money in the state, and voters would approve a new bond issue. Every major group would kick in something and get back more—a larger version of the Chrysler bailout. The whole thing would be run by a "strategic" commission.

On paper, the plan was impressive. (I confess a slightly self-serving bias; the plan's principle author—Ira Magaziner—is an old friend and fellow intellectual traveler.) It was supported by virtually every leader of every interest group in the state.

But when it was put to a vote, the good citizens of Rhode Island rejected the Greenhouse Compact, four to one.

The most plausible explanation: Voters liked the plan but didn't trust their state government to implement it. Government in Rhode Island is roughly analogous to an old septic tank: Although necessary and surely useful, it periodically overflows in a most noxious manner and needs to be drained or replaced. At the same time they were being asked to approve the Greenhouse Compact, Providence voters were seeking a replacement for their mayor, who had been recalled from office after having been convicted of assault. The night before the vote Rhode Islanders were informed on the evening news that a Providence commissioner had been arrested in connection with a wide-ranging corruption probe.

But there may be a deeper lesson here for those who are readying a new version of industrial policy for the next downturn in the business cycle. My guess is that most Americans like the idea of more "cooperation" among business, labor, and government. They also support public financing of research and development, worker retraining, plant modernization, technical education, transportation, industrial parks, and export credits. They would like to ensure that industries that benefit from special tariffs, quotas, and tax breaks use the extra cash to retool their factories and retrain their workers. And they would like to see all these economic-development policies rendered more coherent, more "strategic." (Ubiquitous Harris and Gallup polls bear me out.)

But Americans *don't* like central planning, they don't like complicated plans, and they especially don't trust business, government, and labor elites to do the planning. These predilections are as populist as apple pie, running clear across the political spectrum and rooted deep in our political history.

In other words, "industrial policy" is fine so long as it builds on current policies and institutions. But wrap it in an elaborate plan and assign it to a new "strategic commission" comprised of the Big Shots, and you can stuff it.

Which is what Rhode Island did.

30

COMPETENCE OR IDEOLOGY?

"THIS CAMPAIGN IS ABOUT COMPETENCE, NOT IDEOLOGY," SAID MI-chael Dukakis. George Bush, and apparently most Americans who exercised their right to vote, disagreed.

What, exactly, do we mean by "competence" when it comes to running the American government?

Beneath the daily activities of elected officials, administrators, and their advisers and critics, and beneath the public's tacit decision to accord legitimacy to specific policy decisions, exists a set of first principles that suggest what competent policy making is all about. They comprise a view of human nature, of how people behave as citizens. They also reflect a view of social improvements, of why we think that society is better in one state than another. And they offer a view of the appropriate role of government in society—given human nature, our aspirations for social improvement, and our means of defining and solving public problems.

These principles are often implicit in policy making. They may be invoked to justify a particular policy, but the ground from which these principles spring is usually taken for granted. To state them is to end the conversation, because there seems to be nothing left to say. Nevertheless, they draw on ideas that have been debated for centuries (lat briefly place them in their historical context). The current incart these principles is intimately related to America's present poli ture. As it evolves, so will they.

The prevailing philosophy of policy making in America can be summarized as follows: People are essentially self-interested rather than altruistic and behave much the same way whether they are choosing a new washing machine or voting on a new board of education. The public good, or "public interest," is thus best understood as the sum of these individual preferences. Society is improved whenever some people's preferences can be satisfied without making other people worse off. Most of the time, private market exchanges suffice for improving society in this way; public policies are appropriate only when—and to the extent that —they can make such improvements more efficiently than the market can. Thus, the central responsibility of public officials, administrators, and policy analysts is to determine whether public intervention is warranted and, if so, to choose the policy that leads to the greatest improvements.

These principles are familiar, not because they describe how public policies are actually made in modern America but because they shape the way public policies are typically *justified* and *criticized*. They suggest what is and is not legitimate for government to do, how policy makers should act, how they and those who advise them should think about public problems. Importantly, these principles also sound a cautionary theme: The supposed tendency for individuals to use public policies to get what they want for themselves creates a danger that those who have the greatest stake in a given matter will collude against the rest of us, whose individual interests in any particular policy are apt to be small. This danger can be overcome if policy makers carefully ensure that everyone's preferences are objectively weighed, alternatives are fully considered, and net benefits are maximized.

The ubiquity and robustness of these principles in contemporary America is quite remarkable. They undergird the position papers that stream out of policy institutes and assorted think tanks. They serve as the basis for memorandums of policy analysts in government and academe, editorials in prominent newspapers and magazines, learned treatises on public policy, court opinions crafted by judges schooled in "law and economics," lobbyists' pleadings, and administrative hearings. You hear them even when politicians or administrators talk candidly about what they think they ought (but may not be able) to do. Whenever people who deal in public policy want to be (or to sound) objective and technically rigorous in discussing solutions to public problems, they tend to employ these assumptions—sometimes tacitly, often without further explanation or rationale.

Such assumptions—about human nature, about social improvement, and about the proper role of government—have proven useful in several respects. First, they are appropriate to a heterogeneous society comprising a multiplicity of values and viewpoints, all of which need to be considered in making policy. Rather than assume a single, unifying "public interest," it is often more accurate—and safer—to assume that interests collide and thus trade-offs are inevitable. Second, these premises direct policy making to practical, answerable questions: Who wants this policy and why? How do we know? How much do they want it? Who will lose by it, and how much would it cost to compensate the losers? Why can't the market take care of this? What are the advantages and disadvantages of each alternative way of accomplishing the objective?

The prevailing assumptions also suggest ready means of answering the questions and reaching solutions. It is a matter of measuring what people want and analyzing the most efficient way of satisfying these wants, or of engineering compromises among competing groups purporting to speak for the self-interests of their members. Finally, the assumptions are sufficiently neutral and commonsensical that policies derived from them can gain broad assent, thus avoiding conflicts based solely on ideology or personal rancor. Compromises can readily be reached. For all these reasons, these principles together comprise what is taken for the policy-making ideal in present-day America. They offer a model for what politics should accomplish—would accomplish—if it were less corrupted by special pleadings, money, ideology, and bias.

* * *

But for all its virtues, the prevailing view of competent policy making ignores other important values. In particular, it disregards the role of ideas about what is good for society and the importance of debating the relative merits of such ideas. It thus tends to overlook the ways such normative visions shape what people want and expect from their government, their fellow citizens, and themselves. And it disregards the importance of democratic deliberation for refining and altering such visions over time and for mobilizing public action around them.

The core responsibility of those who deal in public policy—elected ls, administrators, policy analysts—is not simply to discover as

objectively as possible what people want for themselves and then determine and implement the best means of satisfying these wants. It is also
to provide the public with alternative visions of what is desirable and
possible, to stimulate deliberation about them, provoke a reexamination
of premises and values, and thus to broaden the range of potential responses and deepen society's understanding of itself. And here, perhaps,
is where ideology comes in.

Many of the most important policy initiatives of the last two decades cannot be explained by the prevailing assumptions about human
nature or social improvement. Consider the civil rights laws and regulations of the 1960s; the subsequent wave of laws and rules governing
health, safety, and the environment; and the reform of the tax code in
1986. These policies were not motivated principally or even substantially
by individuals seeking to satisfy selfish interests. To the contrary, they
were broadly understood as matters of public rather than private interest. And this perception gave them their unique authority. People supported these initiatives largely because they were thought to be good for
society. Nor were public preferences with regard to these policies stable
or preordained. Public support grew and changed as people came to
understand and engage with the ideas underlying them. The official acts
of policy making—enacting the laws, promulgating the rules, issuing the
court opinions—were embedded within social movements and understandings that shaped them and propelled them forward. To disregard
these motivating ideas is to miss the essential story.

There is ample evidence that the most accomplished government
leaders—those who have achieved significant things while in office or at
least set the direction of public action—have explicitly and purposively
crafted public visions of what is desirable and possible for society to do.
These ideas have been essential to their leadership, serving both to focus
public attention and to mobilize talent and resources within the government. Ronald Reagan perhaps best exemplified this approach to policy
making. His speeches, interviews, and press statements were not simply
devices to muster public support behind a particular initiative or to
glorify the accomplishments of his Administration. They were means of
educating the public in an approach to governance, creating a framework
through which the public would come to support a wide variety of
initiatives and to understand public issues.

The act of raising the salient public question—how to overcome
welfare dependency or Soviet aggression, how to improve American
competitiveness or reduce the budget deficit—is often the key step in the

formulation of policy, because it subsumes the value judgments that declare something to be a problem, focuses public attention on the issue, and frames the ensuing public debate. When questions "catch on" in this way, it is not because those who pose them are especially talented at manipulating public opinion or linking preconceived preferences to attractive agendas. The phenomenon is more interactive than that, and preferences are less defined, more fluid. Even before the question is asked, the public (or a significant portion of the public) seems already to be searching for ways to pose it—to give shape and coherence to events that seem random and unsettling—and thus to gain some measure of control. Rather than responding to preexisting public wants, the art of policy making has lain primarily in giving voice to these half-articulated fears and hopes and embodying them in convincing stories about their sources and the choices they represent.

The prevailing ideal of competent policy making casts government as problem solver, intervening when it can satisfy preexisting preferences more efficiently than the market can. Democratic processes, in this view, are primarily means for alerting policy makers to what people want for themselves. But if I am correct in seeing policy making, inevitably, as a process of posing questions, presenting problems, offering explanations, and suggesting choices, then the prevailing view seriously understates the responsibilities of policy makers, policy analysts, and citizens.

It is not difficult to tally preferences in this era of instantaneous electronic polling and of sophisticated marketing techniques for discovering what people want and how much they want it. It is a considerable challenge, however, to engage the public in rethinking how certain problems are defined, alternative solutions envisioned, and responsibilities for action allocated. The failure of conventional techniques of policy making to permit such civic discovery may suggest that there are no shared values to be discovered in the first place. And *this* message—that the "public interest" is no more than an accommodation or aggregation of individual interests—may have a corrosive effect on civic life. It may invalidate whatever potential exists for the creation of shared commitments and in so doing may stunt the discovery of public ideas. Such a failure may in turn call into question the inherent legitimacy of the policy decisions that result. For such policies are then supported only by debatable facts, inferences, and trade-offs. They lack any authentic governmental character beyond accommodation or aggregation. Those who disagree with the procedures or conclusions on which the policies are based have every reason to disregard them whenever the opportunity arises. Under these circumstances disobedience is not a social act reflecting on one's membership in a community but merely another expression of preference.

To the extent that deliberation and reflection yield a broader repertoire of problem definitions, solutions, and civic responsibilities, society is better equipped to cope with change and to learn from its past. The thoughtless adherence to outmoded formulations of problems, choices, and responsibilities can threaten a society's survival. Policy making should be more than and different from the discovery of what people want; it should entail the creation of contexts in which people can critically evaluate and revise what they believe.

* * *

This suggests a different role for policy makers and policy analysts than that of the prevailing ideal. The responsibility of government leaders is not only to make and implement decisions responsive to public wants. A greater challenge is to engage the public in an ongoing dialogue over what problems should be addressed, what is at stake in such decisions, and how to strengthen the public's capacities to deal with similar problems in the future. Such an explicative process, properly managed, can build on itself: As society defines and evaluates its collective goals, it examines its norms and beliefs; in defining its purposes, it becomes better able to mobilize its resources and achieve its goals.

By the same token, the responsibility of policy analysts is not only to choose the best means of achieving a given objective. It is also to offer alternative ways of understanding public problems and possible solutions and thus to expose underlying norms to critical examination. The analyst can provoke such examination in several ways: by juxtaposing widely accepted but morally or politically inconsistent assumptions about certain public problems and their solutions, by questioning the conventional metaphors and analogies used to justify and explain policies and offering new ones in their place, by providing plausible but novel interpretations of large events, by revealing underlying similarities and patterns in the public's approach to seemingly unconnected situations, and by advancing alternative future scenarios premised on how society might cope with certain problems.

Policy makers and analysts will not spend all their time in such explicative activities; there may be relatively few opportunities for effectively redefining and evaluating social norms. But these responsibilities should be understood as critically important to these jobs. The prevailing philosophy comprises a useful set of precepts for guiding much policy making, particularly where there is wide and enduring consensus about the nature of the problems to be solved, the range of possible solutions, and appropriate allocations of responsibility for solving them; and where solving the problems *as understood* is more useful than understanding them differently. The prevailing philosophy is less helpful—indeed, may forestall social learning—where these conditions are not met. My suspicion—difficult to document, hopeless to prove conclusively—is that many public issues, perhaps most of those considered important enough to be discussed in the newspaper or everyday conversation, fall in the second category, in which definitions, constraints, and responsibilities are centrally at issue.

*   *   *

In a sense, these differences are aspects of a broader debate that has raged for centuries over human nature and the purposes and methods of governance. Do we as citizens dare entrust our collective fates to a government reflecting the demands of self-interested individuals? If not, what is the alternative?

The modern debate had its origins in the Renaissance, in the first stirrings of humanist thought and the beginnings of the bureaucratic state. By the sixteenth century the monarchs of Europe had evolved administrative machinery capable of organizing finance, waging war, and issuing laws and regulations. These bureaucracies were populated by men who owed their positions to specialized training and administrative competence, not to feudal right. They were uniquely skilled in using organization to accomplish complex tasks efficiently. Bureaucratic absolutism was elaborated and refined in the seventeenth century by Louis XIV of France, whose specialized, hierarchical system provided a model for Prussia, Spain, Austria, and Russia. By the eighteenth century "enlightened despots" were firmly entrenched on the continent. Even with the advent of modern parliaments in the nineteenth and twentieth centuries the instruments of central authority and bureaucratic control continued to dominate the core functions of government in continental Europe. As the German sociologist Max Weber described it, "the bureaucratic type of organization . . . is, from the purely technical point of view, capable of attaining the highest degree of efficiency and is in this sense formally the most rational known means for carrying out . . . control over human beings."

The rise of this new, rationally authoritarian form of government paralleled a growing concern about the governability of the masses. By the seventeenth century many thinkers had concluded that moral exhortation and the threat of damnation could no longer be trusted to restrain people's destructive passions. Niccolò Machiavelli, for example, warned that men are "ungrateful, voluble, dissemblers, anxious to avoid danger, and covetous of gain." Thomas Hobbes foresaw the fragility of an order based on human passion and had concluded that the only alternative was a strong central government—a leviathan.

England, however, was evolving another alternative—deliberative government. Victory over the Stuarts had forestalled the kind of bureaucratic absolutism taking root across the Channel. In its place the House of Commons was elaborating what Edmund Burke would call a "deliberative assembly," guided by "the general reasons of the whole." It was through deliberation that common interests and attachments could be discovered and developed and passions thus be restrained. Burke recoiled from the egoistic philosophy animating the French Revolution, whereby

> laws are supported only by their own terrors, and by the
> concern which each individual may find in them from his own
> private speculations, or can spare to them from his own
> interests. In the groves of their academy, at the end of every
> vista, you see nothing but the gallows. Nothing is left which
> engages the affections of the commonwealth. On the principles
> of this mechanic philosophy our institutions can never be
> embodied, if I may use the expression, in persons; so as to
> create in us love, veneration, admiration, or attachment. But
> that sort of reason which banishes the affections is incapable of
> filling their place. These public affections, combined with
> manners, are required sometimes as correctives, always as aids
> to law.

The notion that democratic deliberation would inspire ideas about what was good for society, and thus instill common attachments and constrain selfish passions, was widely discussed in England and America during the late eighteenth and nineteenth centuries. John Stuart Mill saw in democracy a means of developing moral and intellectual capacities "by the utmost possible publicity and discussion, whereby not merely a few individuals in succession, but the whole public, are made, to a certain extent, participants in the government." American Federalists and Antifederalists alike worried about the instability of a society based on selfish passion and spoke of the need for citizens' "attachment" to institutions and "affection" toward one another. After touring America,

Alexis de Tocqueville mused that "the most powerful and perhaps the only means that we still possess of interesting men in the welfare of their country is to make them partakers in the government . . . civic zeal seems to me to be inseparable from the exercise of political rights." And by 1872 the English essayist and critic Walter Bagehot could conclude that "a policy of discussion not only tends to diminish our inherited defects, but also . . . to augment a heritable excellence. . . . No State can be first rate which has not a government by discussion."

* * *

A third alternative for dealing with the passions of a more worldly populace was also being advanced at about the same time. Rather than rely on bureaucratic absolutism to subjugate the passions or on deliberative government to civilize them, this alternative relied on calculated self-interest to constrain them. This third view emerged from the musings of eighteenth-century political economists of the "Scottish Enlightenment," like Adam Smith, Adam Ferguson, and Sir James Stuart, who regarded the discipline of the marketplace as the key to social stability. Stuart argued that a population governed by rational self-interest would be more stable than one susceptible to appeals to general interest, which were likely to ignite the passions. "[W]ere a people to become quite disinterested: there would be no possibility of governing them. Everyone might consider the interest of his country in a different light, and many might join in the ruin of it, by endeavoring to promote its advantages." The British utilitarians—Jeremy Bentham and his progeny—and the economists and sociologists who followed in their wake, shared many of these assumptions. Although, in their view, "every agent is activated only by self interest," egoistic behavior was entirely compatible with the general good. Indeed, they argued, each individual's rational pursuit of his own self-interest would yield the highest utility overall. Government was necessary only as a last resort, a night watchman to guard against encroachments on trade and the freedom to pursue self-interest. Its purpose was entirely instrumental—to help maximize individual utility.

The reigning American philosophy of policy making has drawn on these three currents of thought—bureaucratic expertise, democratic deliberation, and utilitarianism—but in equal parts. Especially in this century, beginning with the Progressives' efforts to insulate policy making from politics and continuing through the modern judiciary's oversight of policy making, there has been a tendency to subordinate democratic deliberation to the other two themes. As the "administrative state" has grown, its legitimacy has increasingly rested on notions of neutral competence and procedural regularity. The "public interest" has been defined as what individual members of the public want for themselves—as such wants are expressed through opinion surveys, data on the public's willingness to pay for certain goods, and the pleadings of interest groups. The ideal of public policy has thus become almost entirely instrumental —designed to maximize individual satisfactions.

* * *

The tradition of democratic deliberation, with its emphasis on what is good for *society* and its concern for citizenship education and social understanding, has been subordinated in part, I think, because of our culture's understandable fear of demagoguery and intolerance. Particularly since the 1930s, we have had ample evidence of the dangers of totalitarianism—of moral absolutism and social engineering toward some monolithic view of the public interest. It seems far safer to assume that people *are* motivated primarily by selfish desires, that social improvement *does* require trade-offs and compromises among such goals, and that the purpose of government *is* instrumental—to accomplish such trade-offs and compromises, particularly when private transactions do not suffice. The great virtue of the American form of government has appeared to lie precisely in its pluralism and ethical relativism, its *lack* of any overarching public ideas about what is good for society.

But there may be greater dangers in failing to appreciate the power of public ideas and the importance of deliberation about them. In an era like the present one—when overall public purposes are less clear than during wars or depressions; when the ways public problems are defined, choices posed, and responsibilities tacitly allocated can make all the difference; when many issues are so technically complex that values are easily hidden with expert judgments; and when "great communicators" can hold center stage on national media geared to visionary appeals— our strongest bulwark against demagoguery is the habit of critical discussion about, and self-conscious awareness of, the public ideas that envelop us. Competence, as it has been understood, is not enough. We also need leadership.

31

GREAT EXHORTATIONS

THE START OF EVERY YEAR INVITES NEW RESOLVE ABOUT HOW WE WILL improve ourselves. The start of every fourth year invites new resolve about how we will improve the nation. With extraordinary regularity Americans begin new diets (having given up on the old one) and become enthralled with new political candidates (having given up on the old). Both recurring urges—toward self-improvement and public improvement—require persistent enthusiasm and unending hope.

To help us in these efforts, we turn to two kinds of improvement books that grace best-seller lists. One kind tells us how to improve ourselves—by losing weight, making money, enjoying sex, getting in contact with the cosmos, getting in contact with eligible members of the opposite sex, getting in contact with ourselves, becoming healthier and fitter, influencing people, managing a successful business, sounding intelligent at parties, and so on.

The other kind of improvement book tells us how to improve society —by cleaning up the environment, ending the arms race, shoring up American defenses, organizing higher education around great books, relieving poverty, and so on.

The two kinds of books begin from different premises. Self-improvement books assume that our private lives are unsatisfactory in some way and that by following some prescribed course of action we can achieve happiness and fulfillment. Public-improvement books assume that certain cherished values are being ignored by the public and that by mending our collective ways we can achieve a good society.

Most of us carry around both sets of aspirations—things we want for ourselves and our families on the one hand, and things we want for our society (or for mankind, future generations, the planet) on the other. The two categories—our personal wants and our public wants—are not always in perfect harmony. The public interest is different than the sum of our selfish wants, the musings of microeconomists and political power brokers to the contrary notwithstanding. The task of improving society involves something more than satisfying the personal desires of some people without making others feel worse off.

Research into political attitudes reveals the difference between the two realms. Although people sometimes vote on the basis of what's good for them personally, they also put aside personal interests to a surprising degree. People's views on busing to achieve racial integration have been shown to depend less on their own experience with busing (or the likelihood that their children will either be bused or go to school with children who are) than on their beliefs about the value of integration in general. People's ideas about the overall level of unemployment and about hardships it causes have more effect on their voting patterns than whether they are unemployed or in danger of becoming so. Attitudes toward the Vietnam War turned much less on whether one (or one's family members or close friends) had experienced it firsthand than on one's general views of American foreign policy. Attitudes toward government programs to provide universal health insurance or guarantee jobs are better correlated with one's general political views than with one's own health or employment status. And so on.

* * *

The two kinds of books that represent these two realms of aspiration are sometimes at war with one another, just as are our selfish and social inclinations. The authors of public-improvement books often decry the selfishness, acquisitiveness, narcissism, greed, and self-indulgence that divert our attention from more noble ideals. They admonish us, in effect, to stop being obsessed with self-improvement. (Professor Allan Bloom, author of a best-seller called *The Closing of the American Mind,* expressed outrage at what he considers to be a modern ethos that recognizes no right or wrong, only problems susceptible to personal counseling.)

Authors of self-improvement books, by contrast, often go to great lengths to reassure us that we shouldn't feel guilty, bad, or otherwise inadequate. We'd be far better off if we stopped listening to all the preaching that is imposed on us and responded instead to personal needs that arise from deep inside. By freeing ourselves from the "oughts," we can become more spontaneous, energetic, sexier, more popular, more influential—whatever we want to become.

(There is a hybrid genre of books whose authors advocate a society in which everyone seeks self-improvement—think of Charles Reich's *Greening of America,* on the left of the political spectrum, or Robert Ringer's *Looking Out for Number One,* on the right. But such antistatist, let-a-thousand-flowers-bloom tracts are less about public improvement than self-improvement. They use the language of public improvement therapeutically, to reassure us that our personal longings are justifiable: Don't feel guilty if you're not involved in political movements and social reform, they seem to say. It's fine to drop out, do your own thing, indulge yourself. Indeed, if everyone did that, we'd have a better society.)

Although most of us hold both self-improvement and public-improvement messages in our heads simultaneously, we tend to be more responsive to one of them at one time in our lives than at another. When we first reach political consciousness—typically between the ages of eighteen and twenty-one, or whenever we first leave home—the self-absorption of our teenage years gives way to a greater concern with the society around us, its aspirations and the inevitable gaps that lie between such aspirations and reality. Then, with the start of our own families, our individual concerns tend to take precedence once again. Our personal wants and public wants cycle back and forth in this way as we live out our lives.

So too with our society. As the historian Arthur Schlesinger, Jr., and the political economist Albert O. Hirschman have both noted, society's passion for public improvement seems to wax and wane over time, alternating with periods in which society is more preoccupied by selfish concerns. Periods of public improvement—like the Progressive era of the first decades of the century, the Depression and war decades, the reformist 1960s—eventually lead to exhaustion and disillusionment when the reforms fail to achieve the exaggerated hopes that fueled them, causing people to turn inward. Self-improvement eras (the 1920s, the 1950s, the 1980s) ultimately lead people to feel empty and disconnected from one another even when their personal ambitions are satisfied, causing a society to turn outward once again.

Not surprisingly, public-improvement eras are often marked by best-selling public-improvement books. America of the 1960s was inspired by the likes of Ralph Nader's *Unsafe at Any Speed*, Rachel Carson's *Silent Spring*, Michael Harrington's *The Other America*, Jonathan Kozol's *Death at an Early Age*, Betty Friedan's *The Feminine Mystique*, and John Kenneth Galbraith's *Affluent Society*. Progressive reforms had earlier been spurred by muckraking accounts like *The Jungle* by Upton Sinclair and Ida Tarbell's *History of the Standard Oil Trust*.

Perhaps society's shifting interests in public and then private improvement are related to our personal cycle. By force of sheer numbers, a huge generation like the postwar baby boomers can turn society inward or outward. It seems more than coincidental that the last great wave of best-selling public-improvement books appeared in the 1960s, just as the early baby boomers reached college age.

*　*　*

Sometimes we're attracted to public-improvement books not because we want to improve society but because we enjoy sharing in the author's indignation about how society has gone off track. Americans have always liked debunking our dominant institutions. (The verb "debunk" itself is as American as apple pie.) We relish exposés. There's nothing quite as much fun as kicking a sacred cow or two. The more venom and vitriol, the more we applaud. In this respect, public-improvement books are just glorified self-improvement books. They may have ponderous titles, but they might as well be hawked as cures for chronic exasperation.

Righteous indignation can also be seductive, however. When public-improvement books are taken too seriously, they can be more dangerous than self-improvement books. Bad advice for improving ourselves will, at worst, disappoint us and cause some of us to have wasted a bit of money. But bad advice for improving society can lead to all sorts of mischief.

What's more, there is a natural check on bad advice about self-improvement. We think we know if we're unhappy or unfulfilled, and if a book doesn't help us much, it won't even make it as a paperback. Self-improvement books are like new shampoos or deodorants. Success is proof enough.

But there's less of a check on bad advice for improving society. Most of us are not very confident about what society's core values really are, apart from high abstractions like freedom and equality (and even these have an annoying way of bumping up against each other when pushed too far). Nor can we simply try out what the author of a public-improvement book advises in order to test it for ourselves, the way we can a new diet or sexual technique.

Often authors of best-selling public-improvement books assert that some cherished value is being subverted and rely on exhortation to convince us they're correct. They scold us, shake us, implore us. They throw around words like "virtue," "honor," "nature," "truth," and "conscience" the way authors of self-improvement books throw around words like "feeling," "bliss," "wonderment," and "delight."

In making their case, public-improvement authors may expose startling facts that we hadn't known before but that run counter to what we have preferred to believe about some aspect of our society. Look at the corruption! Behold the poverty! Witness the ignorance, the cruelty, the decay! Or they may cite a wide range of troubling phenomena, of which we're already dimly aware but had not considered symptoms of the same fundamental crisis: It's all due to our loss of commitment! It's because of our lack of patriotism! It's capitalist greed!

But what often gives public-improvement books particular force—and what makes them especially dangerous—is their one-sidedness. The correctness of the cause is never in doubt. Their authors stand aligned with all that is right, good, and truthful in the world—against the forces of wrongheadedness, false consciousness, and evil. They admit to no shades of meaning, ethical dilemmas, trade-offs, possibilities for unintended consequences. They have no patience for relativism. There is no room for compromise. It is all or nothing: Either we create a perfectly clean environment, abandon all nuclear arms, completely democratize the corporation, eradicate communism, focus all of higher education on the values encoded in the great books of civilization—or we are doomed. Such moral absolutism is understandable. Public-improvement books wouldn't attract our attention unless they conveyed total conviction. The danger comes in treating these exhortations as if they were reasoned arguments for public-policy making, when they are nothing of the sort. They are polemics—single sides of often complex issues.

*　*　*

Provocation of debate about what is good for society can itself result in public good, of course. Democracy depends, after all, on public deliberation. And among the most important subjects we must repeatedly deliberate on are definitions of the problems we face together and understandings of what we need to ask of one another in order to solve them. There is no better means of mobilizing a free people to collective action than through discussion. (Indeed, there's no better check on the bad advice contained in public-improvement harangues than the habit of democratic deliberation.)

Herein lies the real value of public-improvement books. At their best, they goad us into thinking, arguing, questioning our premises, reevaluating what we want society to be. They remind us that we have collective choices—and personal responsibilities for helping make and execute such choices. They inform and stimulate us—as *citizens*.

Beyond their specific admonitions, then, public-improvement books contain a more general but more enduring exhortation: that we become responsible citizens who continuously and conscientiously deliberate our collective future. Public-improvement books thus offer us another goal for our self-improvement—civic virtue, which holds out the possibility of peace between our warring sets of aspirations.

32

THE ONCE AND
FUTURE LIBERAL

IT IS WITH SOME PERSONAL ANGUISH THAT I CONFESS TO MY CLOSEST friends (and now, dear reader, to you) that I spent six months of my life advising Michael Dukakis in his dispiriting run for the Presidency. (I use the term "advising" in the generally accepted sense that I wrote innumerable memos to the candidate, attended an endless series of meetings with other advisers, chatted buoyantly on television and with reporters about the candidate's "new" ideas, and spent hours on the phone, usually very late at night, advising campaign staffers who said they would be talking with the candidate within the week. I actually spoke with Michael Dukakis only twice, and on both occasions he gave a credible performance of having better things to do than listen to my pontifications.)

The campaign was depressing for many reasons, not the least because my candidate lost. There was also "the vision thing," as George Bush so eloquently described it. Bush, in case you have forgotten, accused Michael Dukakis of being a *liberal*. That is, Dukakis was a card-carrying member of the ACLU, he despised the American flag, and he wanted to release black murderers and rapists from prison, among other things.

Dukakis responded less forcefully to these charges than one might have wished. At first, he told the American people that *he*, rather than George, was the real conservative. Not until the last ten days of the campaign, when it looked as though all was lost anyway, did he confess that, yes, he *was* a liberal. George had been right all along. Dukakis threw himself upon the mercy of the American electorate.

George Bush was able to define a *liberal* the way he wanted, because few Americans any longer know what a liberal is. American conservatives now have a clear public philosophy, whereas liberals do not. This chapter is about why that is so. It is also about the need for a new and more coherent liberal public philosophy and the difficulties that may frustrate the development of such a philosophy.

*   *   *

The new conservative public philosophy presents a coherent approach to the world. It proposes explanations for a great deal of our collective experience over the past twenty years, and it embodies these explanations in a vivid core parable about the perils of indulgence and permissiveness. The story line is familiar to postwar America; it is one of doting parents and their spoiled children, of public irresponsibility and social excess. But the parable also tells of a world "out there" grown more ruthless and sternly warns that as individuals and as a nation we are in danger of losing our way. We must impose discipline and responsibility. Through renewed fortitude we can triumph over the forces that threaten us. The parable's power lies in its simplicity and scope, and its evocation of unarticulated fears and hopes.

Consider the new conservative public philosophy's position on social welfare. First, the welfare system is riddled with waste and fraud. Second, when welfare *has* gone to those it was intended for, its effects have often been perverse. It has encouraged poor teenage girls to have babies and discouraged them from marriage and work, trapping children in a lifelong culture of dependency and irresponsibility. At the same time, criminal suspects now enjoy so many rights that our police are incapable of keeping order, so drugs and crime infest our cities. We have forbidden teachers to control their classrooms, so inner-city schools are failing to educate poor children. The three forms of laxness reinforce one another: The easiest path for inner-city youths is to drop out of school, and then for the girls to have babies and live off welfare, and for the boys to live off girlfriends on welfare and the proceeds of crime. The only solution is to reverse course. We should eliminate welfare (except to victims of sudden and unexpected hardships). We should allow our teachers to punish and expel. We should authorize our police officers and judges to mete out swift and certain punishment. In short, we should restore social discipline.

The conservative parable equally encompasses economic policy. For years, the story goes, America has been profligate. The liberal solution to the tendency of the economy to succumb cyclically to recession and underemployment was for the government to spend freely enough to take up the slack. But this Keynesian approach ultimately proved its own undoing. Government went on spending beyond its means, even during times of buoyant growth. Also, it bred expectations that it would always step in to snap the economy out of slumps and slowdowns. The result was a breakdown of social discipline. The lesson of this story, too, is clear. We must restore discipline to the economy. We had to "break the back" of inflation in the early 1980s through tactical unemployment, to remind workers of their vulnerability to joblessness should wage demands get too high, and we must stand ready to do so again. Future economic policy must take the control of inflation as its first priority and relegate unemployment to a lower priority. To control inflation is to impose discipline on the system; the attainment of every other economic goal depends on that basic discipline.

Other strands of the conservative economic philosophy hold that the only way to discipline government spending is to pass a constitutional amendment mandating a balanced federal budget. Others emphasize the discipline of the marketplace and the central importance of rewarding successful entrepreneurialism and punishing failure. According to this view, we should reduce taxes and forswear subsidies and bailouts. The market is *the* source of social discipline—rather than taxes or government regulations. There is a spirited debate between the conservative budget balancers and the supply-siders over whether we should increase taxes to narrow yawning budget deficits. But both sides diagnose our economic ills as the heritage of an overly permissive environment in which no one was held responsible for his economic actions.

* * *

Foreign policy makes up a third aspect of the conservative parable. For years liberals have sought to appease the Soviets, placate the less-developed nations of the Third World, and coddle our allies. As a result, the story goes, we became an easy mark. Our defenses were down; the Soviets surged ahead of us in armaments. Emboldened by our passivity, they viciously subjugated Afghanistan, cracked down in Poland, and expanded their influence in southern Africa, Southeast Asia, and Central America. Simultaneously, the United States was being taken for a ride by Third World nations that demanded our aid but persistently sided with our adversaries and voted against us at the United Nations. Other Third World nations have threatened default on loans from our banks. We were humiliated by Iran and have been easily victimized by international terrorists. In addition, Japan and our European allies have been unwilling to cooperate with us in restricting East-West trade. Worse, they have taken advantage of our open economy by dumping their subsidized goods here. Japan is strongly reluctant to import American goods.

The overarching lesson is the same. We must impose discipline, on adversaries and allies alike. We must regain our credibility, and the way to do that is to get tough. We should maintain a strong military defense, get the Soviets (and their Cuban allies) out of Central America, give aid to Third World nations only when they play on our side, and tighten up on East-West trade so that the Soviets cannot easily take advantage of our technology. The Soviets are ready to make concessions on armaments only because we held tough and built up *our* armaments. We should "play hardball" with our allies on trade and defense. We should threaten to retaliate against Japan if its markets are not fully open to our products. And we should impose austerity on Third World debtors, ensuring that they repay their debts and end their profligate ways.

What is so compelling about all these arguments—drawn from social welfare, economics, and foreign policy—is that they are mutually reinforcing. No conservative public philosopher, and certainly no politician, subscribes to the full complement of these views. But the details of these arguments are less important than the overarching parable. Liberal permissiveness has laid us open to exploitation. Without discipline, there has been no accountability. Without accountability, decadence has crept in, irresponsibility has become endemic, the system has lost its "moral fiber," and we have let ourselves become victims.

The conservative parable embodies a subtle but important distinction between two forms of social discipline—one applying to *us*, the other to *them*. *They* are the poor, the workers who demand unjustly high wages, our trading partners, Third World debtors, and the Soviets. We must discipline them. To do so, we will need to be strong and resolute.

In a curious way bundling such disparate issues together into a single parable of decadence, slackness, and assertiveness gives comfort.

The larger explanation suggests a way of comprehending, and thereby eventually reversing, the decay. Lessons can be learned, steps taken. It is simply a matter of recognizing the prevailing pattern and applying the moral. The new conservative public philosophy offers an easy formula.

* * *

The liberal response to the new conservatism has been unconvincing —and not because Walter Mondale, Tip O'Neill, John Kenneth Galbraith, or even Michael Dukakis has been lacking in imagination. Even in recent years liberals have shown no end of cleverness in devising new schemes and programmatic solutions to all manner of problems. Those who bemoan the liberals' dearth of "new ideas" have not been paying attention. The failure has lain deeper, with a liberal public philosophy that no longer embodies a story in which most Americans can believe. The liberal parable does not explain. It does not yield clear lessons. It does not ring true.

The prevailing liberal public philosophy rests on notions of altruism and conciliation. The parable is that of wise and generous parents who skillfully accommodate the conflicting demands of their children, help their poorer cousins, and seek reconciliation with wayward relations. The modern liberal hero is a combination of Jesus and Robert Young in *Father Knows Best*.

This parable generalizes across issues as easily as the new conservative fable does. It requires no great elaboration here, because it is so familiar to us. The needy should be helped. The less fortunate should have the opportunity to become as prosperous as the richest among us. Those who are members of groups that have been discriminated against in the past should be given special help. People who commit crimes should be rehabilitated, not merely punished. Economic policy should favor full employment even at the cost of some inflation, for joblessness is an awful burden to impose on anyone; inflation can be restrained by an incomes policy that will cause no increase in unemployment, unlike the conservative remedy. Taxes should be progressive. Poorer nations deserve our aid, to encourage land reform and the growth of democratic institutions. As to our allies, we should work in concert with them, all the while recognizing that their needs and priorities may be different from ours. And we should persistently seek a structure of peaceful co-existence with the Soviets, through trade, cultural exchanges, summit meetings, and arms control.

The liberal public philosophy has its own coherence. Only through altruism and conciliation can we maintain domestic tranquillity and global peace. Only through peace can we gain prosperity. Only through prosperity can we afford to be charitable and conciliatory. The logic is internally consistent. And this philosophy contains a moral vision no less compelling than that of the disciplinarians.

But the parable of the generous and wise parent seems to many Americans disconcertingly naive in a world grown colder and crueler. Popular wisdom now teaches that the welfare system does not reduce poverty, "full-employment" budgets cause inflation, Third World aid merely generates corruption and profligacy, détente merely promotes Soviet aggression. The new conservatives did not invent these relationships; they just pointed them out. Charity and conciliation are worthy goals for our personal lives, but such sentiments cannot sustain a nation in the world as it is. They are no longer reliable pillars for a public philosophy.

* * *

Yet the fact is that pure altruism never figured prominently in the liberal public philosophy of the period from the New Deal to the end of World War II—the gestation period of modern liberalism. The New Deal was concerned primarily with social insurance rather than with the redistribution of wealth. The stronger precept of social solidarity was born not of specific legislation or programs but of certain experiences— the Depression and World War II—that profoundly affected almost all Americans. The goals of reviving the economy and winning the war, and the sacrifices implied in achieving them, were well understood and widely endorsed. The public was motivated less by altruism than by its direct and palpable stake in the outcome of what were ineluctably *social* endeavors.

This distinction between social solidarity and altruism parallels the conservative penchant for disciplining others but not necessarily ourselves. The liberalism of the New Deal and World War II partook of an inclusive spirit of generosity toward ourselves. Society was not seen as composed of *us* and *them*; it was the realm of *we*. We were all bound together, fundamentally dependent on one another's compassion and common sense.

The liberal idea of common dependence even found its way into thinking about national defense and international trade. While conservatives sought to isolate America from the world, the liberals who emerged from the Depression and the war designed a system of "collective security" in which we and our allies would work collaboratively. These earlier liberals forged the United Nations and other structures for mediating international political disputes, and they created a parallel system for working out the rules of world trade.

* * *

The liberalism of the 1960s was quite different. By this time many Americans were experiencing the exhilaration of rapidly rising incomes, along with the new mobility and privacy that went with cars, highways, and suburban homes. There was less occasion in everyday life for social solidarity. Generosity still claimed the liberal conscience, but circumstances had transformed this sentiment into altruism. Thanks to liberal altruism, the hitherto ignored lot of the poor was brought to the public's attention. Gradually, however, our poorer citizens, and the inhabitants of other, poorer nations, became *them*.

The special conditions of the time allowed *us* to be generous to *them* with little identifiable sacrifice. The extraordinary growth of the American economy during the 1960s made it possible for the nation to wage a war on poverty, and then another on North Vietnam, and even enjoy a rise in living standards. Keynesianism, the dominant economic school of the time, asserted that such public spending, far from impoverishing the middle class, would serve to keep the vast economic machine going at full throttle. Extending civil rights to blacks also cost the majority of Americans relatively little. Segregation in Southern schools, luncheonettes, and hotels could be forcefully attacked without causing unpleasant side effects elsewhere. The United States was preeminent in the world economy, with no serious trade competition from overseas. So the nation could afford to indulge its allies and the Third World; boosting foreign purchasing power could only result in more American export sales. In short, the liberal public philosophy of the 1960s and early 1970s entailed a peculiarly low-cost form of charity.

This easy altruism was reinforced by prevailing pluralist ideas about American democracy. By the 1960s pluralism had come to serve both as a description of the American political system and as a prescription for its continued health. American politics was thought to be powered by shifting and overlapping groups whose leaders bargained with one another over the shape and purpose of public action. The result was assumed to be a stable but responsive political system. To many Americans, these features helped explain why democracy had continued to survive so well in the United States in contrast to its fate in other nations.

In the pluralist view, the "public interest" was nothing more (or less) than an accommodation among group leaders, with no substantive content apart from what these leaders sought. Policies that could placate a greater number of interest groups were by definition the most conducive to the public good. Pluralism thus contained no principled limits on what compromises should be reached or how far government should go to accommodate the various groups that made up the public.

These two intellectual currents—Keynesianism and pluralism—were easily combined. Just as Keynesianism legitimized the idea of activist government as a way to stabilize the economy, pluralism legitimized it as a way to stabilize politics. Both currents were ultimately propelled by the comforting notion that some people could be helped without imposing costs on others. Full employment in the economic sphere, coupled with the ongoing accommodation of interest groups in the political sphere, would ensure that everybody got his over the long term. Public issues were subtly transformed into private claims, all of which could eventually be satisfied. Hard choices and the setting of priorities could be avoided; the logic of public action could be left vague. Social altruism knew no bounds and had no strict definition. There was no finely honed and rigorous liberal public philosophy, because there seemed to be no need for one.

As a result, postwar liberalism was doomed to excess. Its fullest flowering, in the 1960s and early 1970s, occurred in an anomalous moment of history during which the United States was particularly unconstrained. It was a sheltered and rich environment, a cultural hothouse unlike anything America had experienced before or is likely ever to experience again.

* * *

Any public philosophy so germinated would be enfeebled once it left the hothouse. Liberalism was no exception. As the economy began to slow and American economic preeminence came under challenge, it was no longer possible for some groups to benefit without the burden manifestly falling on others. But because liberal pluralism lacked any definition of the public good apart from the sum of individual claims, and also lacked a system of principles for screening and balancing such claims, conflicts grew harsher and claims more insistent. By the late 1970s liberalism and, inevitably, the Democratic party, too, appeared less the embodiment of a shared vision and more a tangle of narrow appeals from labor unions, teachers, gays, Hispanics, blacks, Jews, the handicapped, the elderly, women. Of course, these demands were no more parochial than those from Republican claimants—bankers, oil companies, insurance firms, doctors, and corporate bureaucrats, among others. But the perception remained that the Democratic party was dominated by "special interests," because by the late 1970s the liberal public philosophy conveyed no central theme to organize and legitimate the claims of its diverse constituencies. It failed to explain the new reality in which we found ourselves and to prescribe clear lessons. It offered nothing but a feeble and unconvincing call to charity and conciliation. Without an integrating philosophy, these fractious Democratic constituencies, each promoting its own agenda, were all that liberalism had to show to the citizenry.

The philosophical watershed, where conciliation gave way to discipline, came with the Administration of Jimmy Carter—the Democratic President who carried into policy many of the central precepts of the new conservative public philosophy. Carter understood the public's growing disdain for Washington. He had campaigned as an outsider, against the Washington "insiders." He decried "fraud, waste, and abuse" in the burgeoning welfare system and sought its overhaul. (Carter's abortive reform effort adopted the model of the negative income tax, first proposed by conservative economists to minimize administrative complexity and purge the system of its presumed incentives against work and family.) Carter's conservative tendencies became particularly apparent in the last years of the Administration. He appointed Paul Volcker chairman of the Federal Reserve Board and supported the Fed's decision, in October 1979, to limit the nation's money supply in order to combat inflation, even though interest rates and unemployment were predicted to rise as a result. And it was Carter, and his national security adviser, Zbigniew Brzezinski, who ended détente with the Soviets. In the wake of the Soviet invasion of Afghanistan, in December 1979, Carter embargoed grain sales to the USSR; and in response to the Soviet deployment of SS-20 missiles in Eastern Europe, Carter moved to install U.S. missiles in Western Europe.

All these departures from liberal public philosophy were understandable: Many Americans resented the growth in welfare spending; inflation was soaring; the Soviets were becoming more aggressive. The point is that Jimmy Carter—and the American public—embraced the new conservative public philosophy because it seemed to offer the only comprehensible guide to what was happening and what to do about it. The world was already divided into *us* and *them*—that is, greedy workers, the poor, Soviets, and other foreigners. The choice was to be either charitable and conciliatory or assertive and tough. The first alternative had proved to be tragically misguided. That left only the second. Absent any other option, the public's efforts to discern what was at stake and the lessons to be learned inevitably began to be shaped by the conservative parable.

*   *   *

Every public philosophy that gains credence, every story about our lives together that strikes a chord of recognition among the public, contains some truth. If it did not, the parable would not resonate so powerfully in our collective consciousness. But a public philosophy is a simplification of reality. Without some simplifying fables, citizens would be awash in disconnected data. The world is too complex for wholly empirical politics.

The new conservative public philosophy contains an important element of truth. America's permissive policies of the 1960s and early 1970s, and the larger failure to define goals and limits, of which the permissive policies were a consequence, did contribute to the growing problems of welfare dependency, inflation and economic drift, and Soviet aggression. Permissiveness—that is, an overwhelming preference for smoothing over rather than settling conflict—contributed to an environment in which unaccountability flourished, both at home and abroad. In abdicating public authority, America issued an invitation to irresponsibility, at home and abroad.

But the skeins of cause and effect are far more tangled than anything dreamt of in the conservative parable. The 1960s liberal public philosophy can be faulted for ignoring the harsh realities of the late 1970s and the 1980s. But the new conservative public philosophy is open to criticism for denying their underlying causes. However much public laxity may have contributed to our troubles, it was not the principal culprit. A far deeper transformation was occurring across all three realms of immediate concern—domestic poverty, the national economy, and the Soviet threat. The transformation is still going on, even if we can discern only its outlines.

Before turning to first causes, consider some salient symptoms: By 1988 the average weekly earnings of American production workers, adjusted for inflation, were just about the same as they had been a full twenty years before. Women and baby boomers streamed into the workplace—some nineteen million of them over the 1970s, and millions more since then. But many of these new entrants have been driven by the need to prop up stagnant or declining family incomes. Young workers, in particular, have fallen behind. Many can no longer afford to buy their own houses nor aspire to the standard of living enjoyed by their parents.

The poorest among us have fared the worst. America's poverty rate —the fraction of the population officially listed as controlling too little cash to tend to their minimal needs—stopped declining in 1973 and then slowly began edging up again. When the income of the median American family stopped rising, so did that of the poorest.

The pernicious lure of welfare dependency cannot be blamed for the continuing plight of America's poor, as conservative sociologists would have us believe. Subtract payments to the middle class and the elderly from the nation's growing social-welfare bill and it becomes apparent that the needy have received surprisingly little public help during this long period of stagnation. In fact, from 1970 to 1980 annual case assistance for each nonelderly poor person in the United States rose by just ninety-three dollars—hardly a sum to tempt crowds of Americans away from honest labor. Adjusted for inflation, benefit levels for Aid to Families with Dependent Children, which is the largest cash-assistance program for the poor, actually declined during the decade, and they have continued to decline since 1980.

Most "welfare" has gone to the middle class, through programs like Medicare and Social Security, not to the poor. By 1980 the aggregate of these benefits was more than three times larger than that for programs based on need.

* * *

Just as conservative sociology provides the wrong explanation for the persistence of poverty, conservative economics gives the wrong explanation for our long-term industrial problems. Our economy has suffered less from inflation and underinvestment than from a long-term slowdown in productivity. For nearly two decades before 1970 the average working American had produced around 3 percent more goods and services at the end of each year than at the start. But in the 1970s the annual increase in the rate of productivity fell dramatically. Not even the 1980s economic recovery has returned productivity to its former level of growth. Almost no growth of productivity in America has meant almost no rise in the real incomes of Americans. This stagnation has been particularly apparent in comparisons between the United States and other nations. From 1973 to 1988, for example, while American productivity improved by an average of just 2 percent a year, the Japanese were producing 6 percent more each year. Even the troubled economies of Western Europe raised productivity more rapidly than we did.

No one can fully explain why our rate of productivity growth has declined, especially relative to that of other nations. But we know that productivity depends on social organization—on how our firms are managed and our workers motivated and trained, and on how quickly our enterprises adapt to new possibilities and challenges. Adaptation is the key, because the terms of global competition have changed dramatically.

And here we have come to the heart of the matter. The stresses Americans began experiencing in the 1970s are intimately connected with the transformation of the global economy. The two oil shocks of the 1970s, the flood of Japanese automobiles and consumer electronics into America, and the loss of American jobs in basic manufacturing—much of this story is painfully familiar. Other aspects of the transformation are less well understood. Our difficulties competing in the world actually became apparent in the early 1970s. American manufacturers were able to stay competitive during the 1970s only with the help of a drop in the value of the dollar, which produced a drop in the foreign prices of American exports. No degree of toughness with our trading partners would have altered this outcome much.

* * *

This transformation is not limited to the patterns of trade between the United States, Japan, and Western Europe; it is far more international than that. In fact, our economic fate is being played out ever more centrally in the Third World—in particular, Latin America, the Middle East, and Southeast Asia. The planet's population balance is tipping precipitously in the direction of the Third World. In 1950 two thirds of mankind lived in less-developed nations. By 2020 the proportion will be five sixths. The implications for our economy and our politics are profound.

Step by step, the nations of the Third World are climbing toward industrialization and a higher standard of living, though each one is pursuing its own path to development. Far from halting this migration of mass production to the Third World, automation is actually accelerating it. Sophisticated machines are readily transported to countries where wages are low. Robots and computerized machines are substituting for semiskilled workers. And all the while, ever greater numbers of Third World citizens are flooding into the work force. The vast majority will be willing to work for a small fraction of the wages of an American. More than two billion people now live in countries where the per capita income is the equivalent of $400 or less. Some of these nations are already stepping onto the first rungs of the industrial ladder.

While this transformation is causing strains in industrialized nations, as workers in basic industries face the loss of traditional jobs, it is leading to upheaval in much of the Third World. Some developing nations have sunk deeply into debt, and many are awash in severe inflation. Rapid industrialization has contributed to urban poverty, corruption, and social unrest; the unrest has encouraged extremist left-wing and right-wing regimes and, on occasion, religious zealotry.

This unrest brings us to the last realm of the new conservative public philosophy, which concerns the Soviet threat. There can be no doubt that the Soviet Union has taken advantage of Third World instability wherever possible. But these Third World tensions are manifestations of an economic and social transformation; their connection to the East-West rivalry is in most cases derivative and wholly secondary. Our national security is surely affected by religious fanaticism in Iran, sectarian violence in Lebanon and India, the ability of the oil-producing nations to raise oil prices, the flow of advanced weapons to all manner of semi-sovereign groups, South Korea's and Taiwan's advances in high technology, and China's convulsive drive toward modernization. But these developments are not the result of Soviet machinations, and to view them as such, to treat them as occasions for secondhand warfare between the United States and the Soviet Union, leads to tragically myopic prescriptions. Yet the conservative parable holds no other role for the poor majority of mankind than as a pawn in the East-West struggle.

The Soviet Union has been brought to the peace table, not because of American toughness, but because of the fragility of the Soviet economy, no longer able to support its huge military commitments. To this extent, America and the Soviet Union share a common problem, which, if unaddressed, will lead them to a common fate. The military machines of both nations are undermining their respective economies at a time when Japan, South Korea, and West Germany are surging ahead. The East-West struggle has not disappeared, but it is rapidly becoming a sideshow to a more profound realignment of world wealth and, accordingly, world power.

* * *

The new conservative philosophy is comforting to an America confronted by a newly intractable world—mostly poor and nonwhite—in which America is no longer preeminent. The parable of permissiveness and indulgence invites us to deny the wholly natural loss of an unnatural postwar economic and political supremacy and to reject our new interdependence. It lets us blame our trials on liberal indulgence and promises renewal if only we forswear the flabby principles of altruism and conciliation. It charges us to summon our power and exercise it boldly to reclaim our hegemony.

But the conservative parable virtually ignores the fundamental transformation of the world economy and society. It overlooks the key relationships between domestic poverty and the stagnation of family incomes, between this stagnation and changes in the global economy, between these changes and political instability around the globe, between this instability and Soviet opportunism, and between Soviet overextension and our own overextension. Its message of social discipline and pugnacity, in other words, does not so much seek preeminence as presume it. This is an invigorating but reckless vision.

The first objective of our public policy, and thus the first concern of a durable public philosophy, must be to redefine America's place in a transformed world. The overriding goal is not to resist change by clinging to dangerous notions of world mastery but rather to embrace change as inevitable and to ease the dislocations it causes. Our other goals—reducing domestic poverty, maintaining a buoyant national economy, and deterring Soviet aggression—are attainable only insofar as we achieve this basic reorientation to reality. But the new conservative public philosophy fails to comprehend the scope or importance of the global economic changes we have been discussing and the force they exert on our goals, and thus many of the policies that it inspires are being pursued without any attempt to assess their unintended effects. In being tough with the Soviets, with our trading partners, and with Third World debtors, therefore, we run the risk of frustrating global adjustment. The ironic result is that we also make worse the problems of domestic poverty, our national economy, and Soviet adventurism.

* * *

Whatever form it might take, a new, liberal philosophy would embrace a much more informed and strategic approach to global change. Its parable would evoke dynamism and diversity. Above all, the new philosophy would reject the notion—so deeply embedded within both liberal altruism and conservative pugnacity—that the central struggle of our age is over the division of a fixed quantity of global wealth. It would suggest instead the possibility of an enhanced quality of life for all, contingent on mutual adaptation. It is crucial to understand that such an approach would be neither a matter of charity nor a ploy in a competitive struggle for survival but an expression of a larger and more enlightened self-interest—akin to the ideal of social solidarity that modern liberalism abandoned for altruism. The easier the transition is for any one group or nation, the smoother and more rewarding it will be for everyone else.

The new public philosophy would lead to policies that embrace the reality of interdependence in all three realms—economics, foreign affairs, and social policy. Preceding chapters advanced a number of specific proposals. To summarize: Our trade policies would welcome the transfer of basic industries to poorer nations; we would reject the grim choice between deindustrialization and protection. Simultaneously we would relieve Third World debtors of their burdens and offer the Third World access to the kind of long-term financing they desperately need. So far as these measures ameliorated the trauma of global change, right-wing generals and left-wing revolutionaries would have fewer occasions to exploit despair. We thus could feel more secure about reducing our military support to Third World countries. And exquisitely mindful of the crippling effects on our economy of our military burden, we would respond to Soviet troop reductions and offers to reduce arms expenditures with bold reductions and counteroffers of our own.

A central domestic task would be to ease the transition of our own work force out of low-skilled standardized businesses of the sort that Third World nations are beginning to enter. This would require not only more money for education, but a different approach: Rather than stress routinized learning, which prepares our children for lives of routinized work, our schools would train young people to discover problems and solutions for themselves, and give them skills in collaborating with others. It would also require that, once prepared for a lifetime of learning, our workers be given on-the-job experience designing and producing complex technologies—regardless of whether the firm they work for is headquartered in New York, Tokyo, or Bonn. Thus it is that education, training and retraining, and the nurturing of technologically intensive businesses would become central goals of public policy.

Simultaneously, hostile takeovers, leveraged buyouts, and other feats of transactional daring would be curbed. Fewer of our young brains would gravitate to Wall Street and to corporate law; more would be attracted by the challenges of inventing, manufacturing, and marketing new products worldwide, and of discovering new cures for dread diseases, better ways of cleaning our environment, and improved means of delivering public services. Worker ownership would become common-place, as everyone connected with the enterprise shared in its profits and bore the burdens of its losses. Government would help spur new tech-nologies, but no longer through the Department of Defense; a civilian research and development agency would provide seed money to groups of firms willing to pool their efforts and put up the bulk of the funds.

A more adaptable national and world economy would help restore the long-term upward direction of American incomes, including those of poorer Americans. A new public philosophy would also embody the recognition that we have a direct stake in the poor themselves, in their increasing productivity and adaptability. In an era in which capital and technology flow around the earth at the speed of an electronic impulse, national economic vitality depends to an ever greater extent on the health and readiness of *all* our people. Domestic spending on the pre- and postnatal care of poor infants, and on the nutrition and preschool edu-cation of poor children, would come to be seen as an extension of poli-cies for guarding our nation's long-term security and prosperity.

* * *

Clearly the transition to a new public philosophy will not be easy. We are entering a paradoxical era. At a time when technology is render-ing geographic borders almost irrelevant, there is an upsurge in nation-alism—in chauvinistic posturing and sectarian violence. At a time when global collaboration can yield huge benefits, we are witnessing a with-drawal from international institutions and multilateral negotiations, save for joint military commands and banking consortia. And just when we need bold leadership in Washington, we elect politicians who want to avoid hard choices and who regard government as fundamentally inept. In all these dimensions resistance to change is mounting precisely as—and largely because—the change is becoming more convulsive. The con-servative mind wants to preserve and protect, to restore and to reclaim: back to traditional values, back to basics, back to old-fashioned patri-otism and the simplicities of a local market economy. But there is no turning back, and efforts to cling to the past will only render change more painful.

If it is to be useful to us, a new liberal philosophy must explain reality and yield palpable lessons for the future. But if it is to be accepted, it must do so in a manner that simplifies and reassures. Sadly, these two conditions are sharply at odds in this age of turbulent change and baf-fling complexity. Hence, the resurgent liberal's greatest challenge.

INDEX

ABOUT THE AUTHOR

Robert B. Reich, a member of the faculty of Harvard's John F. Kennedy School of Government, is one of America's foremost political economists. He served as Assistant to the Solicitor General in the Ford administration and Director of Policy Planning for the Federal Trade Commission in the Carter administration. He is a contributing editor of *The New Republic*, chairman of the editorial board of *The American Prospect*, a frequent contributor to the *Harvard Business Review* and the *Atlantic*, and a regular commentator for both National Public Radio and public television. He is also the author of *Tales of a New America, New Deals: The Chrysler Revival and the American System, The Next American Frontier*, and *Minding America's Business*. His next book, *The Work of Nations: Capitalism in the 21st Century*, will be published in March 1991 by Knopf. Reich lives in Cambridge, Massachusetts, with his wife and two sons.